Fighting Hitler's Jets

Fighting Hitler's Jets

The Extraordinary Story of
the American Airmen Who Beat the
Luftwaffe and Defeated Nazi Germany

Robert F. Dorr

ZENITH PRESS

First published in 2013 by Zenith Press, an imprint of MBI Publishing Company, 400 First Avenue North, Suite 400, Minneapolis, MN 55401 USA

© 2013 Zenith Press

Text © 2013 Robert F. Dorr

Zenith Press titles are also available at discounts in bulk quantity for industrial or sales-promotional use. For details write to Special Sales Manager at MBI Publishing Company, 400 First Avenue North, Suite 400, Minneapolis, MN 55401 USA.

To find out more about our books, join us online at www.zenithpress.com.

Library of Congress Cataloging-in-Publication Data

Dorr, Robert F.

Fighting Hitler's jets : the extraordinary story of the American airmen who beat the Luftwaffe and defeated Nazi Germany / Robert F. Dorr.

pages cm

ISBN 978-0-7603-4398-2 (hardback)

1. World War, 1939-1945--Aerial operations, American. 2. World War, 1939-1945--Aerial operations, German. 3. Messerschmitt 262 (Jet fighter plane) 4. Jet planes, Military--Germany--History--20th century. I. Title.

D790.D666 2013

940.54'4943--dc23

2013027952

Editor: Erik Gilg
Design manager: James Kegley
Cover design: Karl Laun
Layout: Helena Shimizu

Printed in the United States of America

Contents

ONE

THE AIR SHOW, NOVEMBER 26, 1943

When the war was over, when there was no going back to change any part of what happened, a large American man named Valmore Beaudrault sat in a barber shop, awaiting his turn.

"Hitler Is Alive—Prepares to Return," was the title of an article by George McGrath in the June 1953 issue of *Police Gazette*.

Beaudrault later told a friend about reading an article with those shocking first three words in its title. The *Police Gazette*, sold in drugstores and always in barbershops, published stories titled "Hitler Is Alive" at least three times. Other stories in the magazine told how the Führer had escaped from Berlin and was living in exile in Argentina (December 1960), Colombia (June 1968), or in Antarctica (in several editions). In one issue, referring to Antarctica, the term SECRET NAZI BASE was spelled entirely in capital letters throughout.

Paradoxically, in other issues the *Police Gazette* reported that Hitler had died in his bunker in the German capital, but that the magazine had gotten a copy of his will (March 1955), found proof that he was a Jew (August 1959), or that his previously unheard-of daughter had married a Jew (December 1966).

Beaudrault, who had been a P-47 Thunderbolt pilot during the war and who had found himself fighting Hitler's jets, read one of these stories while awaiting a trim of his reddish-brown locks near his home in Nashua, New Hampshire. He shook his head, and the story took him back. For just a moment he was no longer at home but back again above the battlefields of Europe. For just a moment he again heard the rumble of piston engines, the howl of jets, and the chatter of machine guns in cold, clear skies high above Nazi Germany.

"I don't believe this stuff," said Beaudrault, one of 165 Americans who racked up an aerial victory fighting Hitler's jets. "I don't believe any of it. We won the war."

AIR SHOW FOR ONE

It may have been one of the largest air shows ever held. Certainly, it was the largest ever for an audience of one.

On Friday, November 26, 1943, a collection of the Third Reich's most advanced weapons stood ready—almost—to be demonstrated to Adolf Hitler. The location was the German military airfield at Insterburg in East Prussia. The weather in the region is usually lousy, but this was a cold but clear day.

En route with the Führer from Berlin aboard a Junkers Ju 52 tri-motor transport plane, Reichsmarshall (Marshal of the Empire) Hermann Göring hoped his orders to set up an impressive display had been followed to the letter.

Göring knew he was in disfavor with the Führer, even though the German air force, the Luftwaffe, of which he was in charge, appeared to be winning the war. German fighters and fighter pilots were shooting down American bombers right and left. A month ago, during one mission, the Americans had lost sixty bombers, each with a ten-man crew aboard. Göring kept telling the Führer that the Americans would not be able to continue to lose bomber crews at this rate, that the Allies would never be able to launch an invasion of

Nazi-occupied Europe because German fighter pilots commanded the sky.

Hitler heard this, was encouraged by it, but saw Göring, grotesquely overweight and addicted to morphine, as an asset of declining value. The Führer ardently hoped that what he would witness today would alleviate any doubts about Göring and Göring's Luftwaffe, and ensure that Germany's airmen would continue to command the skies.

In fact, Göring was very much a hands-on leader of the air force he loved, and despite his flaws—he was grossly overweight, had a reputation for enjoying fine food and wine, loved partying, and was publicly pledged to blindly follow Hitler—he was more complex than his latter-day image suggests. He had counseled against Germany starting the war because he felt its forces were not ready. In *Hitler's Charisma*, Laurence Rees wrote:

> Göring was a more complex character than the bluff, bullying caricature that is so often presented, and his views about the road Hitler was traveling were complex. It wasn't that Göring was against Nazi aggression—quite the contrary. What Göring worried about [in 1938]—as did Hitler's generals—was a wide-ranging conflict that involved Britain, France, and potentially America and the Soviet Union as well.
>
> Göring was happily married to the actress Emmy Sonnemann and was father to a daughter, Edda, who was just over a year old. They lived in epic splendor at his vast estate in Carinhall in the Schorfheide Forest and at his grand house in Berlin. Life for Göring was good.

Göring feared Hitler's temper. Even though he was officially the second-ranking figure in the Reich, he had never really been an insider. Jittery about what would happen on this day, Göring also saw this as his day to shine.

Göring looked "like a child with a new toy," one observer commented, as he prepared to claim credit for Germany's recent scientific advances. The Führer was especially interested in a new jet aircraft called the Messerschmitt Me 262 *Schwalbe* (Swallow). Today Göring would be certain it was showcased to good advantage. This was his chance, he believed, to restore his on-again, off-again status in good standing with the Führer. It was also a grand opportunity to outshine his rival, Generalfeldmarschall (Field Marshal) Erhard Milch, who held the title of air inspector general.

Several "black," or secret, aircraft and items of equipment were ready for Hitler's inspection. None looked more dull or deadly basking in the winter sun than the Me 262, the *Wunderwaffe* or "wonder weapon" that was soon to be touted as the world's first operational jet fighter. Göring had been singing the praises of the Me 262 for months. For today's show, two prototypes of the Me 262 were dismantled and shipped by rail with a crew of the Messerschmitt company's most experienced mechanics. The trip took them five miserable days through Czechoslovakia and Poland.

Although he was his country's highest-ranking military officer, wearing an elaborate uniform of his own design dripping with awards and decorations, Göring was not as well informed about the Me 262 as he thought.

This soon became apparent after the Ju 52/3m landed at Insterburg just past noon, taxied to a halt in front of the top brass at the military airbase, and disgorged its very important passengers. Emerging from the transport were Hitler, Albert Speer, Göring, Milch, and an entourage of officers of the Luftwaffe. Hitler's personal pilot, and the only pilot Hitler would fly with, SS-Brigadeführer (Major General) Hans Baur, said that he flew all of these notable people from Berlin, taking off from Tempelhof and making the short flight in good weather, so there was no problem in having the transport plane overloaded with so many notable persons. Hitler, it should be noted, did not like flying on a crowded plane, and always kept a seat for himself and his painting of Frederick the Great, the great German military leader he admired so much, in a case. He did not talk during flights, since flying scared him. Baur's recollection notwithstanding, some of the other luminaries may have traveled from Berlin aboard other airplanes or arrived by other means.

Karl Baur, chief test pilot for Messerschmitt and no relation to Hans, remembered Hitler arriving "with a flock of Generals and grim-looking SS guards at his side." Karl Baur was a virtuoso in the cockpit of the new aircraft being developed with those new engines. He had no idea that within the short span of a couple of years he would observe his Me 262 at displays in two places with similar-sounding names—Insterburg and Indiana.

The other Baur, Hans Baur was one of the few people genuinely close to Hitler. Hans had nothing but contempt for Göring, whom he called "a thick-headed glutton." Others felt that while Göring was far from brilliant, he was also the jolly-fellow-well-met in any of Hitler's frequent and bloated travel entourages.

Today's showcasing of German air power was meant to be Göring's day.

THE OPPORTUNIST

Waiting to greet them on arrival was Germany's most important aircraft designer, Professor Wilhelm "Willy" Messerschmitt. The tall, thin, balding Messerschmitt wore his title handily even though he possessed no academic degrees. He had made certain his name was indelibly attached to the new Me 262 jet, even though he hadn't worked on the engineering team that designed it. In fact, Messerschmitt had had almost nothing to do with the wonder plane that was going to ensure the Reich's salvation. "I'm more an artist than a mechanic," Messerschmitt once said, as if to denigrate those who labored over drawing boards and blueprints. "I might be the right person to be in charge, but I'm not right for the working details."

The record does not show whether the designer of the Me 262, Ludwig Bölkow, who worked for Messerschmitt, was in attendance.

One of Messerschmitt's detractors called him an opportunist. A less partisan view is that he should be best remembered as an aviation visionary and organizer. Although Messerschmitt unquestionably wanted to ingratiate himself with the hierarchy of the Third Reich, his situation is perhaps best summarized by another expert who was interviewed about him: "They needed him as much as he needed them."

Author James Neal Harvey wrote in *Sharks of the Air* of how Messerschmitt fit into the Third Reich, noting his friends "urged Willy to join the [Nazi] party. Although Messerschmitt believed in most of the party's principles, he was not anti-Semitic." It appears Messerschmitt never did officially become a Nazi—a formal process that involved several steps and included carrying an identity card. His job today was to show off his new and potentially game-changing aircraft, not talk politics.

"We have the jet you asked about," Messerschmitt told the Führer.

"The jet. Show me the jet."

THE AMERICAN SIDE

While the Führer was enjoying the airshow, most of the Americans who would soon be fighting Hitler's jets were at bases in the United States, part of an American war machine that seemed to have inexhaustible time and resources to prepare men for battle. Valmore Beaudrault, a gentle giant from New Hampshire, was learning the nuts and bolts of a not-so-gentle giant called the P-47 Thunderbolt, the largest single-engine American fighter of the war. It wasn't beautiful, it wasn't graceful, and it wasn't always forgiving, but like Beaudrault himself the P-47 was big, tough, and dependable.

Urban L. Drew, later to be known by the nickname Ben, was another young American pilot, a very young one who had gotten his wings just after his nineteenth birthday. Expecting to be sent overseas, he was instead retained at Bartow, Florida, and made a flight instructor in the P-51 Mustang. Drew did not want to be a flight instructor. He wanted to be in combat. He said as much to everyone he could find who would listen. It never occurred to him that he was getting the best possible preparation for fighting Hitler's jets. As an instructor, he logged seven hundred hours in the very new and not yet proven

P-51 in just a few months. The typical American pilot went into combat with sixty hours.

James L. "Jim" Vining had a twinkle in his eyes and showed up at the recruiter's office in Livingston, Louisiana, weighing 135 pounds dripping wet. He was a little past his eighteenth birthday, younger even than Drew. " 'No way are you going to become a pilot,' " Vining remembered the recruiter telling him. "No way I'm not," he replied. Looking into the stern face of a doubtful and disbelieving senior sergeant who happened, paradoxically, to like him a lot, Vining flashed his brilliant blue eyes and said, "My ambition is to fly the biggest thing available." Beaudrault, Drew, and Vining were all going to be fighting Hitler's jets.

At that very moment, in late afternoon in Germany, when Messerschmitt was sucking up to the Führer, an American private was joining a morning reveille formation at Scott Field in Illinois. William R. Wagner, known as Bill, was having a tough time. "I'm really good with code because I have a musical ear," Wagner said to a buddy. "But the mechanics of the radio are too much for me. I just don't have the mechanical aptitude."

Wagner wanted to fight. Being of Jewish heritage, he hoped especially that he would be permitted to fight in Europe, where he was hearing terrible things about the Nazi regime. But his bosses at this airfield in Illinois seemed to be wondering whether they'd done the right thing, sending him to radio operator school. "You might be the right person to be a gunner," one of his buddies said to Private Wagner in the morning. "But you're clearly having problems with the radio stuff."

Adolf Hitler was fifty-four years of age. He was five feet eight or nine inches tall with a manner that often seemed unfeeling or callous, a likely defense against his discomfort with virtually every other human being in his circle. He began the afternoon at Insterburg in the subdued and businesslike way that was often his manner when his temper was in check. No photograph appears to have survived of his visit to Insterburg, but it seems certain he was wearing his peaked cap and gray winter military overcoat, without the swastika armband that he'd stopped wearing when he began the war on September 1, 1939. There is no known photograph of the Führer wearing the swastika after that date.

Aircraft and weapons were ready and on display around the German airfield. Pilots were preparing to fly for the Führer. It would be little exaggeration to say that every man on the airfield on that bright November day was looking to ingratiate himself with the leader and chancellor of the Reich.

There is every reason to believe that the Führer was here only because of his interest in the Me 262. The Heinkel He 280 jet aircraft was nowhere to be seen; Milch had been asked by Göring to organize the display and did not include the He 280 or 280a because Milch himself had struck off this aircraft from the development list (on March 3, 1943) in favor of the Me 262. Worse, Göring had nationalized the Heinkel airplane company and detained Ernst Heinkel, who would not be fully rehabilitated until the postwar era. Worse yet, Göring had seized the Arado company, maker of the Ar 234 jet bomber, after its chief, Heinrich Lübbe, refused to join the Nazi party. It was up to Willy Messerschmitt, the perfect sycophant, to stay out of jail and appear more loyal than the Reich's other plane makers by putting on a super show for the Führer.

MESSERSCHMITT ME 262

The Messerschmitt Me 262 *Schwalbe* (Swallow) is almost always billed as the world's first operational jet fighter and sometimes as the first jet aircraft designed for operational military use. As this narrative will relate, those statements could as easily be applied to the American Bell XP-59A Airacomet. It's important to look at dates to understand why the Me 262, especially the one Hitler saw at Insterburg, was far less than it appeared to be.

The prototype Me 262, the Me 262V1, made its initial flight on April 18, 1941, but used a piston engine for that foray into the sky. An attempt to fly the same airframe with both piston and jet power took place on November 25, 1941, but the jet engines failed. The *Schwalbe* did not fly as a jet-powered aircraft until the third plane in the series, the Me 262V3, went aloft on July 18, 1942, using Jumo 004 turbojets. Fritz Wendel, who was the premier German test pilot of the era, flew the craft. But wait a minute. That flight was made with a tail wheel and without a full kit of military equipment. The first flight of an Me 262 with its intended tricycle landing gear and military gear did not occur until the *sixth plane in the series, the Me 262V6, flew on October 17, 1943*—five weeks before the Insterburg show—with Jumo 004B-O engines. That happened more than a year after Robert Stanley made the first flight of the XP-59A at Muroc, California, on October 1, 1942, and the XP-59A was fully equipped as an operational fighter from the beginning.*

None of that detracts from the brilliance of Ludwig Bölkow's Me 262 design. The Me 262 evolved slowly and painfully. Still—although this happened long after Insterburg—it became a world-class war machine while the XP-59A never even matched the performance of propeller-driven fighters. The Me 262 is one of a handful of true greats, and it reflects an area of science and technology where the Germans were far ahead of the rest of the world.

Hitler looked at the two Me 262s on display "like a kid looking at a new toy," Göring said later, but the Insterburg airshow did not take place with the flawlessness Göring had hoped for. Generalleutnant (Major General) Adolf "Dolfo" Galland, the thirty-four-year-old fighter ace who had flown a tailwheel-equipped Me 262 six months earlier and famously recommended that priority be given to the aircraft on production lines—for this, in postwar years, he would be better known in the United States than in Germany—now watched as an Me 262 took off as part of the demonstration, flamed out, and had to limp back to the runway for a dead-stick landing. Galland

---

*That's right. It can be argued that the Americans, not the Germans, made the first flight of a jet fighter. Britain's Gloster Meteor did not fly until March 5, 1943, but it, too, was a fully capable fighter from the beginning as the Me 262 was not.

thought the Führer was fairly calm when this failure occurred in front of him, but Hitler's expression was beginning to change.

Hitler appeared impatient as a second Me 262 (the Me 262V6, which was then the only example approaching a production configuration as the first plane with tricycle landing gear and MK 108 cannon ports) prepared to take off. Piloted by Gerd Lindner, the 262 lifted away with its imperfect Jumo 004 turbojet engines howling, circled over the visitors, and flew overhead with no apparent flaw. Galland heaved a sigh of relief. Undoubtedly, Göring did too.

Because some of it still lay ahead, no one at Insterburg that day could know that early Me 262 developmental flying would be plagued by burst tires, electrical and mechanical malfunctions, and persistent engine flameouts.

Hitler had had a question in mind ever since he'd learned about the new weapons. Now, he posed the question not to Göring but to the ever-servile Messerschmitt. The pair walked side by side. "Tell me," Hitler said. "Is this aircraft able to carry bombs?"

Messerschmitt was clearly uncomfortable but had a quick answer: "Yes, my Führer. It can carry for sure a two hundred fifty–kilogram bomb, perhaps two of them."

No one involved in the design of the Me 262 had ever considered such a thing.

"Well!" Hitler beamed. "Nobody ever thought of this!" He was certainly right on that point. "This is the Blitz bomber I have been requesting for years."

It was the right moment for Messerschmitt to add, "This aircraft is a fighter, my Führer. It has the potential to reinforce our command of the air over the Reich. It can halt the American bombing campaign in its tracks and prevent the Allies from landing in Europe."

"No one thought of this," the Führer repeated. "I'm going to order that this 262 be used exclusively as a Blitz bomber, and you, Messerschmitt, have to make all the necessary preparations to make this feasible."

Watching this exchange, Galland felt his heart sink. Galland had met Hitler previously and knew the Führer wanted a Blitz bomber that would halt an invasion by the western Allies. Willy Messerschmitt, who knew less about the aircraft bearing his name than Hitler realized, was making it sound all too easy. Converting the Me 262 into a bomber required structural changes, a relocation of its center of gravity, and new internal wiring. It was not easy, but it was also not quite so much a challenge as the engines were. Messerschmitt's engineering team already knew—and had demonstrated—that the Jumo 004 turbojet was cantankerous and unreliable. The fixes were going to take longer than anyone imagined.

While no one else appears to have noticed anything odd about the Führer, Karl Baur would later say that Hitler could not lift one arm and appeared to be sick, as if he had suffered a stroke. He would later say Hitler appeared to have a mental disability.

The tough-minded, often argumentative Galland was approaching the end of a prolonged period when he believed the Luftwaffe could prevail and Germany could actually win the war. The previous month, October 1943, Luftwaffe fighters had shot down sixty American B-17 Flying Fortress bombers over Schweinfurt, a devastating blow to the U.S. Eighth Air Force, to the daylight bombing campaign, and to Allied hopes for an invasion to liberate Nazi-occupied Europe.

With that recent success in mind and with "wonder weapons" arrayed all around him and Hitler talking of support for the military, Galland should have been riding high and thinking big. But although he was quite young, Galland was, like many of his peers, already exhausted from the war. The Battle of Britain, which took place more than three years ago, left the Luftwaffe with enormous losses. Hitler's invasion of the Soviet Union, begun two years ago, began easily enough, though quickly became a meat grinder. The sheer number of aircraft the Russians kept throwing at the Germans was beginning to wipe out the Luftwaffe's best. This very month—November 1943— the Americans were beginning to field a new fighter that the Reich hadn't planned for, hadn't wanted at first, and did not yet quite know how to use. The P-51 Mustang wasn't a wonder weapon, but it was an accidental triumph of engineering.

Galland watched the Insterburg display for the Führer and was quietly grim. Even in the best of times, Galland was grim, and for Galland's beloved Luftwaffe this was a better time than any that would occur ever again.

OTHERS AT INSTERBURG

Except to Karl Baur, who saw a sick man approaching a life change, Hitler appeared unremarkable when Messerschmitt and others began showing him other weapons and aircraft on display. Soon, though, he began to appear impatient again. He may not have been that interested in the V-1 robot bomb, two antishipping missiles called the Hs 293 and Fritz-X, and film of the new panoramic radar sets and the Korfu receiver stations tracking British bombers by their radar emissions during a night attack on Berlin a few days earlier. Another aircraft the engineers displayed for Hitler was the Dornier Do 335, which wasn't a jet, but a very odd pusher-puller aircraft with propellers at both ends of the fuselage.

A six-engined Junkers Ju 390 V-1 was also displayed, but was largely ignored. It was one of the largest German landplanes of the war and might have made a superb transport or bomber, but Hans Baur saw it as too big and too economical for executive duty with the Führer's personal fleet. Immediately after the display, the Ju 390 V-1 was flown immediately from Insterburg to Prague. There, it took part in a number of test flights, which continued until March 1944, including rare tests of in-flight refueling. The big Ju 390 was cancelled the following spring after just two airframes had been built; most historians discount a wartime claim that one of the aircraft made a 32-hour reconnaissance flight that took it within eyesight of Long Island, New York.

A four-engined Junkers Ju 290 A-5, an early version of another big aircraft that could be used as a transport or a bomber, was also part of the display. Hitler paused in front of it. "I want one for my personal use," he said. It would happen a year later when a similar Ju 290 A-7 was assigned to his personal flight unit as a Führermaschine—although Hitler would never fly in it. Both the Ju 290 and the Ju 390 would later be identified by conspiracy theorists as the aircraft in which Hitler escaped from Berlin in 1945 in order to take refuge at the SECRET NAZI BASE in Antarctica, or in Argentina, or Colombia, or somewhere.

The Ju 290 that Hitler never flew had a special passenger compartment in the front of the aircraft for the Führer, which was protected by a half-inch (12mm) of armor plate and two-inch (50mm) bulletproof glass. A special escape hatch was fitted in the floor, and a parachute was built into Hitler's seat. In an emergency, he could put on the parachute, pull a lever to open the hatch, and roll out through the opening. This arrangement was tested using life-size mannequins. The escape seat for the Führer has appeared several times in speculative fiction.

Hitler never assigned a high priority to large aircraft and seemed to have no further interest in this one. The Third Reich would reach the end of the war without ever having any significant number of four-engined bombers, while the United States and Britain would employ more than sixty thousand. At this juncture in the war, those Allied four-engined bombers were nothing more and nothing less than fat, inviting targets for German fighters, and Hitler had no reason to think that would change. He could not have known that the real wonder weapon of the European air war was not going to be the Me 262 but another plane that looked and acted far less wondrous: the North American P-51 Mustang.

Eager to increase Hitler's interest and to upstage Milch, Göring attempted to take the Führer's arm. Hitler shook off the gesture but could not prevent Göring from acting as chief guide, speaking loudly, claiming credit for many of the technical achievements for his own staff. Göring talked while Milch looked on, infuriated and embarrassed.

In *The Rise and Fall of the Luftwaffe*, historian David Irving described the debacle that followed:

[The Reichsmarschall] took the printed program out of Milch's hands and began introducing each aircraft to Hitler, working his finger down the list. He was unaware that one of the fighter prototypes had had a mishap at Rechlin [the German flight test base on the south shore of the Müritzsee] and as a result one aircraft was missing; the remaining aircraft had each been moved along one place in the line. Milch saw what was going to happen and took his revenge: he stepped tactfully back into the second row. Where the missing fighter should have been, there was now a medium bomber. Göring announced it to Hitler as the single-seater; for several more exhibits this farce continued until the Führer decided that enough was enough, and pointed out Göring's error.

One aircraft that aroused little interest on Hitler's part was the Feiseler Fi 103 flying bomb, a manned version of the V-1 "buzz bomb." The leader of the flying-bomb experimental unit at Peenemünde-West, Hermann Kröger, explained to the Führer how the weapon worked. An awkward conversation about when the Fi 103 could become available caused Hitler to stomp away in a huff while one of the Führer's lackeys asked, "Who was the pessimist who arranged this demonstration?"

Recollections of the Insterburg event differ, but it appears Hitler did not personally look at the small, buglike Messerschmitt Me 163 *Komet* that was the world's first rocket-propelled fighter. Göring did. Or at least, as Rudolf "Rudy" Opitz related later, Göring did. Göring supposedly stopped by each aircraft to personally speak with pilots and crews. The small and plain-looking-looking Opitz apparently was mistaken for a mechanic, and it took some explaining for Göring to grasp that he was chief test pilot for the 163 program. Once Göring got it right, their brief exchange went something like this:

Göring: "Young man, were you drafted to serve in the rocket fighter squadron or did you volunteer to fly this aircraft?"

Opitz: "I am in charge of it, sir."

The Me 163 may not have been an important factor that day—it was not possible to find any record of the Führer ever speaking of it—but the wobbly little rocket craft was destined to be put in combat very soon.

The star of the show was the Me 262 jet fighter, but the Insterburg exhibit also included an Arado Ar 234 twin-jet bomber and reconnaissance aircraft, which was transported to the event with great difficulty. While the Me 262 was at the event to show its flying skills, the third airframe in the Arado jet series, the Ar 234 V-3, was dismantled and transported by road to Insterburg, where technicians hurriedly pieced it back together for static display. The Arado was parked unceremoniously between a pair of Junkers Ju 88 twin-prop warplanes, one of which carried special equipment for laying smoke screens.

According to Arado company records, Hitler immediately gave the plane maker Arado carte blanche to obtain factory personnel, raw materials, and funds so that the company could build two hundred Ar 234s by the end of 1944. Some former members of Luftwaffe bomber units, who had been scheduled for reassignment as ground troops—possibly to the horrors of the Soviet front—were diverted to Arado to become workers on the project.

HANS BAUR

Hans Baur, Hitler's personal pilot and known for his cheerful personality, was savoring the display of new flying machines.

"Baur was a decent person in many ways," said his biographer, G. G. Sweeting, in an interview. "He was a good husband and loyal family man with a pleasant disposition, but he never wavered in his stalwart support for national socialism and for Hitler. He was busy running his private squadron, which was not a part of the Luftwaffe. He told me he was really impressed by the jets, especially the Me 262, but also by the Ju 290 A-5 transport."

Baur's outfit was dubbed *Die Fliegerstaffel des Führers*, or the Führer's personal squadron, and was marked with a special insignia that was painted on the nose of all planes: a black eagle head on a white background, surrounded by a narrow red ring. Unlike Galland,

Baur was still optimistic about the war. He pictured himself squiring Hitler about in a sky made safe by the sharklike, jet-propelled Me 262s.

In *The Me 262 Stormbird*, authors Colin D. Heaton and Anne-Marie Louis recount what Baur told them:

> Hitler was always excited about new things, like a child at Christmas, you could say. If there were any new ideas in tank, U-boat, or aircraft designs, he wanted to see all the blueprints and have them explained to him. His memory was photographic and he forgot nothing. I remember we were having lunch in Berchtesgaden in March or so, this was 1943, and Hitler was discussing this Messerschmitt project with Göring and Speer. [Heinrich] Himmler and [Martin] Bormann were there also.

In the meeting, Göring expressed support for the Me 262 and named some prominent German pilots who might conduct test flying of the revolutionary jet. Speer pointed out that the Reich was facing a shortage of raw materials for war projects. It would probably not have occurred to him to mention the American daylight bombing campaign, which, so far, was achieving little in its own efforts to stymie aircraft production. Hitler told Speer that he would have a letter prepared authorizing procurement of whatever was needed to acquire the materials. Speer concurred. As Bauer remembered it:

> I then remembered that the next day Hitler called his secretary, Fraulein [Trudl] Junge, into his study where he composed the letter. I know because I was discussing the flight plan with him for us to go to the Ukraine for a visit. Later Speer came by, picked up the letter, gave party salute, and left. The funny thing was that later that day some gauleiter from somewhere had called, demanding to speak with the Führer. Well, Bormann took the call and I remember him telling the man on the other end of

the line to just 'shut his mouth and give Herr Professor Speer whatever the hell he wanted,' and his life would be much easier. 'Bothering the Führer with this complaint would not be advised.' And then he hung up the phone.

According to Heaton and Lewis, Hitler's secretary Junge later remembered the letter. It was for Speer, one of only two such letters Junge (1920–2002) ever typed for the Führer. Once Speer had the letter in hand, no one hesitated to provide the materials needed for Me 262 production.

DECEMBER 20, 1943

As for Baur, sixteen months later one of his last acts was to fly the Ju 290 intended for Hitler's use to Munich-Riem airport on March 24, 1945. Baur parked the aircraft in a hangar and went to his home. The next morning, he learned that Allied bombing had destroyed the magnificent four-engined transport and its hangar. In a Monday, December 20, 1943, speech to Wehrmacht officers, Hitler revealed the priority he placed on the Me 262 as an anti-invasion weapon:

> Every month that passes makes it more and more probable that we will get at least one *Gruppe* of jet aircraft. The important thing is that they [the enemy] get some bombs on top of them just as they try to invade. That will force them to take cover, and in this way they will waste hour after hour! But after half a day our reserves will already be on their way. So if we can pin them down on the beaches for just six or eight hours, you can see what that will mean to us.

This was the speech in which Hitler predicted an Allied invasion two or three months hence, much sooner than it actually happened. This was also the date of a "president to prime" letter in which Franklin D. Roosevelt agreed with Prime Minister Winston Churchill that an announcement could be made on the first of the year that Gen.

Dwight D. Eisenhower would command Overlord, the code name of the invasion the Führer was preparing for.

Hitler's "wonder weapon" show lasted just ninety minutes. At 1:30 p.m., the Führer entrained for his Rastenburg headquarters.

Heinrich Himmler followed him within the hour. But a thought process was forming in Himmler's mind. He was seeking new ways to expand his security apparatus into a military formation. He was just a year away from snatching away the ownership and management of some of the Führer's wonder weapons from the Reich's military staff. Heinrich Himmler, much like Hans Baur but in a different way, would soon be in charge of his own air force.

TWO

"WHAT'S A PEARL HARBOR?"

It was peacetime. It was a balmy evening in Spokane, Washington, in 1941. A very young Gwendolyn Yeo had mixed feelings about the fellow escorting her to the cinema. She could not guess that one day he would be fighting Hitler's jets or that he would become her husband of seventy-plus years.

He was clean-cut, eager, and nineteen years old. To her he was a force of nature. He filled any room he entered. She knew quite a bit about him, but what Gwen knew most about Clayton Kelly Gross was that she didn't want to go to the movies with him.

"I'd rather try a picture with a little romance in it," she told him, shaking her head at the marquee. These were the days when a single theater offered a single film.

"You'll love this movie," he said.

She didn't. She was still saying so decades later. But she liked him. It was mutual. Both of them soon abandoned other steadies in order to be together.

Against Gwen's wishes, the couple sat through all 135 minutes of *I Wanted Wings*, starring Hollywood newcomers William Holden and Veronica Lake. It was Clayton Kelly Gross's choice. He was smitten with Gwen, but the aviation bug had gotten to him first.

Gross told her that like the men in the movie he wanted to fly fighters for the army.

The newsreel that night included footage of Adolf Hitler giving a speech. It was something about a newly begun operation on the eastern front to "crush our opponent in the east." To Gwen, to Kelly, to most Americans, this was far away, on the far side of a vast ocean.

Months later, Americans were looking toward the other ocean on December 7, 1941, when Japanese carrier planes attacked Pearl Harbor. Clayton Kelly Gross looked around among his friends in Spokane and saw shock and anger. "I knew the U. S. fleet was there," said Kelly. "I knew what the attack meant."

DECEMBER 7, 1941

Urban L. Drew was at the movies, at a Sunday matinee in Detroit, with his brother Earl and his mother, Olive, on December 7, 1941. Drew, better known by his nickname Ben, was just seventeen years old. Years later, he was unable to remember which motion picture they saw that day. *I Wanted Wings* was still in theaters and is a possibility.

When he and his family came out of the theater, people on the street were talking on the radio about the news. Ben's mother told him the obvious: he would soon be wearing a military uniform. Ben had no doubt what he wanted to do in the military.

"I had piles of books with lurid drawings of Spads and Fokkers splashed in color on their covers," he remembered later. "I had all the pulp adventure stories of the era, including G-8 and His Battle Aces [stories]. I knew that G-8's wingmen were Nippy Weston and Bill Martin. I read 'Smilin' Jack' in the comic strips. I visited an airport whenever I could. I built tissue-covered airplane models and balsa wood airplane models. I was hooked."

Ben Drew's first experiences in the cockpit of an airplane were not encouraging. The Detroit youngster was not a natural, an instructor told him. He was more than good enough to instruct, though, which is why he found himself in Bartow, Florida, instead of the war zone.

Yet soon moviegoers Clayton Kelly Gross and Urban L. "Ben" Drew would have plenty in common, including the fact that the Messerschmitt Me 262 jet fighter was part of their future.

An army flying cadet named Edward B. Giller said there was nothing remarkable about December 7, 1941, for him. "We knew there was trouble in Europe and we knew that trouble was centered in Berlin. I was an aviation cadet in flying class 42-D at Lubbock Field, Texas. I was in the barracks that Sunday when somebody came through and announced that Pearl Harbor had been attacked. Somebody told me, 'We're going to be in the war, too,' and he was right." Giller was from Jacksonville, Illinois. He would later pilot the P-38 Lightning and P-51 Mustang and find himself fighting Hitler's jets.

A huge number of Americans didn't know much about Hawaii or Pearl Harbor on December 7, 1941, but eighteen-year-old Robert Des Lauriers knew it firsthand.

Des Lauriers was a product of the Los Angeles basin. Though he had been born in Illinois, he grew up near Covina—at that time partly residences and partly potato fields—and went to high school near Watts. He was ordinary in appearance and remarkable in his achievements: Bob played the trumpet, raised homing pigeons, became an Eagle Scout, and—of course—built model airplanes. When the battle for France ended and the Battle of Britain raged between July and October 1940, Des Lauriers and other Los Angeles boys learned the recognition features of the Supermarine Spitfire and Messerschmitt Bf 109. At a time when Adolf Hitler's fighter pilots were arguably at the peak of their prowess, Des Lauriers built replicas of their planes out of balsa wood. But flying was only one of his many interests. He wanted to be an architect.

"We lived across the street from a movie theater so we went to the shows on Saturday," Des Lauriers recalled. "I loved Tom Mix western movies. We had radio and newspapers at home, of course, but we got our visual news from the Saturday newsreels. We looked at that guy Hitler delivering fiery speeches and we thought he was very far away and very distant from our lives."

In September 1941, the Des Lauriers family received passage to the American territory of Hawaii, where Bob's dad was under contract from the U.S. Engineering Department to build bomb storage facilities at Wailoa. A buildup of sorts had been taking place in America's distant territory in the Pacific and bomb storage was going to be needed for the new, four-engined bombers that were going to be key to American air power policy.

Bob was just short of his eighteenth birthday when he began working at Wheeler Field, where Curtiss P-40B Tomahawk fighters were stationed.

On December 7, 1941, Bob was in the family home at Wailoa. When it began, he was in bed. He heard aircraft. The previous day, people had been talking about a mock war unfolding between the army and navy on the adjacent island of Kauai, so he assumed a war game was under way. Bob rolled over in bed and went back to sleep. Hours later, soldiers were stringing up barbed wire around the compound where his house was located. While Admiral Chuichi Nagumo's First Air Fleet was attacking Pearl Harbor, Hickam Field, Wheeler Field, and other places in Hawaii with 135 Mitsubishi A6M2 Zero 21 fighters, 135 Aichi D3A1 "Val" dive bombers, and 144 Nakajima NB5N2 "Kate" torpedo bombers, killing 2,403 Americans, Robert Des Lauriers slept through it all.

His brother Jerry was among agricultural workers in a nearby pineapple field that morning and saw Zeros approaching at low level. For a moment, Jerry ran a race with a Zero that came up alongside him, accelerated, and kept going. The family saw the aftermath of the attack and listened to President Franklin D. Roosevelt on the radio, and for the first time in his life Robert Des Lauriers wanted to fight. He had never been one of those kids who built models or read *Air Trails* magazine, "but now I wanted to fly and fight," he said. Des

Lauriers would one day find himself in a B-17 Flying Fortress under attack from a Messerschmitt Me 262.

BUSH AND BUSCH

Before Hitler's tanks went grinding into Poland, before the Battle of Britain, before Pearl Harbor, two boys with similar names, Robert Bush and Hans Busch, celebrated their fourteenth birthdays in 1938. Robert thought he wanted to be a fighter pilot. Hans thought he wanted to be a sailor on a submarine.

Robert lived in a community called Hillcrest, where southeast Washington, D.C., butts up against the Maryland state line. His father worked downtown for the government, a fortunate situation at the height of the Great Depression, and after a long commute via streetcar and bus Dad sometimes had a gift in hand when he arrived home at the end of the day. Sometimes it was a copy of the aviation magazines, a major investment at twenty-five cents. Sometimes it was a Strombecker wooden model airplane, which could cost a dollar or more and which father and son built together, paying careful attention to authenticity and detail. A member of the Boy Scouts, Robert found it difficult, when the model was almost finished, to apply the decals properly using water and thumb pressure. Sometimes, he carried a finished model around with him.

He thinks he remembers reading in a science magazine about Nazi Germany's Ritscher Expedition to Antarctica around this time. For a few months (between December 17, 1938, and April 12, 1939), the merchant ship *Schwabenland*, with two Dornier Do 16 flying boats on board, lingered in the Antarctic region now known as Dronning Maud Land. Approved by Hermann Göring, the expedition was publicly aimed at improving German prospects for whaling, but conspiracy theorists later said its real purpose was to establish beneath the ice shelf a secret Nazi base, which in postwar U.S. writings would become the SECRET NAZI BASE.

In years to come, a veteran of German naval service would claim that the expedition left people and equipment in a very special natural ice cave, the entrance to which was reinforced with steel walls and stairs. Großadmiral (Grand Admiral) Karl Dönitz, the veteran would claim, is supposed to have referred to the location in Antarctica as having been built for the Führer in "a Shangri-La on land, an impregnable fortress." But nothing like this was reported at the time. "I think it was just an article about a scientific expedition," said American youngster Robert Bush.

German youngster Hans Busch lived in a rural area not far from Lübeck. He got good grades in school. His father encouraged him to be busy in activities with other boys. He and a friend were working on a model submarine when he joined a group that was building an actual aircraft, a glider called an SG-38. It was a high-wing, cable-braced, single-seat primary-training glider in which the pilot sat completely out in the open. Once exposed to what flying was all about, Hans abandoned his dream of sailing beneath the sea. He left his submarine model at home when he went to meetings of the *Flieger* (aviation) group of the Hitlerjungen, or the Hitler Youth.

"I knew we had a strong leader in Adolf Hitler," said Hans. "I didn't know about politics or about the dark side of things in Berlin. I just knew that our country was on the rebound from difficult times and it was a good time to want to fly."

Germany had risen to "become a favorite vacationland," Busch would later write—and be accused by a critic of being a political naïf. He also noted, "During the Olympic Games in Berlin many people came to Germany and found that the country that had been in shambles [just years earlier] was now flourishing, was very industrious, and was friendly and open to visitors. The world-famous aviator Charles Lindbergh, who crossed the Atlantic in a single-engined aircraft, was very much impressed. Later, when he said that American should not get involved in a war in Europe he was black-balled for his politically-incorrect statements."

Busch appears to have regarded the Third Reich as nothing worse than "politically incorrect," but he would become very much involved in the war in Europe. He would eventually fly the Me 262 jet fighter.

TOO SMALL, TOO BIG

December 8, 1941

After Pearl Harbor, everybody was mad as hell at the Japanese. Everybody wanted to fight. Jim Vining was pretty sure he would get into the fight, even though he was a little guy and was too young to sign up. Born in Louisiana in 1925, Vining was a small youngster, a veritable bantamweight. He had something in common with Clayton Kelly Gross, though. He wanted to fly.

"My dad, too, was interested in flying, but he was a farmer and I was the oldest of ten kids: We were poor and I knew that if I wanted to fly I would have to do it in the army. When I first inquired at age fourteen in 1939, they told me you had to have a minimum of two years of college and had to be twenty years old. That seemed so far away it was all but out of reach," he said.

"I graduated from high school in 1942 and won a four-year scholarship to Southeast Louisiana College in Hammond," he continued. "Just when I was about to go into pilot training, I ran into my next obstacle. They put a freeze on new student pilots. The freeze was lifted on January 1, 1943, when they announced that 'We need twenty thousand aviation cadets each in the army and navy.' But then, the doctor told me that I was ten pounds under weight to become a pilot! I was then five feet nine inches in height and weighed one hundred twenty pounds, while a pilot was required to weigh one hundred thirty.

"The doc sympathized. He gave me three weeks to gain weight. I went home and ate up an extra plate and had an extra jug of milk every day. My mom made a lot of extra heavy biscuits for me. I really, really wanted to fly."

With bright blue eyes and looking something like an eager puppy, Vining had instant appeal for girls and he knew how to ingratiate himself with guys. He had real charm. And he used it on the flight surgeon.

"I went back to see the doc just before my eighteenth birthday. I had gained eight pounds, but he gave me a break and called it ten! As soon as I became eighteen, they sent me off to preflight in San Antonio, Texas. I was a member of flying class 44-A."

It was not until January 4, 1944, that Jim Vining pinned on his pilot wings and lieutenant's bars and became, at eighteen, the youngest airplane commander of a B-26 Marauder medium bomber in the U.S. Army Air Forces. "The first time I flew a B-26, it was a religious experience. I've been a believer ever since," he said.

If Jim Vining was a little guy who could, Val Beaudrault was the big guy who almost didn't. Valmore J. Beaudrault, also known as Val, looked big and gruff but was as good-natured as they come. A product of Nashua, New Hampshire, when that location epitomized small-town living, Beaudrault was, the town's historian wrote, "big, husky, burly and formidable. He looked like a north woods lumberjack or a football lineman, which he was at Milford High School." He became a machinist at the Abbott Machine Company in Wilton, where the foreman always asked him to move heavy machinery when needed. Beaudrault began dating his Nashua girlfriend, Priscilla Pero, right after the Japanese attack on Pearl Harbor. They later got engaged. To his fiancée, Beaudreault was a little like the portly P-47 Thunderbolt he was soon to fly—"big, sturdy, imposing, and yet easy to get along with," she said.

On December 7, 1941, Priscilla Pero was at a church event with friends in Nashua. "That Sunday afternoon, we were talking about church events and people that I didn't know started coming up to me and saying, 'Have you heard?' The local newspaper's office was just up the street, and they always put the latest issue in their display window. We ran up to the paper's offices and saw the headline telling us that our country had been attacked by Japan," she said.

Priscilla Pero, later to be Priscilla Beaudrault, was just fifteen years old.

Val Beaudrault, who did not remember having met Priscilla as a child—"his mother took care of my grandmother," she recalled—was busily working at Abbott Machine. Like Clayton Kelly Gross on the other side of the American continent, Beaudrault had already logged some air hours. On weekends he begged, cajoled, and sometimes paid to get flying lessons at Nashua Airport. He wanted to be a fighter pilot. On December 7, 1941, Val and fellow machinists were gathered around a radio listening to the news and one of them asked the question that so many Americans were asking: "What's a Pearl Harbor?"

Beaudrault told a recruiter he wanted to fly fighter planes.

"You're too big," the recruiter responded.

"What?"

"You're too big. You won't fit in the cockpit."

At that moment, it's possible neither the recruiter nor Val knew that a fighter called the P-47 Thunderbolt came with a very roomy accommodation for its pilot. They also probably didn't know that throughout the war the U.S. Army Air Forces were always inconsistent about how they applied height and weight restrictions.

"I'll find a way," Beaudrault told the recruiter. Ahead of him lay the same long, seemingly almost leisurely training that American pilots would undergo—and, after that, an encounter fighting Hitler's jets.

EARLY JET POWER

During the years 1938 to 1942, when they were being hastily transformed from boys into men, the future combat pilots of this narrative—Gross, Des Lauriers, Bush, Busch, Beaudrault, and others—possessed the means to know about jet propulsion and other new technologies, but none of them remember being exposed that early. It also appears unlikely that Roosevelt, Winston Churchill, or Adolf Hitler received briefings on jet power until long after the first jet research aircraft had completed their maiden flights.

All the way back in 1928, a junior Royal Air Force cadet named Frank Whittle submitted his ideas for a turbojet engine to his superiors. On January 16, 1930, at age twenty-two, Whittle applied for his first patent, for a two-stage axial compressor feeding a single-sided centrifugal compressor. Whittle would later concentrate on the simpler centrifugal compressor only, for a variety of practical reasons, while his German counterparts would take the riskier route of the axial-flow configuration. Whittle had his first engine running on a test stand in April 1937. It was loud, powerful, and unreliable, and at times it would simply stop working for no visible reason. Still, Whittle told a visitor that his primitive turbojet meant that "we're now in a new age of propulsion."

In 1935 Hans von Ohain started work on a turbojet engine design in Germany, unaware of Whittle's work. Ohain held meetings with Ernst Heinkel, one of the great aviation industrialists of the era—albeit, one soon to be out of favor with Hitler—and the way was set for what would become the Heinkel He 280 jet fighter. First, however, Ohain and Heinkel teamed up on their first—and the first—aircraft to be propelled by jet power. The simple, compact, and very plain-looking Heinkel He 178 accomplished its maiden flight in the hands of pilot Erich Warsitz on August 27, 1939, at Rostock-Marienehe aerodrome on the Baltic coast. This was the world's first flight by a jet aircraft.

Italy flew its Caproni-Campini CC.2, resembling a long cigar with wings, on August 17, 1940. The Italian aircraft had no propeller, relying on a piston-powered ducted fan to push it through the air. It was a "jet" in a sense, but different in design from the gas turbine–powered planes being developed in Germany and Britain. The ducted-fan concept never led anywhere. No air force in the world ever fielded a warplane with this form of power.

The first British aircraft to fly under jet power, the Gloster E28/39, made its maiden flight on May 15, 1941, piloted by Lt. Gerry Sayer.

The Messerschmitt Me 262, so much a vital part of this narrative, first flew on March 25, 1942, but using a reciprocating engine. The evolution of the Me 262 into a tricycle-gear, jet-powered, combat-ready fighter was destined to be incremental.

Pearl Harbor had not yet happened when the Me 262 took flight, so the Americans were not yet in the war. Nevertheless, they were contemplating building not one but two jet military aircraft, starting with the Bell XP-59A Airacomet (it would take to the air piloted by Robert Stanley on October 1, 1942). The early Heinkel and Gloster planes were research craft while the XP-59A was arguably the first of the jets that was equipped and ready for a combat mission, although it would turn out not to perform very well at it. Britain would fly its first jet fighters, the Gloster Meteor and De Havilland Vampire, on March 5, 1943, and September 20, 1943, respectively.

At Lockheed, young engineer Clarence "Kelly" Johnson had proposed a jet fighter way back when Hitler's tanks were first grinding into Poland and the Army Air Forces (AAF) had ignored his proposal. Designed in a Burbank, California, facility that would later be called the Skunk Works, Johnson's L-133-02-01 was a futuristic canard that would have relied not on a British import for power but on two company-designed L-1000 turbojet engines. If the AAF had invested in it when Johnson first mooted it in 1939, the entire war might have unfolded differently. But Johnson would not produce a jet aircraft until his spinach-green XP-80, wearing the name *Lulu Belle* on the nose, flew on January 8, 1944, with Milo Burcham in the cockpit. It wouldn't see combat in this war, but would shine in Korea as the F-80 Shooting Star.

READY TO FLY

Getting a chance to fly, even during wartime, was a real draw for many of the young Americans, who had already experienced a lot of sacrifice as children of the Great Depression. At least that was how Don Bryan saw it: "We didn't have high expectations, but we were drawn by the glamour of aviation." They were young men who wanted to fly and who felt their heartstrings drawn by sleek, silvery new planes like the magnificent P-38 Lightning—which captured the imagination of every young air enthusiast but later proved to be the wrong fighter in Europe. "When I saw a P-38, I knew I wanted to fly something like that magnificent fighting machine," said Bryan, who ended up at the controls of a P-51 Mustang instead.

They wanted to fly, but it seldom occurred to them that they might have to kill. "I always aimed at the enemy airplane, not at the man in it," said Bryan, who was gifted with flawless eyesight and eye-hand coordination. And, yes, Bryan had seen *I Wanted Wings* at the cinema, too.

Bryan was a California boy, eager, handsome, smiling. If he had anything other than a routine West Coast, middle-class upbringing, his buddies never discerned it. A friend called him a "loveable crank" and a "philosopher," but he was mostly just an ordinary very young man who may have been less impacted by the economic hardships of the era than many. Like so many who went through the rigorous flight training regimen described in later paragraphs, Bryan was devastated when he got it all behind him only to find himself in the cockpit of a P-39 Airacobra.

"I had such wonderfully high expectations and then I was assigned to the P-39 and I thought, 'Oh, no. This was not what I was meant to do.'"

Roscoe Brown grew up in Washington, D.C., and he was inspired by famous aviators like Charles Lindbergh and Roscoe Turner and grabbed every opportunity to visit airports and see airplanes. A decade before the author of this book did the same three things, Brown visited Bolling Field, visited Naval Air Station Anacostia, and made his first flight in a transport aircraft at Bolling, all before finishing high school. Not everyone who became a pilot in World War II was a near fanatic about aviation at an early age, but Brown was. He was fixated on just two things: flying and sports.

The Americans introduced in this narrative came from all over a country that still had regional differences, dialects, customs, and cultures. But all those introduced so far in this narrative had one characteristic in common: They were white.

Brown was black. He took segregated military officer training while still in all-black Dunbar High school in Washington. He read about a training program for black pilots that had been launched (in early 1941) in Tuskegee, Alabama. "They were accepting only the 'best of the best' into the program, and I felt I could become one of them," said Brown. He knew that the U.S. military would not relax its requirement for a bachelor's degree for black pilots—although it eventually did for everyone else—so he enrolled in Springfield College in Massachusetts.

"On December 7, 1941, I was listening on the radio to a game between the New York Giants and the Brooklyn Dodgers," Brown said. The two *football* teams were competing at the New York Polo Grounds and celebrating Tuffy Leemans's Day in honor of the Giants' star running back who was himself intending to become a pilot.

"They interrupted the radio coverage of the game to tell military service members to report to their units because the Japanese had attacked Pearl Harbor. Because of my military training in high school and in my first year of college, I knew that the U.S. Fleet was in Hawaii. I knew we would be at war," Brown said. "I also knew that if I wanted to become a pilot, I would have to finish college." He would eventually graduate in 1943 and surrender a reserve commission in order to become an aviation cadet—a Tuskegee Airman.

Clayton Kelly Gross had ninety hours in his logbook. Under the Civilian Pilot Training Program (CPTP), Gross made his first solo flight in a Porterfield 75-C aircraft at Felts Field in Spokane in March 1941. CPTP was a product of its time and was responsible for giving a start to many of the best pilots destined to fight in the war ahead. The backstory goes like this:

During the Great Depression, the number of pilots trained by the U.S. Army Air Corps decreased until in 1937 only 184 graduated from pilot training. In 1939, responding to a call for expansion by Roosevelt, the air corps announced a plan to graduate 4,500 pilots in the following two years. It was too ambitious by half.

Lacking facilities to train so many cadets, in mid-1939 the air corps contracted with nine of the best civilian flying schools to begin training pilots. When France fell to Germany in 1940, the air corps increased the number of pilots to be trained to seven thousand per year. By December 1941, the air corps had contracted with forty-five civilian flying schools. Only 257 new pilots graduated at Randolph Field, Texas, in 1939—while *I Wanted Wings* was being filmed there—but two years later 2,000 were enrolled in each class. When the Army Air Forces (AAF) was formed on June 20, 1941— two days before a proclamation by Hitler announced an attack on the Soviet Union—the U.S. air arm was beginning a training effort that would graduate 250,000 pilots from its schools during the war ahead.

The training that Clayton Kelly Gross underwent is outlined here as being typical for all American pilots of the era. The scheme, which included three stages of flight training—primary, basic, and advanced—suggests that an American nation rich in both resources and manpower could afford the luxury of taking its time to preparing a pilot for combat duty. In early days, the Third Reich exercised the same luxury—Hans Busch's pilot training would be lengthy and exhaustive—but as the war progressed men would be climbing into Messerschmitts with fewer and fewer logbook hours.

Gross's Army Air Forces Flying Class 42-H underwent weeks of preflight training in Alabama before shipping to the small town of Coleman in the Texas panhandle to begin flying. There, Gross encountered the Fairchild PT-19, an open-cockpit, mostly-fabric, low-wing trainer with a tail wheel. Already experienced in a cockpit, Gross said he stepped down from his first PT-19 flight feeling like Rickenbacker himself.

"We were warned that the PT-19 had a wooden center section, and if you made a hard landing, you could break the aircraft," said Gross. "Our instructors told us that if we broke a PT-19, we'd be carrying a rifle as close to Germany as they could send us. We were jealous of student pilots who flew the Stearman PT-17 biplane. I don't remember anybody disliking the PT-19, but I don't remember anybody loving it like pilots loved the Stearman."

After a brief stay in Waco, Texas, Gross continued his leisurely training at Randolph Field in San Antonio, where the cadets met Veronica Lake. Gross flew the relatively rare North American BT-14 basic trainer, powered by a 450-horsepower engine. After four weeks of basic flying, he transferred again to adjacent Kelly Field and flew the AT-6 Texan advanced trainer. The course lasted several more weeks and included sixty-five hours of flying time in the AT-6, a nearly all-metal monoplane that may have been the best trainer in the world at the time. When Clayton Kelly Gross pinned on his silver pilot wings and gold second lieutenant bars on September 6, 1942—and married eighteen-year-old Gwen Yeo the following day—the American taxpayer had invested some fifteen months and almost $100,000 into making him a pilot. Every man who followed him would have similar training. By the time they got overseas, American pilots were ready for what came next.

Gross's first assignment was to the 329th Fighter Squadron at Hamilton Field, north of San Francisco. The squadron was flying the Bell P-39 Airacobra. "It was said that your first one hundred hours in the Airacobra were dangerous because it had characteristics unlike any other plane," Gross said. It had tricycle landing gear, a cannon in the propeller hub, an automobile-style door, and an engine behind the pilot. "We did lose a lot of pilots in training in the Airacobra and a lot of them disliked the airplane intensely. I didn't feel that way. In fact, I loved the aircraft," he said.

He may have been almost alone in that feeling, and he was not modest about being a fighter pilot. Few were. On a typical flight he took off from Hamilton Field and headed toward San Francisco. "I leveled out and searched the sea to the horizon for an invasion fleet. By God, the Japanese will not make a sneak attack while I am up here defending the coast! When I rolled out straight and level, I caressed the gun handle switches," Gross said. "I would have charged them, but I wasn't sure how to uncharge them. I flew back to make what I thought was another perfect landing. I was sure the powers that gave me this job had made the right decision. This is where I belong."

Also assigned to the 329th Squadron at Hamilton Field after fourteen months of training was 2nd Lt. Robert Bush, from Washington, D.C. "I was like everybody else," Bush said. "I wanted being a fighter pilot to be glamorous. And then they put me in a P-39 and I thought, 'There's nothing glamorous about this!' "

The Army Air Forces operated fifty-five civilian-operated primary flying training centers across the country.

According to records that were kept but not released at the time, more than twenty thousand men died in stateside aviation accidents while training to participate in a war they never reached. It's impossible to remember these men without thinking of Nile Kinnick, the Iowa running back who received the Heisman Trophy in 1939 and was killed in the 1943 crash of an F4F-3 Wildcat fighter on an aircraft-carrier training flight off the coast of Venezuela. He was a naval aviator who never reached the war. Another naval aviator hopeful, football's Tuffy Leemans, was sidetracked by a playing field injury before he could ever climb into a cockpit.

From December 1941 to August 1945, the Army Air Forces lost 14,903 pilots, aircrew, and other personnel, plus 13,873 airplanes, inside the continental United States. These losses were the result of 52,651 aircraft accidents (6,039 involving fatalities) in forty-five months. As author Barrett Tillman wrote in a blog, that's 331 men and 308 aircraft lost in a single month, or eleven men and ten planes in just one day. In addition, almost one thousand AAF aircraft simply vanished while being ferried from the United States to locations overseas.

Others got there but never came home. There was enormous attrition from the AAF, which reached its peak strength in 1944 with 2,372,000 personnel. No fewer than 43,581 AAF aircraft were lost overseas, including 22,948 on combat missions (18,418 in fighting in the Mediterranean and Europe) and 20,633 attributed to non-combat causes in the overseas combat zones. U.S. forces suffered 291,557 battle deaths and 113,842 other fatalities during the war, including total AAF combat casualties of 121,867. A little-known fact is that more U.S. airmen were killed in World War II than U.S. Marines were.

THE P-39 AIRACOBRA

Of the five principal fighters flown by Army Air Forces pilots during World War II (the P-38, P-39, P-40, P-47, and P-51), only one does not have an association for pilots who meet to share their experiences at reunions. Only one is not included in the fighter memorial at the U.S. Air Force Academy in Colorado Springs. Only one is the brunt of almost universal disparagement by those who flew it—even though almost none of them flew it in combat. And it was, in fact, a far better fighter than is generally acknowledged. At low altitude it was faster than, and as maneuverable as, the Messerschmitt Bf 109 or Mitsubishi A6M2 Zero.

The Bell P-39 Airacobra was also the best pursuit ship to have if you needed to travel on a highway rather than in the sky. Robert Bush fantasized about "driving" a P-39 down the two-lane highway from Hamilton Field and across the newly built Golden Gate Bridge to San Francisco, where he planned to use the Airacobra's menacing nose 37mm cannon to stick up a grocery store. The idea may have had its genesis when another 329th Fighter Squadron pilot followed up an emergency landing on a dirt road in northern California by taxying twenty miles to a filling station where he pulled in and phoned for help. Another 329th pilot, 2nd Lt. Nathan Serenko, really *did* fly *under* the Golden Gate Bridge and was rewarded with an assignment to the infantry.

"Having the engine behind the pilot created an unpleasant smell that we never forgot," said Bush. The P-39 Airacobra was the first army single-seat fighter with tricycle landing gear. Its undercarriage was dictated by the desire to mount an American Armament Corporation's T-9 37mm cannon (later built by Oldsmobile) in the nose. The decision to locate the cannon to fire through the propeller hub meant that the engine had to be mounted within the fuselage, directly above the rear half of the wing with the propeller driven by an extension shaft, which passed beneath the cockpit floor. Bush, Gross, and other Airacobra pilots feared the damage the drive shaft might inflict if it should break loose or be damaged in combat. In fact, the arrangement proved safe.

The Allison V-1710 was a 1,300-horsepower liquid-cooled, twelve-cylinder inline engine, which also propelled the Curtiss P-40 Hawk series. At the core of its problems was the fact that the Airacobra lacked a supercharger for high-altitude performance.

The XP-39, progenitor of eight thousand Airacobras to follow, made its first flight at Wright Field, Ohio, on April 6, 1938. Twelve months later, following extensive evaluation by the U.S. Army, twelve YP-39 preproduction versions were ordered, plus a planned YP-39A that did not materialize. At first designated P-45, the Airacobra (based on an XP-39B test ship) went into production on August 10, 1939. The army then ordered 369 P-39Ds in September 1940. The first operational squadron was the 39th Pursuit Squadron, 31st Pursuit Group, at Selfridge Field, Michigan.

Great Britain signed contracts for 675 planes initially dubbed the Caribou and later known as the P-400. Britain quickly rejected the fighter and sent examples to Russia via convoy. Others returned to U.S. hands and ended up on Guadalcanal.

Although Bell incorporated changes in the P-39F, P-39J, P-39K, and P-39L, essential features of the Airacobra remained unchanged over the war years. The P-39M, P-39N, and P-39Q, the latter two earmarked for Soviet use, had only minor changes.

The Airacobra was introduced to combat by the 8th Fighter Group, which flew P-39Ds in New Guinea in 1942. On April 30, 1942, Lt. Col. Boyd D. "Buzz" Wagner led a battle against Zero fighters. The magazine for Bell employees sang the praises of pilot 1st Lt. Paul G. Brown, the first Airacobra ace, according to an August 1942 article. Brown is officially credited with three aerial victories, but Wagner attained ace status with five aerial victories (one of only two Americans to rack up that many in the Airacobra, which, again, saw little combat in American hands).

September 14, 1942

At embattled Henderson Field on Guadalcanal, P-39D-2s and repossessed P-400s (British export Airacobras) fought Japan's best, including the vaunted Zero. First Lieutenant Wallace L. Dinn Jr. of the 67th Fighter Squadron, 58th Fighter Group, pioneered the use of the Airacobra as a dive bomber to attack Japanese shipping, a role for which the P-39 had never been designed, but at which—with proper technique and tactics—it excelled.

On September 14, 1942, fourteen P-39Ds and Fs of the 54th Fighter Group flew from a steel-planking Aleutian airstrip as part of a force that made the first counterstrike on the Japanese in the region. Airacobra pilots strafed antiaircraft gun positions with their nose cannons and shot down two floatplane fighters.

It's unlikely, as was claimed, that Lt. Clyde G. Rice shot down a Zero with a single 37mm round high over the Aleutians. (Rice was said to have gotten several Airacobra victories in a 1942 article, though he is not officially credited with any). However, Lt. Gerald R. Johnson scored half a dozen Zero kills in the Aleutians at the controls of a P-39D Airacobra of the 42nd Fighter Squadron, 54th Fighter Group, before raising his total to twenty-two elsewhere.

Most combat operations in the Airacobra were carried out by the Soviet air force in support of the Red Army. Radio newsman Robert Magidoff on the NBC News roundup on May 25, 1942, spoke about the Airacobra in Russian hands: "The squadron I visited brought down eighty-six enemy planes since the outbreak of the war. Twenty-nine of these were laid down by flying Tommyhawks [a reference to the Curtiss Tomahawk], Kittyhawks, and Airacobras." Magidoff added that the Airacobra would be the key to victory over Hitler in 1942.

Russian pilots had opportunities to engage the Messerschmitt Bf 109 at low altitude, where the American-built fighter performed best. Flying the *Cobrastochka* (Dear Little Cobra), Lt. Col. Alexandr I. Pokryshkin became the Allies' second-ranking ace of the war with fifty-nine aerial victories, forty-eight of them accomplished in his Airacobra.

Some 4,924 P-39s were sent to the Soviet Union, of which 4,758 reached their destinations. Between 1939 and 1944, 9,529 Airacobras were produced. The U.S. Army Air Forces reached a peak inventory of P-39 Airacobras in February 1944 with 2,105 aircraft. Production ended with assembly on July 25, 1944, of the final P-39. Most army Airacobras remained stateside for use as trainers, and nearly all pilots who achieved fame in other fighters flew the P-39 Airacobra at home first.

That was true of the Americans who later found themselves fighting Hitler's jets.

THREE

WONDER WEAPONS

Could Nazi Germany have gotten a jet fighter into action earlier than it did? What if the Third Reich had rushed the Heinkel He 280 into service rather than waiting for the similarly jet-powered Messerschmitt Me 262 that came later?

A sky full of He 280s, faster and deadlier than any fighter in Allied colors, might have prevented the U.S. Eighth Air Force from building up its bombing campaign over Europe—and might have forced the Allies to postpone the invasion of occupied Europe that took place at Normandy on D-Day, June 6, 1944. Maybe even, in the wildest imaginations of a few leaders in the Third Reich, squadrons of He 280s might have turned the tide and won the war.

Or maybe not. Today, the history of the He 280 is buried in obscurity; the aircraft is not as well known as some of Adolf Hitler's other *Wunderwaffen* (wonder weapons).

The very term "wonder weapons" was a hopeful proclamation that the miracle of advanced science would save the Reich, the Führer, and the German people. By late 1943, subjected to bombing every day and night, food shortages, electrical blackouts, and frequent reports of new successes by the Allies, the German people seized the term and shortened *Wunderwaffe(n)* to *Wuwa*, a meaning-less pair of syllables that resembled the name of a children's cartoon. The people used the term to belittle not only the projects but also the Führer himself, although it was always necessary to be on guard when doing so.

On the field of battle, on the ground, and in the sea and air, the issue was still in doubt. Scientists, engineers, and pilots still knew the Reich could win the war. They truly could achieve a miracle. They knew it, they said later, and didn't doubt it. No other nation had anything like the V-1 robot bomb. No other nation had the V-2 rocket that terrorized London. The V-1 and V-2 were in Hitler's wonder-weapon subcategory of *Vergeltungswaffe*, or retaliation or vengeance weapons, developed at the secret northeastern German rocket facility Peenemünde.

Hitler wanted to call the V-1 the Maikäfer, May bug, but engineers on the program almost never uttered the term. The V-1 was a straightforward, straight-wing design from the engineering team of Robert Lusser, chief designer and technical director at Heinkel, although production of the V-1 was turned over to the Fieseler aircraft company after Ernst Heinkel fell into disfavor. The V-1 was powered by a simple pulse jet engine that pulsed fifty times per second, producing the unique and, to some, terrifying sound that prompted those on the receiving end to call it the buzz bomb. The pulse jet engine had just one moving part, a shutter assembly in the front air intake. This was not a jet engine as the term is used today, and it didn't have a great deal of power. However, it was sufficient to push along a powered projectile with a lethal, 1,900-pound warhead in the nose, a welded steel fuselage, and wooden wings. Apart from an autopilot, the flying bomb had no guidance system: when the engine cut out, the V-1 dropped from the sky.

The V-1 was manufactured at various sites in the Reich, but the main production facility was the notorious underground SS slave-labor complex known as Mittelwerk at Nordhausen in the Harz Mountains. An estimated total of twenty-four thousand V-1s were built in 1944, with, as many as ten thousand built in 1945, though quantities tend to vary from source to source.

The V-1 was called a doodlebug, a robot bomb, or a buzz bomb. But "buzz" is not really the right sound that emanated from this crude cruise missile and terrorized those in its path. The grinding drone of the V-1's pulse jet engine sounded something like a washing machine struggling to find its pace. When the V-1 reached its target and dived, the sound of the propulsion unit spluttering and cutting out, followed by an eerie silence before impact, was nothing but terrifying, although the silence at least provided a warning to seek shelter. If you were a customer at a certain retail shop near the King's Cross tube station in London, a cheery sign let you know that you could shop there and have enough time, with this warning, to make it to the station to take shelter.

Many Londoners became victims without ever making it to the underground. Clouds and rain in summer 1944 aided the effectiveness of the V-1, and casualties mounted. By late summer a million and a half people had evacuated London, and the rate of work production declined. The Royal Air Force would eventually respond to the V-1 by fielding something new and different—a jet fighter called the Gloster Meteor. Looking like an upended rifle bullet with small fins, the V-2 rocket, also known as the Aggregat 4, or A-4, stood to a height of forty-five feet eleven inches when on its launching stand, weighed almost 28,000 pounds, and carried a nose-mounted 2,200-pound Amatol explosive warhead.

Inspired by Germany's Hermann Oberth and America's Robert Goddard, who did early studies and tests of rocketry—although Goddard (1882–1945) was largely ignored in his own country—the V-2 was developed by a scientific and engineering team at headed by Wernher von Braun at Generalmajor (Maj. Gen.) Walter Dornberger's Peenemünde Army Research Center. It was the world's first successful ballistic missile and it had a futuristic look that seemed relatively benign when, in reality, it was the most malignant kind of weapon—an indiscriminate one.

Some historians question whether von Braun had as significant a role in developing the V-2 as he later claimed. He was one of four section leaders at Peenemünde, and writings from another section leader, Paul Schröder, suggest that von Braun's role was minor, at most.

What is not in dispute is that Von Braun had full knowledge and completely acquiesced to the use of slave labor. He was a willing member of the Nazi party. A postwar musical spoof by Tom Lehrer called von Braun a man "whose allegiance is ruled by expedience." And who, claimed Lehrer, didn't care where his rockets came down.

Even after the first launch of a V-2 prototype on October 3, 1942, when the new missile exceeded the speed of sound and rose to an altitude of sixty miles—the first man-made object ever to fly in space—Hitler was unimpressed. He viewed the V-2 as merely a larger and farther-reaching version of an artillery shell. He groused about its apparent high cost (although not about the slave labor that eventually enabled its production).

Hitler's view changed over time. He authorized mass production of the rocket. After the Allies began bombing Peenemünde, production shifted to the underground slave labor camps known as Dora-Mittelbau (the Mittelwerk), located in impenetrable gypsum tunnels under Mount Kohnstein at Thüringen near Nordhausen.

The Mittelwerk—which will be discussed in chapter ten on the Heinkel He 162 *Volksjäger* jet fighter—was, plainly put, a hellhole. Construction of the V-2 rocket factory claimed the lives of six thousand slave laborers. Building the rockets cost fourteen thousand more lives, or about four human beings for every V-2 produced. The slaves were pulled mainly from Buchenwald, a German concentration camp, and were mostly French, Polish, and Russian prisoners of war. Hitler specifically banned Jews from working on his wonder weapons for fear of sabotage. Von Braun made visits to the Mittelwerk, and in May 1944, he went to Buchenwald and asked the commandant for 1,800 skilled French prisoners of war.

When the V-2 became operational (on September 2, 1944), Allied boots were already on the ground in Europe and Paris had been liberated.

JET FIGHTERS

Unlike the crude V-1 and V-2 rockets, everything about the brilliant, fearsome, and flawed Messerschmitt Me 262 was different. With its sleek, sharklike fuselage, mottled ocre and olive green colors, and razor-thin swept wings from which huge turbojet engines hung, and with its hot, paraffin-tainted blast and high-pitched whine, the Me 262 was like nothing that had been in the skies before. When black-helmeted pilots began taking it into combat at snow-covered Rheine-Hopsten in 1944, the Me 262 was a cantankerous and unreliable mount so long as it was taxiing or flying in the airfield pattern. But once freed of the bonds of its airstrip, the Me 262 flew brilliantly and wielded awesome firepower. No other warplane could defeat it, its pilots were told.

It didn't have to happen that way. Ernst Heinkel's company was ahead in jet-plane development in the late 1930s, with Messerschmitt struggling to hold second place.

Heinkel was an arrogant figure who had little regard for the Nazi party (which he joined only under pressure), nor for other aircraft designers, whom he saw as not sufficiently willing to take risks in order to advance technology. Heinkel's grandest decision was taking into the fold Hans von Ohain, a twenty-four-year-old engineer, who met with Heinkel at the latter's villa estate overlooking the beach at Warnemünde and pulled out engineering drawings of something he called a turbojet device. No other figure in German industry would give von Ohain the time of day. When von Ohain admitted that there were weaknesses in the revolutionary engine—high fuel consumption was a problem and it wasn't clear the engine's combustion could be contained—Heinkel was smitten by the young engineer's candor. He and his company embraced von Ohain and set forth to build a new aircraft around the new powerplant. At the time no one in

Heinkel's company knew that a British pioneer, Frank Whittle, had secured a patent for his own version of a turbojet engine. The high-wing Heinkel He 178, using a 992-pound thrust HeS 3 engine drawn from a patent by Ohain, became the world's first aircraft to fly under turbojet power on August 27, 1939, piloted by Erich Warsitz (who'd also been the first to fly under liquid-fueled rocket power in a different Heinkel test ship). That was the month a U.S. scientist named Albert Einstein wrote to President Franklin D. Roosevelt warning of U.S. inaction in harnessing atomic fission.

On September 1, 1939, Hitler's tanks grinded into Poland—and invaded Luxembourg, the Netherlands, Belgium, and France soon afterward on May 10, 1940—so what had been a research project was now a war machine effort.

The Reich's aeronautical future now belonged to the twin-engine Heinkel He 280, which qualifies as the world's first jet fighter, although it appears never to have been fully armed. The He 280 took to the air with Fritz Schäfer in the cockpit at Rostock-Marienehe on September 22, 1940. That was an unpowered glide flight, but Schäfer completed the first flight of Germany's first definitive jet fighter at the same location, using the He 280V2 second proto-type, on March 30, 1941. Noteworthy in the appearance of the aircraft were its twin engines, twin fins and tricycle landing gear, all of which gave it a superficial resemblance to the B-25 Mitchell medium bomber. The aircraft used Heinkel-designed 1,852-pound thrust Junkers Jumo 004A turbojets in lieu of Heinkel's troubled He S8. If surviving recordings are to be believed, the engines throbbed in a louder version of what might be called purring, rather than emitting the thunderous roar of later turbojets. The first flight was smooth and unremarkable.

Schäfer reportedly told Ernst Heinkel that the He 280 was a little difficult to control in turns but that an experienced pilot should be able to fly it easily. He also reported the He 280 to be a little sluggish on landing but said that otherwise it handled well.

Designers credited the He 280 with a top speed of 508 miles per hour, making it in every respect a formidable competitor to the Messerschmitt Me 262.

The He 280 offered a compressed-air power ejection seat to enable the pilot to escape in an emergency, the world's first aircraft to be so equipped. It became the first to be used, ever, on January 13, 1942, when a pilot found himself in trouble due to icing conditions, jettisoned his canopy, and made the first-ever emergency ejection from an aircraft.

Unfortunately, Generalfeldmarschall (Air Marshal) Ernst Udet, whose opinion then held considerable sway, was unimpressed by the aircraft.

Colin Heaton and Anne-Marie Lewis, authors of *The Me 262 Stormbird*, speculate the following: "This is where history took a strange course. Had Udet been impressed enough to approve continued development, Heinkel would have received the extra funding they needed. This infusion of capital and political support would likely have led to the firm solving all of the problems they were having with the engines."

In tests, the He 280 proved itself speedier than the best German fighter, the Focke-Wulf Fw 190. During a demonstration, the He 280 completed four laps on the oval circuit course before the Fw 190 could complete three. The maximum weight displacement of the He 280 was 4,296 kilograms (9,470 pounds) compared with 7,130 kilograms (15,720 pounds) for the Me 262. The He 280 could have gone into production by late 1941 and maintained the air superiority, which the Fw 190 had been designed and built for. The initial teething experience with the He S8 engine would have plenty of time to be ironed out just as production of the fighter airframe had begun.

Udet and Air Inspector General Erhard Milch saw the He 280 as an aircraft that could be in frontline service as a stopgap in anticipation of the Me 262. Equipped with three 30mm cannons and capable of 512 mile-per-hour speeds, the He 280 would have provided a bridge between the Fw 190 and Me 262 and would have enabled the Luftwaffe to maintain superiority in Europe at a time when the Allies had no comparable aircraft. Heinkel, of course, had even grander aspirations. This is intriguing speculation, but it fails to go far enough. With a smaller footprint, greater ease of maintenance, and better reliability than the Me 262, the He 280 *could* have become operational by, one speculates, mid-1942. At that point, although the Royal Air Force was bombing Germany at night, the Allies did not yet have a full-fledged air campaign over the continent. The fledgling U.S. Eighth Air Force was still struggling merely to come into existence. The Americans were going to change everything with their own four-engine heavy bombers and with high-altitude precision daylight bombing of military and industrial targets. Yet as late as October 1943, they lost sixty bombers on one mission and had not yet fielded a true escort fighter, the P-51 Mustang. General Dwight D. Eisenhower was telling anyone who would listen that the Allied air campaign would have to succeed or plans for the invasion of Europe would have to be put on hold. If hundreds of He 280s had been in the field before the bombing campaign even began, before the first P-51 arrived or even before the first American bombers reached Berlin as late as March 1944, B-17s and B-24s would have been swept from the skies.

The He 280 would have reigned supreme. Battered by their losses, unable to command the air, the Allies would have needed to sue for a peace agreement that would allow Hitler to keep much of Western Europe, turn his guns to the east, and overwhelm the Soviet Union.

Or maybe not. From an engineering perspective, the He 280 was more complex and may have had less growth potential in its design. The Me 262 with good engines would have been better tailored for air defense.

Was the Heinkel effort deterred in part by Ernst Heinkel's misguided effort to develop an advanced four-engine bomber—something the Germans would never do successfully?

The failure of the German air arm to equip itself with long-range bombers goes hand in glove with the failure of the Heinkel He 177

Greif (Griffon), a towering symbol of unrealized possibilities. Rarely has an aircraft been so despised by the men who maintained and flew it. Rarely has an aircraft with so many technical problems gotten as far as the He 177.

The He 177 was a four-engine bomber that looked like a twin-engine bomber. It had "twinned engines" in each of two nacelles, making it a four-engine bomber—sort of. The concept relied on the Daimler Benz DB 606 twin engine, which took two 2,950-horsepower DB 601A-1/B-1 inverted V inline engines and placed them side by side, with the inner cylinders almost vertical, producing an inverted W. The engines were prone to overheating, and in-flight engine fires were common. Six of the original eight aircraft were lost, most due to engine fires, and many of the first thirty-five production aircraft (built mainly by Arado) also suffered the same fate.

"Why has this silly engine suddenly turned up, which is so idiotically welded together?" asked Hermann Göring. "They told me then, there would be two engines connected behind each other, and suddenly there appears this misbegotten monster of welded-together engines one cannot get at!" Göring, the Reich leader who was Ernst Heinkel's greatest adversary, wouldn't have liked the He 177 if it had come with an apple strudel.

The He 177 made it into service. As engineers kept redesigning the He 177, they introduced new versions of the bomber, which were then modified further in the field. Front-line armorers at Stalingrad, which was resupplied at great cost by a half-dozen He 177As used as transports, installed a 50mm BK-5 antitank gun under the nose. A separate effort to install a 75mm cannon produced new aerodynamic problems and was cancelled after five He 177A-3/R-5s received the guns.

None of the changes could overcome the inherent faults in the He 177, including a tendency to swerve sharply sideways on take-off. Troops called it the "Luftwaffe Lighter" (referring to a cigarette lighter) or the "Flying Tinderbox."

Until manufacture of all aircraft other than fighters was virtually halted in October 1944, Heinkel and Arado built about 1,100 He 177s, including 826 examples of the He 177A-5 model, which was much improved over earlier versions. The usefulness of the bomber did not improve. On one occasion, Göring watched fourteen aircraft taxi out for late-war attacks on London. Thirteen took off. Eight returned immediately with overheating engines, one diverted elsewhere, and four actually reached London, but one was shot down.

The He 280, that promising jet from the same builder as the He 177, never did become operational. Ultimately, the He 280 faced an insurmountable obstacle. Dour-faced, bespectacled, Nazi party member Ernst Heinkel had objected to a Hitler decision in 1933 to fire Jewish designers and staff, while tall, muscular, strong-jawed non-Nazi-party member Willy Messerschmitt, although mostly interested in aeronautics and technology, was always willing to show his unwavering support for the Führer. Ernst Heinkel never used slave labor. There is no indication Willy Messerschmitt, like von Braun, viewed using slave laborers as anything but the price of being permitted to pursue his advanced projects.

The idea of making the Me 262 a bomber had genuine consequences and possibly owes less to Hitler than to Messerschmitt. On September 7, 1943, granted a rare audience with the Führer, Messerschmitt expressed mixed feelings about the jet and repeated his longstanding request that top priority be accorded to his Me 209 propeller-driven fighter.

The Me 209 was close to Messerschmitt's heart because it was a derivative of the Bf 109, which Messerschmitt did design. The Bf 109 was the world's most manufactured fighter with about thirty-three thousand copies, but it is sometimes called the only product from Messerschmitt's drawing board that was truly successful. The Me 209, even though it had established a world air speed record of 469 miles per hour in its original configuration on April 26, 1939, was in its production form very fragile, longitudinally unstable, and riddled with its own panoply of technical problems.

During his conversation with Hitler, Messerschmitt, never hesitant to curry favor, touted the Me 209 vigorously and also suggested to the Führer that the Me 262 be modified to carry bombs. This was fully two months before the Insterburg demonstration and before the conversation in which the Führer famously asked if the jet aircraft could do exactly that. During their earlier meeting, Hitler had not yet received a detailed briefing about, or seen, the jet and, in fact, had only a little interest at most.

THE AMERICAN SIDE

While the Third Reich was securing its hold on occupied Western Europe and launching an offensive against the Soviet Union, the Americans were arriving in England with the fledgling beginning of what would become the mighty Eighth Air Force. They arri holding the firm belief that high-altitude daylight precision bomb of military and industrial targets would enable them to expand the aerial offensive and pave the way for an Allied invasion. Very likely, the nascent Me 262 was the last thing on their minds.

On January 19, 1942, seven U.S. airmen set up VIII Bomber Command at Daws Hill, England. They did not yet have troops or bombers, but they brought with them a body of knowledge about strategic bombing that didn't exist elsewhere. Within months, VIII Bomber Command became a component of the Eighth Air Force, which set up headquarters at High Wycombe. In the early spring of 1942, the first three heavy bombardment groups were activated. B-17 Flying Fortresses began to arrive at new bases being built for them on British soil but owned by the Americans. Brigadier General Ira C. Eaker famously told his British hosts: "We won't do much talking until we've done more fighting. After we've gone, we hope you'll be glad we came."

On May 5, 1942, Lt. Gen. Carl "Tooey" Spaatz assumed command of the Eighth Air Force. Eaker retained responsibility for VIII Bomber Command while Brig. Gen. Frank O. "Monk" Hunter ran the newly forming VIII Fighter Command, initially with American-crewed Spitfires and newly arrived P-47 Thunderbolts. At first, they were going to have plenty of trouble with Messerschmitt Bf 109s and Focke-Wulf

Fw 190s. We can only imagine the greater challenge had the Heinkel He 280 begun to enter squadron service to challenge them.

The U.S. bombing campaign over Europe began on a small scale, with both the brass and the bomber men pinning their prospects on a firm belief that the bomber would always get through to the target. Hardly anyone was doing enough thinking about fighter escort. Eaker was among those to whom the belief was almost religion: the bomber would always get through.

On August 17, 1942, eight B-17E Flying Fortresses attacked marshalling yards at Rouen-Sotteville in France. A sign on the flight line egged bomber crewmembers on by imploring "Ruin Rouen." The bombers ran into a few German fighters, dropped a few bombs, and didn't accomplish very much.

On September 6, 1942, Fortresses attacked an aircraft factory at Meaulte, France. Crews flew part of the mission without fighter escort, after the fighters and bombers failed to meet up on time. This time, the bomber did not always get through. Two B-17Es were lost.

Soon, B-17F Flying Fortresses and B-24 Liberators were venturing deeper into occupied Europe, escorted part way by P-47 Thunderbolts. But German fighter defenses were formidable, and a typical bomber crew faced heavy odds against completing its assigned twenty-five missions.

The Luftwaffe began making head-on attacks from ten degrees above the centerline flight path of each bomber, the position the Americans called twelve o'clock high. A frontal attack required nerves of steel and unparalleled skill on the part of a Luftwaffe pilot. Later in the war, maintaining skill levels would become the greatest challenge facing Adolf Hitler's air force. But if a Messerschmitt or Focke-Wulf pilot could ignore all the instincts that were shouting at him to peel off, and if he could stay on course for a closeup shot from the front, he had a strong chance of killing both of a bomber's pilots. Even if the pilots survived, a frontal attack could confuse and break up a bomber formation. The B-17E had no real defense against a head-on firing pass, while a B-17Fs carried two cheek guns that were ineffective until their position in the nose was changed.

On December 1, 1942, Eaker replaced Spaatz as commander of the Eighth Air Force and pinned on a second star. On a December 20, 1942, mission, six B-17s were lost attacking a target without fighter escort.

Consultations between the British and the Americans became frequent as both tried to carve out a joint policy for using heavy bombers against the Third Reich. For almost a year, Britain's Royal Air Force had been operating under an air ministry order directing RAF Bomber Command ". . . that the primary objective of your operations should be focused on the morale of the enemy civil population and in particular the industrial workers." This was the highly controversial policy of area bombing, or bombing that made no allowance for sparing civilians, and it was a striking contrast to the American doctrine of daylight precision bombing of military and industrial targets. Already, bomber crewmembers were caught up in a controversy that would remain with them forever: Were they carrying out a legitimate mission against an enemy's military under the law of war or were they (as the British were often all too ready to admit) engaged in terror bombing aimed at breaking the will of the German people?

This was one of many issues debated at the January 14 Casablanca Conference in French Morocco attended by U.S. President Franklin D. Roosevelt, Britain's Prime Minister Winston Churchill, and France's Gen. Charles de Gaulle. Large military staffs accompanied the leaders. Notably absent was the Soviet Union's Premier Josef Stalin, who was preoccupied with the fighting at Stalingrad. It was at this conference that the Allies issued a declaration demanding the unconditional surrender of the Axis powers. This would become a controversy all its own. Was it really necessary? Could the war have been ended some other way, perhaps with lesser loss of life?

General Henry H. "Hap" Arnold was most concerned with this thought. He was an administrator, a leader who delegated authority.

At Casablanca where he could have stood beside Air Chief Marshal "Arthur Bomber" Harris, Arnold chose instead to exert influence in the background but to allow Eaker (the most important advocate of precision bombing) to convene meetings and conduct briefings. The British and the Americans clearly had very different ideas about how to use four-engine airplanes to deposit bombs within the Third Reich. Eaker proved an excellent spokesman with his mix of modesty, knowledge, and persuasiveness.

It would be tempting to imagine Arnold's and Harris's lieutenants rolling up their sleeves, putting on their green shades, and squinting at reconnaissance photos taken by Allied camera planes, especially the nimble De Havilland Mosquito, which will reappear on these pages as the first victim of the Me 262. In fact, there is no evidence that these high-level meetings included lower level intelligence-sharing sessions. The Americans and British knew their plan to push bomber formations deeper into the Reich would be met by formations of flak and fighters that were plentiful, well equipped, and well manned. But even while searching for a formula to combat the Luftwaffe's propeller-driven fighter force, did Arnold and Harris know that a second generation of jet fighters was being developed? Did they realize how fortunate they were that the Germans had not fielded the He 280 and that the Me 262 was taking longer than it should have? We do not know. The top brass responsible for paving the way for an Allied invasion of Europe appears to have paid little attention to German, British, or American development of jet aircraft.

Following the Casablanca conference, on January 21, 1943, the British area bombing directive was replaced by the Casablanca directive, which was approved by the combined chiefs of staff and was a key part of the British-American combined bomber offensive (CBO). The critical language in the Casablanca edict established the CBO's prime objective as " . . . the progressive destruction and dislocation of the German military, industrial, and economic systems and the undermining of the morale of the German people to a point where their capacity for armed resistance is fatally weakened.

Every opportunity to be taken to attack Germany by day to destroy objectives that are unsuitable for night attack, to sustain continuous pressure on German morale, to impose heavy losses on German day fighter force, and to [divert] German fighter strength away from the Russian and Mediterranean theatres of war." The short version: the British would conduct area bombing at night, the Americans precision bombing by day.

And the air arm of the Third Reich would do its very best to knock them out of the sky.

THE ME 262'S BACKGROUND

The revolutionary design emerged from a 1938 Reichsluftfahrt-ministerium (Reich Air Ministry, the RLM) request for an aircraft to use two turbojet engines then being developed by the engine maker BMW, which was exploring the same technology that belatedly interested the Americans and the British. Optimists imagined that the BMW engine would offer 1,320 pounds of thrust and would be ready to be joined to an airframe by December 1939.

These, it must be remembered, were aviation people, not military people. Mostly anonymously, the men at RLM headquarters on Frederichstrasse in Berlin were civilians. While they were not immune to sucking up to Hitler or Göring, they did not come from military careers. It would have been unthinkable for a true military man such as Generalleutnant (Maj. Gen.) Adolf "Dolfo" Galland to perceive his role in the Luftwaffe as a stepping stone to a cushy job in the aviation industry. Hitler enforced an ironclad rule against military men going to work in the air industry or air ministry. In that era, unlike today, the United States had a similar proscription, but it was exerted by peer pressure, not by any written rule. In 1944, a general in either German or American forces would have deemed it beneath himself to accept employment in the civilian aviation world. Erhard Milch, the State Secretary for Aviation, was a military man, but after 1943, the RLM came under Albert Speer. Milch and his colleagues—mostly civilians—were mostly responsible for Me 262 development, and it is easy to wonder whether it might have happened more quickly had Milch not been a bitter enemy of Willy Messerschmitt.

The Messerschmitt team, initially headed by Woldenmar Voigt, envisioned an all-metal, low-winged monoplane with retractable landing gear and two turbojet engines mounted in the wing roots. Messerschmitt built a mockup in 1940. By then, of course, Germany was embroiled in war. It had at its disposal prospects for a truly revolutionary warfare, which, if it were developed on a timely basis, would almost certainly guarantee victory.

The Me 262 was a swept-wing design with the degree of sweep being modest at 18.5. This configuration addressed a range of aerodynamic considerations and offered the best prospect for a higher speed than conventional aircraft.

Perhaps the lack of initial enthusiasm was linked to the dismal performance of early jet engines. The BMW engine failed to materialize as planned. Junkers began developing the Jumo 004 turbojet, created by Anselm Franz. During its first run-ups in November 1940, the Jumo, too, performed poorly.

Test pilots Karl Baur and Fritz Wendel were on hand at the Messerschmitt facility at Augsberg, but no urgency was attached to the flight development of the Me 262. Of far greater concern to Messerschmitt were improvements to the Bf 109 and Bf 110 propeller-driven fighters (although Galland would soon recommend discontinuing production of both). The BMW engines initially meant for the new aircraft prototype arrived from Spandau in mid-November 1941, just in time for Wendel to attempt to fly the aircraft under both jet and prop power: he experienced a double flameout and cannot be said to have completed a jet flight.

Fortunately, an alternative to the touchy BMWs was available. Always under consideration in any event was the Junkers Jumo 004, developed by Dr. Anselm Franz's engineering team.

In their adherence to axial compressors, German engine designers showed much courage and foresight. This type of compressor was difficult to construct and balance, and was susceptible to vibration and could be damaged far more easily than the tough centrifugal type of compressor. It became apparent that the acceleration rates, fuel efficiency, power output, and drag coefficients of axial-flow turbojets far exceeded the figures attained by the tougher and somewhat more reliable centrifugal types.

By August 1941, the Jumo 004 was giving 1,323 pounds of static thrust and many of its teething problems were being cured. Technicians installed Jumo 004s on the Me 262 V3, and this aircraft, bereft of piston engine but still with tail-wheel gear, made its first flight on July 18, 1941, in Wendel's experienced hands. It looked correct in every way except for the absence of the finalized landing gear design; it flew beautifully, and henceforth the fortunes of the Me 262 were to rise at the expense of its nearest rival, the He 280. To the end, many German air experts felt certain a combat-ready He 280 was capable of being fielded earlier. Still, the project was eventually canceled in March 1943.

Service test pilots of the Erprobungsstelle (testing center) at Rechlin were enthusiastic about the Me 262 from the beginning. It was largely because of the urging of these pilots that Messerschmitt received contracts to produce prototypes for weapons and engines tests. The experienced Maj. Wolfgang Späte had already reported his findings when Galland flew the Me 262 V4 on May 22, 1943, and issued his celebrated written recommendation that the piston-engined Messerschmitt Me 209 A be cancelled and that the Focke-Wulf Fw 190 and Me 262 become the only fighters being produced in the Reich. (The Bf 109 does not appear in Galland's memorandum to Göring, but Galland clearly intended that the Bf 109 be discontinued).

Despite cancellation of the He 280, it was curiously true in both the United States and Germany that industry was designing, building, and testing a far wider variety of aircraft than would ever contribute to new knowledge, find any purpose, or fight any battles. The United States invested heavily in three pusher-engined, propeller-driven fighters, the XP-54, XP-55, and XP-56, which never were able to match the performance of prewar fighters and did little to advance technology. As we shall see, the Reich had a variety of fighter designs on the drawing boards long after Germany should have searched harder for priority and focus. Experimenting with weird and wonderful designs of little practical value was a luxury the Americans could afford and the Germans could not.

Speer seemed to have this on his mind in a famous quote late in the war, referring to the Reich's diversity of wonder weapons:

> We possessed a remote-control flying bomb, a rocket plane that was even faster than the jet plane [this, a reference to the Messerschmitt Me 163 *Komet*], a rocket missile that homed on an enemy plane by tracking the heat rays from its motors, and a torpedo that reacted to sound and could thus pursue and hit a ship fleeing in a zigzag course. Development of a ground-to-air missile had been completed. The designer Lippisch had jet planes on the drawing board that were far in advance of anything so far known. *We were literally suffering from an excess of projects in development* [emphasis added]. Had we concentrated on only a few types we would surely have completed some of them sooner.

Speer was on record as favoring concentration on the V-2 rocket.

Galland's recommendation was discussed at a conference in Berlin on May 25, 1943, but was not followed. Against its own best interest, Nazi Germany continued to manufacture too many aircraft of too many kinds until the final day of the war. That included the Bf 109. It had been a breakthrough when it first appeared in 1936 and had been the most advanced warplane in the Spanish Civil War, but by 1944 the Bf 109 was a design that couldn't be improved upon any further. The Berlin conference achieved little in terms of focusing the Reich's aircraft production priorities, but it did yield an all-important contract for one hundred Me 262s.

There was a good-news, bad-news story for the Reich's air defenses on August 17, 1943. The good news for Hitler's side was that the day marked a massacre of American bomber crews—losses the Eighth Air Force would not have been able to sustain. The bad news was that the bombing inflicted a setback on the Me 262 program.

For bomber crews, Schweinfurt-Regensburg—on the anniversary of the first, puny bombing mission dispatched by the Eighth Air Force—was a horror. Two hundred thirty bombers launched against Schweinfurt and another 146 against aircraft factories in Regensburg. Sixty were lost before returning to base, and another eighty-seven had to be scrapped due to irreparable damage.

Over Regensburg, supremely experienced German pilots attacked, slashed through the bomber formations from the front, and shot down twenty-four Flying Fortresses. Many of the attacks came from twelve o'clock high. German gun camera film portrays the majesty of a Flying Fortress under attack, but it also depicts B-17s catching fire, breaking up, sometimes tumbling end over end, the crewmembers inside often pinned by gravity forces and sometimes burned by flash fires. In addition to the shootdowns, the Luftwaffe defenders damaged fifty more bombers during the first stage of the day's fight over Regensburg. At this stage of the war, Germany had plenty of battle-seasoned pilots, the Americans were still feeling their way, and the battle was one-sided. Despite all the years the Americans had spent forging their daylight precision-bombing doctrine, the Germans were winning a mighty battle high in the freezing sky and seemed closer to winning the campaign. Some Luftwaffe pilots talked of halting the American bomber offensive in its tracks. Having begun their air campaign so recently with such spirit and optimism, the Americans were being defeated.

Unknown to the Americans, the Regensburg portion of the air attack destroyed most of the manufacturing jigs for the Me 262. Anything that delayed the German jets was a huge plus for the Allies. The results at Regensburg were better than just anything: the Reich's air industry was forced to disperse Me 262 production into small, crude factories hidden in deep forests. This imposed a requirement to transport assembled components for final assembly amid chaos in the German transportation network, and this hurdle significantly delayed completion of the first jets.

In the second phase of Schweinfurt-Regensburg, the day's fighting, 183 Flying Fortresses attacked Schweinfurt's ball-bearing plants. Ball-bearing factories were vulnerable and losing them would cramp the Reich's war effort. But the execution was flawed. Again, Messerschmitts and Focke-Wulfs ripped into the bomber formations. The Luftwaffe extracted a horrendous toll—thirty-six Flying Fortresses shot down, including two that ditched in the frigid North Sea. Total B-17 losses at Schweinfurt-Regensburg were 60 aircraft lost, 4 damaged beyond repair, and 168 damaged.

U.S. planners rated Schweinfurt-Regensburg a disaster and as a warning that the entire plan for bombing Germany might be a prescription for failure. This first of two disastrous missions to Schweinfurt removed any doubt that bombers needed help protecting themselves and that some way would have to be found to extend fighter cover all the way to the target.

To the great satisfaction of everyone of high rank in the Third Reich, the Americans now took their next step in the deadly confrontation unfolding in the high blue over occupied Europe.

They backed off.

FOUR

TWIN-ENGINE FIGHTERS

The American fighter pilot spotted two shapes cutting diagonally across a road just slightly above and in front of him. They were blemishes in motion.

Twelve o'clock high, he thought.

He rechecked his armament switches, rammed his throttles to full power, and went down, low, as low as he dared, hugging treetops. The afternoon shadow of his P-38 Lightning raced across French hedgerows and fields, the pilot trying now to identify the other two aircraft, wanting them to be Focke-Wulf Fw 190s falling so nicely into the crosshairs of his nose-mounted 20mm cannon and four .50-caliber machine guns.

Captain Robin Olds applied left rudder, slid his pipper across the nearest plane's left wing, and, in an instant of epiphany, saw the Iron Cross painted on the rear fuselage. Until that instant, he hadn't been certain the planes were German.

Olds shot down one Fw 190 in a few seconds, followed the second into a violent left break, fired, and watched the pilot bail out. It was August 14, 1944, and Olds had just used his heavy, robust, fast P-38 to rack up the first two of his sixteen air-to-air combat victories.

"I loved the P-38, but I got those kills in spite of the airplane, not because of it," Olds said. "There were a lot of advantages to having two engines. But the fact is, the P-38 Lightning was too much airplane for a new kid, and a full-time job for even a mature fighter pilot. Our enemies had difficulty defeating the P-38, but, as much as we gloried in it, we were defeating ourselves with this airplane."

It was, Olds hastened to add, "the most beautiful plane of our generation." And it fought well in the Pacific and the Mediterranean. So what happened in northern Europe, and how did things go so wrong?

LIGHTNING LESSONS

The P-47 Thunderbolt was proving effective against the German air arm, and the P-51 Mustang would become decisive. However, during the critical late months of 1943—the period when the Eighth Air Force suffered heavy losses and both the air campaign and the future invasion of Europe appeared in doubt—the P-38 was the bulwark. Although its effectiveness as an escort was a bit of a myth, the P-38 was beloved by bomber crews perhaps because they, too, like fighter pilots, were simply so infatuated with its looks and style. The fact that it had two engines was important. Exactly as the designers of the Messerschmitt Me 262 were in the process of demonstrating, two engines meant greater reliability. If you lost one engine, you had another to keep you aloft. By the end of the twentieth century, nearly every fighter in the world would have two engines.

One advocate for twin-engine powerplants was none other than Adolf Hitler. He spoke favorably of the Messerschmitt Me 410 *Hornisse* (Hornet) twin-engine fighter developed from the Bf 110. He had high hopes for the twin-engine Dornier Do 335 pusher-tractor. In a military staff meeting, the Führer expressed the need for "a fast aircraft with an absolutely superior speed and great security, so they can land even when one engine fails, in order to fight the

Mosquito attacks that are looming more and more frequent." Hitler also said, "A twin-engine aircraft is better than a single-engine aircraft—there's no doubt."

Just as the Heinkel He 280 was a twin-engine fighter, from its very inception the Me 262 was not intended to have anything but twin engines. On the Me 262, the matched powerplants would be slung in pods beneath a wing with a slight sweepback of 18.5 degrees. The original plan was to use turbojet engines from BMW that would confer 1,323 pounds (600 kilograms) of thrust. The subsequent Junkers Jumo 004 would offer up to 2,000 pounds thrust. The Me 262 would never be as complex to operate as the P-38, but as a comparative heavyweight at 14,272 pounds (6,473 kilograms), it would have more in common with the P-38 than with the Americans' single-engine warplanes. At the juncture when the P-38 was crucial in the European war, the Me 262 was still being brought up to operational standard.

MUCH-LOVED LIGHTNING

A survey of stateside training bases in 1941 showed that 87 percent of prospective pilots requested to be assigned to the big, sleek, twin-engine, twin-boom Lockheed P-38 Lightning. "We were in awe of the P-38," said future air ace Jack Ilfrey. "It looked like a beautiful monster." "If you were a boy in America, you wanted to fly it," said another future ace, Lt. Gen. Winton "Bones" Marshall. "If you played with Dinky metal toys and balsa wood airplane models, you wanted to fly it."

The P-38 captured the imagination of young Americans on the eve of Pearl Harbor in a way that other fighters could not. Eighth Air Force commander Lt. Gen. James H. "Jimmy" Doolittle called the P-38 "the sweetest-flying plane in the sky."

With tricycle gear, twin booms, and a centerline fuselage pod brimming with guns, the P-38 was pulled through the air by two 1,600-horsepower Allison V-1710-111/113 liquid-cooled piston engines driving three-bladed, nine-foot Curtiss Electric propellers.

Although a fully loaded P-38 weighed more than ten U.S. tons, or nearly twice as much as a single-engine P-51 Mustang, a skilled pilot could fling the P-38 around like a lightweight. The problem was that while American pilots were generally well trained, they weren't well trained for a complex fighter with more than one engine.

Struggling to keep the air campaign over Europe alive in the face of unspeakable bomber losses, the Army Air Forces rushed two P-38 combat groups to England. The 55th Fighter Group became the first to conduct operations on October 15, 1943. On November 6, the Lightning men mixed it up with Bf 109s and Fw 190s and racked up their first aerial victories. "We were arrayed against the Luftwaffe and they were facing us head-on," one of the pilots said, "and we were not winning."

The P-38 and P-47 Thunderbolt performed usefully, but not use-fully enough. The P-38's Allison engine had a tendency to blow up, and its GE turbo-supercharger could get stuck in overboosted or underboosted mode. This occurred mainly when the P-38 was flown in the freezing cold above thirty thousand feet, which was the stan-dard situation in the European air war (the P-38 was more successful in the Pacific; the weather was warmer and Japanese planes did not operate at such high altitudes). Another difficulty was that early P-38 versions had only one generator. Losing the associated engine meant that all the pilot had available for power was the battery. Historian Roger Freeman described how bravery plus the P-38 was not enough on the November 13, 1943, mission to Bremen:

> . . . An unlucky day for the 55th. In typical English November weather, damp and overcast, forty-eight P-38s set out to escort bombers on the target leg of a mission to Bremen; one turned back before the enemy coast was crossed and two more aborted later. At 26,000 feet over Germany, pilots shivered in bitterly cold cockpits, flying conditions were unusually bad, and the probability of mechanical troubles at that temperature did not help. Again outnumbered, the 55th was heavily engaged near

the target as it strove to defend the bombers, for which it paid dearly. Seven P-38s fell, five to enemy fighters and the others to unknown causes.

Two weeks later another sixteen Lightnings limped home with battle damage. Things did get better, but the P-38 Lightning had to claw its way toward reaping successes that had been expected to come easier and earlier. Lightning pilot 2nd Lt. Jim Kunkle of the 370th Fighter Group remembered that the Lightning was big, but not roomy. "The cockpit was a little tight," Kunkle said. "I would find my head rubbing up against the top of the canopy. You had fairly long travel on the rudder pedals, but you got used to it. The critical problem with us was we didn't have much heat in the cockpit. On high-altitude missions, it was very cold. And we didn't have the engine in front of us to help keep us warm. Bomber guys had those heated blue union suits that they wore, but we tried heated clothing and it didn't work for us."

It was actually worse than that. Rather than being merely uncomfortable, Lightning pilots were sometimes in near agony. Wrote Freeman: "Their hands and feet became numb with cold and in some instances frost-bitten; not infrequently a pilot was so weakened by conditions that he had to be assisted out of the cockpit upon return." The only source of heat in the cockpit was warm air ducted from the engines, and it was little help. The fiery commanding general of VIII Fighter Command wondered, as so many others did, why the P-38 wasn't producing the results everyone wanted and what to do about it.

Asked to provide a written report, 20th Fighter Group commander Col. Harold J. Rau put pen to paper (and had the report typed up) only with reluctance and only because he was ordered to. He wrote: "After flying the P-38 for a little over one hundred hours on combat missions it is my belief that the airplane, as it stands now, is too complicated for the 'average' pilot. I want to put strong emphasis on the word 'average,' taking full consideration just how little combat training our pilots have before going on as operational status."

Rau wrote that he was being asked to put kids fresh from flight school into P-38 cockpits and it wasn't working. He asked his boss to imagine a pilot fresh out of flying school with about a total of twenty-five hours in a P-38, starting out on a combat mission. Rau's young pilot was, according to him, on "auto lean and running on external tanks. His gun heater is off to relieve the load on his generator, which frequently gives out (under sustained heavy load). His sight is off to save burning out the bulb. His combat switch may or may not be on." So, flying along in this condition, wrote Rau, the kid suddenly gets bounced by Germany fighters. Now, Rau wrote, he wonders what to do.

"He must turn, he must increase power and get rid of those external tanks and get on his main [fuel tank]," Rau wrote. "So, he reaches down and turns two stiff, difficult gas switches (valves) to main, turns on his drop tank switches, presses his release button, puts the mixture to auto rich (two separate and clumsy operations), increases his RPM, increases his manifold pressure, turns on his gun heater switch (which he must feel for and cannot possibly see), turns on his combat switch and he is ready to fight." To generations to come in the future, this would be called multitasking, and it was not what you wanted to be doing when Luftwaffe fighters were pouring down on you.

"At this point, he has probably been shot down," Rau wrote, "or he has done one of several things wrong. Most common error is to push the throttles wide open before increasing RPM. This causes detonation and subsequent engine failure. Or, he forgets to switch back to auto rich, and gets excessive cylinder head temperature with subsequent engine failure."

Another P-38 pilot described the multitasking challenge this way: "When you reduce power, you must pull back the throttle (manifold pressure) first, then the prop RPM, and then the mixture. To increase power you must first put the mixture rich, then increase prop rpm, then increase manifold pressure. If you don't follow this order, you can ruin the engine." This is a lot to think about when under attack!

Rau added that in his own limited experience, his P-38 group had lost at least four pilots, who, when bounced, took no evasive action.

"The logical assumption is that they were so busy in the cockpit trying to get organized that they were shot down before they could get
going," Rau wrote.

Rau described part of the solution: "It is standard procedure for
the group leader to call, five minutes before [rendezvous with the
bombers being escorted] and tell all pilots to 'prepare for trouble.'
This is the signal for everyone to get into auto rich, turn drop tank
switches on, gun heaters on, combat and sight switches on, and to
increase RPM and manifold pressure to maximum cruise. This procedure, however, will not help the pilot who is bounced on the way
in and who is trying to conserve his gasoline and equipment for the
escort job ahead."

Pointing to advisory visits to his fighter group by representatives
from plane maker Lockheed and engine maker Allison, Rau wrote
that among their suggestions, the most-needed was a unit power
control, incorporating an automatic manifold pressure regulator
(which would control power), RPM, and mixture by use of a single
lever. He may not have known that in the P-51 Mustang a pilot could
perform all of these functions with one hand—something that never
became possible in the P-38, even in later versions.

Rau also pointed to the need "to simplify the gas switching system in this airplane. The switches [valve selector handles] are all in
awkward positions and extremely hard to turn. The toggle switches
for outboard tanks are almost impossible to operate with gloves on."
That last issue was no small thing. P-38 pilots were always so cold
that a pilot without gloves was all but dead anyway.

Critics and champions of the P-38 alike often failed to remark on
the obvious—that it was a multiengine aircraft while most fighters
were single-engine.

Long after the war, former 1st Lt. Arthur W. Heiden, in an out-
burst that made Rau seem tame by comparison, wrote: "The quality of multi-engine training during World War II bordered on the
ridiculous. I am convinced that with training methods now in use
we could take most of civilian private pilots who might be about to

fly the Aztec or Cessna 310, and in ten hours, have a more confident pilot than the ones who flew off to war in the P-38. A P-38 pilot usually got his training in two ways. The first way, of course, was twin-engine advanced training in Curtiss AT-9s, which had the unhappy feature of having propellers you couldn't feather. After sixty hours of this, the student received ten hours of AT-6 gunnery, although he might get his gunnery training in the AT-9, since AT-6s were in short supply."

Frank E. Birtciel, who flew seventy-two combat missions in the P-38 and forty-nine in the P-51 Mustang, said that near the end of training in the AT-9, the usual practice was to give a student pilot a piggyback ride in a P-38 with a second seat, and then check him out in the RP-322, a version of the same fighter with simpler systems. Birtciel said that procedures were so lax that a training instructor simply appeared amid a group of students one day and asked, "Anyone want to fly a '38?" Britciel raised his hand, expecting to be a back-seater, and found a fully operational, single-seat P-38—not an RP-322—waiting for him on the ramp. "The crew chief told me how to start it up, and I took off and flew it without any instruction," said Birtciel.

Edward Giller joined the 55th Fighter Group in time to fly the P-38 in combat and to hear rumors that the Germans were developing a new generation of warplanes with a new kind of engine. "We didn't think much of it at first," said Giller. He was busy being annoyed by other aspects of the P-38, including its need for constant attention and the fact that it was the only Allied fighter that emitted two contrails—a quick way for the foe to identify the type of aircraft approaching and to plan accordingly.

Giller felt the P-38 needed to be more nimble: "If you got on a German fighter's tail, he would do a split S, meaning he would flip upside-down and then go straight down at four hundred miles per hour or faster. We couldn't do that in the P-38." Giller piloted a series of planes named *Millie G.*, after his wife, Mildred, and practiced his skills to anticipate what German fighters would do before they did it. He did not want to be caught unawares in his P-38.

Every pilot interviewed for this book agreed that it was difficult to learn to fly the P-38 and easier to fly the P-51 Mustang. Even the most ardent supporter of the P-38—and it inspired support like no other war machine—knew that the Lightning was neither numerous enough nor capable enough to turn the tide.

So what of the closest German equivalent to the P-38, the comparatively lackluster Messerschmitt Bf 110?

The ability of the Bf 110 to haul heavy metal into the battle space was nothing to scoff at. Air-to-air missiles were a relatively new concept, and the Germans had worked on them earlier and more than anyone else. Combining missiles with the Bf 110 initially produced a formidable tool for the defense of the Reich.

The first air-to-air rocket projectiles carried into battle by Bf 110s were Werfer-Granate Gr. 21s, which required launch tubes that added to aerodynamic drag and were awkward to use. The Luftwaffe replaced these with the better-known R4M air-to-air rocket projectile. With the R4M, the Bf 110 lived up to its name as a destroyer. It could approach a combat box of American bombers and fire rockets without drawing in range of gunners.

Another Bf 110 weapon was Schräge Musik (Jazz Music)—the name given to installations of upward-firing autocannons mounted in night fighters by the Luftwaffe. Other Reich warplanes, including the Junkers Ju 88, also used upward firing guns, but the Bf 110G-4 may have been the most numerous. In the fall of 1943, when it was unclear whether the bombing campaign would be able to continue or whether an Allied invasion of Europe would be possible, Schräge Musik–equipped Bf 110s were wreaking havoc with Royal Air Force bombers in Germany's nocturnal skies. The upward-firing guns were responsible for dozens of air-to-air kills, including many Avro Lancaster four-engine heavy bombers, but their success was short-lived. Sighting the guns using mirrors was a cumbersome process, and bringing the guns into firing position exposed the Bf 110 to fire from the bombers' gunners. Whatever its merits, Schräge Musik demonstrated that imitation is the sincerest form of flattery: like many German ideas, the concept was copied and tested—with little success—on an American Lockheed P-80A Shooting Star jet fighter in the postwar era (see chapter 12).

The Bf 110 wasn't especially maneuverable and wasn't ever likely to prevail in a close-quarters dogfight. Once escort fighters began to accompany bombers into the Reich, the Luftwaffe wisely withdrew the Bf 110 from daylight operations. More than one Allied pilot remarked that a Bf 110 in daylight was "meat on the table" for his gunsight and guns.

As the fighting wore on, the Bf 110 was ever more likely to face opposition it couldn't contend with. Giller said he was piloting a P-38 on February 25, 1944, when he was credited with shooting down a twin-engine, propeller-driven German fighter—his recollection and the record are unclear whether it was a Bf 110 or a Me 410—"but it didn't amount to much," Giller said. "It was an airplane that I stumbled onto with my flight. Since I was the flight leader, I got there first. I just came up on him from behind and started shooting and shot him down," he added.

Useless in daylight after the early part of its era, the Bf 110 was more effective during the hours of darkness. It was beautifully configured to carry an aerial search radar unit and a radar operation, which it did to good effect during nocturnal fighting. Major Heinz-Wolfgang Schnaufer, the Reich's successful night fighter pilot, flew the Bf 110 and claimed 121 aerial victories.

Another pilot with experience in twin-engine, propeller-driven fighters was Hans Guido Mutke, an imposing, six-foot-two looming presence of a man. If fighter pilots were supposed to be loud and crude, Mutke did not fit the bill. He was something of an intellectual who was always brimming with ideas and was intrigued by the Reich's scientific advances. Before flying jets, Mutke flew combat missions in the Dornier Do 217, which he did not like, and the Bf 110, which he did, although he readily admitted that neither could hold its own against a P-38.

Mutke's experiences were similar to those of former Hitler Youth member Hans Busch. Both logged extensive combat hours in twin-engine fighters. Both bailed out of an aircraft once without significant injury—Mutke, from a Bf 110 at night in the middle of a snowstorm. Both also survived serious crashes—Mutke in a Dornier Do 217 after hundreds of night-intercept missions in the Bf 110 and Do 217. Both expressed agreement that their twin-engine Messerschmitts were in a far more sluggish category than the more powerful, more nimble P-38. Both would eventually strap themselves into the cockpit of the Me 262 jet. Neither was an ace and neither held high rank, but both fought for the Reich from early in the war until its final days.

The advantage of having two engines and the capabilities of the Bf 110 inspired Messerschmitt to develop the improved Me 210. But while it looked like a winner, the Me 210 was plagued with poor flight characteristics and technical glitches. After extensive redesign, it morphed into the Messerschmitt Me 410 *Hornisse* (Hornet), which came late to the war, joining the Defense of the Reich around the beginning of 1944. The Me 410, too, carried both guns and rocket projectiles. On April 11, 1944, Me 410s achieved a spectacular success, shooting down ten B-17 Flying Fortresses while sustaining no losses. It was a fluke. Although Hitler personally expressed his admiration for the Me 410, it was an easy target for P-38, P-47, and P-51 pilots.

"There were reports available to us about what was going on with the Germans in aviation," said American ace Giller. "They analyzed intelligence data at Wright Field and we had a steady flow of feedback. We also received a monthly publication that told us about technical developments." Giller was referring to the pictorial *Impact* magazine, published between April 1943 and December 1945 and classified confidential. It came to troops with a warning from Army Air Forces boss Gen. Henry H. "Hap" Arnold: "*Impact* is highly classified. It should be handled with due regard for its classification, yet it is desired that this information about our operations be disseminated to those of our forces to whom it may be of value."

"We had very good intelligence on the German fighters," said American ace Capt. Robin Olds, who flew numerous combat missions in the P-38 and P-51 (and many more in Vietnam in the F-4 Phantom II, another fighter with the advantage of two engines). "We were briefed on their capabilities and we felt knew how to fight them." That was particularly true of the entire range of German twin-prop fighters—the Do 17, Do 217, Ju 88, Ju 388, Bf 110, Me 210, and Me 410—because examples of nearly all were captured intact in an early stage of fighting. By mid-1944, found to be too vulnerable to American fighters, nearly all Me 410s were withdrawn from operational service.

While the Americans struggled to make the P-38, P-47, and P-51 ready and able to wage war high over Europe—taking a breather after the disastrous bombing missions in August and October 1943 and still trying to sort out how to make their air campaign work—the Germans were missing opportunities to bring about a revolution in air combat.

Testing of the jet Me 262 continued. Flight testing of the Me 262 dragged out more than a year and a half. The notorious reliability problems of the early jet engines were so severe that some had to be replaced after a single flight. A quantum leap in technology was coming, but it did not arrive until the beginning of combat operations in April 1944. Long before that, many P-38 Lightning pilots learned that their planes were going to be replaced. Even though the P-38 faced challenges in the freezing skies of northern Europe, pilots such as Olds were not initially pleased that they were getting a new fighter called the P-51 Mustang. Inspiration died hard.

At the end of 1943 and the start of 1944, with the U.S. daylight bombing campaign still moving in fits and starts, the first P-51 Mustangs were in service, not with one of the experienced fighter groups such as the 4th or the 56th but with the 354th Fighter Group. Its airmen never experienced any other fighter once they reached England.

MUSTANG MEN

Arrival of Mustangs in Britain altered every aspect of the Americans' aerial campaign against Hitler's "Festung Europa," or Fortress Europe. Whatever Lightning or Jug pilots might have said then, or might say today with a half-century of hindsight, the Mustang's combination of speed and maneuverability was superior to other U. S. fighters, and it had the legs to go deep into enemy territory. A P-51B could carry four hundred gallons of fuel, almost as much as the bigger P-47 Thunderbolt, but the Mustang got 3.3 miles per gallon while the P-47 (and P-38 Lightning) got less than 1.8. Its lower rate of fuel consumption gave the P-51 a combat radius of more than seven hundred miles, enough to reach any target the bombers could. Additionally, unlike the P-38 and P-47, the P-51B's performance was superior to all German fighters. The P-51 was thirty to seventy miles per hour faster than any German piston engine fighter and had better acceleration, while its maneuverability and climb rate matched or exceeded anything the Luftwaffe could offer.

The 55th Fighter Group was the first to get the new P-51D, trading in its old P-38s for the new bubble canopy fighters. The change from the torque-less twin-engine P-38 to the single-engine P-51 caused some initial problems, and the lack of directional stability (caused by the presence of a full fuselage tank) took some getting used to. However, once the pilots became fully adjusted to their new rides, they found that the P-51D gave them an edge in both speed and maneuverability over all Luftwaffe piston-engine fighters at altitudes above twenty thousand feet. Luftwaffe pilots considered the Mustang to be rather vulnerable to cannon fire, particularly the liquid-cooled Merlin engine, which could be put out of action with a single hit. The Mustang was the only Allied fighter with enough range to accompany bombers on their "shuttle" missions, in which landings were made in Russia after deep-penetration targets had been attacked from bases in England. The Mustangs also participated in low-altitude strikes on Luftwaffe airfields, a rather dangerous undertaking as these fields were very heavily defended by flak. Heavy losses were

suffered by American airmen in these raids due to Mustang's comparatively poor ability to withstand battle damage.

The 20th Fighter Group's official history tells us that the P-38
"was not equal to the extreme cold and moisture conditions that
prevailed at operating altitudes [of] 20,000–30000 feet [over]
northern Europe."

Warren M. Bodie, author of *The Lockheed P-38 Lightning* wrote
that the P-38 should have been converted from Allison to Merlin
power, exactly as was done with the P-51. "Neither P-38 pilots,
mechanics, facilities or logistics were prepared to operate efficiently
in one of the bitterest European winters on record [1943–1944],"
Bodie wrote. "No other Allison-powered aircraft ever operated at
altitudes of more than twenty thousand feet over the Continent for
even a half hour." Still, Bodie was a staunch advocate of the P-38, but
in a 1991 interview he acknowledged that it achieved mixed results
in air-to-air battle with the Luftwaffe in northern Europe.

The P-38 Lightning inspired young men, fought a great war, and
established its place as one of the greats of all time. In the European
Theater of Operations, it was miscast, misused, and severely chal-
lenged. Only one fighter group in northern Europe, the 474th, flew
the Lightning from arrival in Europe until war's end on May 8, 1945.
It remained, as always, the mount of preference for great men who
loved this aircraft like no other. Twin-engine fighters drew mixed
reactions from both sides, and except for the Lightning, none was
ever truly loved by the men who flew and maintained it. Many
German pilots in Bf 110s and Me 410s wondered if they would be
stuck in the cockpits of their inadequately performing twins until
the war was resolved.

FIVE

WONDER WEAPONS, PART II

After the unsuccessful Schweinfurt-Regensburg raid of August 17, 1943, which resulted in 60 aircraft lost, 4 damaged beyond repair, and 168 put out of commission, the Americans paused, pondered, and debated how to build the daylight bombing offensive that would have to succeed later that year if the Allies were going to invade occupied Europe in 1944. On both sides of the war, aircraft engineers and builders worked on new ideas in order to give themselves an advantage, but many of these ideas never became reality.

Today, it's easy to believe that the United States might have benefited from putting newer aircraft into production. Shifting P-47 Thunderbolt production lines to build the P-72—an experimental heavy fighter—might have provided the Eighth Air Force a much needed escort fighter sooner than it received one. Or the United States could have stopped manufacturing P-38s, P-39s, P-40s, and concentrated its production line on the P-51 Mustang and, subsequently, the P-80 jet fighter. It didn't happen that way. Instead of attempting to field small numbers of the most advanced weapon systems, the United States made a subconscious choice to put into the fray vast numbers of systems that were good enough.

In both the United States and Germany, the aircraft industry enjoyed the luxury of experimentation—even when a practical outcome was uncertain. Both sides designed dozens of aircraft that never got off the drawing board.

With hindsight, it's obvious that the defense of the Reich would have been more effective had the Reichsluftfahrtministerium (Reich Air Ministry, the RLM) accepted a proposal from air ace Generalleutnant (Maj. Gen.) Adolf "Dolfo" Galland that Germany concentrate its manufacturing capacity on just two aircraft types— the Focke-Wulf Fw 190 and Messerschmitt Me 262 fighters.

Instead of taking Galland's advice, German industry continued manufacturing outdated warplanes such as the Messerschmitt Bf 109 and experimenting with new ideas that had merit, but also with many that clearly didn't. This book now looks at one aircraft design in the latter category. Depending on how you look at it, the Blohm und Voss P.170— an attempt at a high-speed warplane that wasn't a jet—was either a brilliant mistake, or just a mistake.

The design of the P.170 fighter-bomber dates to 1942 but was still being developed at the time of Schweinfurt-Regensburg raid in 1943. Simply put, it was both forward-thinking and strange looking.

If the P.170 with its three engines, broad wing, and cockpit astride the tail was a brilliant aircraft design, credit belongs to Dr.-Ing. Richard Vogt of Hamburger Flugzeubau, the aircraft company owned by the shipyard founded by Hermann Blohm and Ernst Voss in 1877. The company produced many unusual aircraft, including the BV 141, an asymmetrical reconnaissance aircraft, and the BV 222 *Wiking* (Viking), a giant flying boat. The BV 141 carried a three-man crew in a gondola mounted atop the wing to the right of an unmanned fuselage that was off-center to the left. The BV 238 was an even larger flying boat that had an appointment with U.S. pilot Ben Drew.

In a design that was either daring or foolish, the P.170 employed a forward-mounted, very broad rectangular, constant-chord wing spanning fifty-two feet six inches with one engine mounted in the nose and two more in gondolas at the wingtips. The gondolas mounted rudder fins, giving the rear fuselage a clean, tailless look. Each gondola, including the center fuselage, contained a fifty-two– U.S. gallon fuel tank that could feed only the engine ahead of it. The fuselage was forty-six feet eleven inches in length and wing area was 473.60 square feet.

It was intended that three 1,600-horsepower BMW 801D radial engines, each with a three-blade propeller fully eleven feet five inches in diameter, would power the P.170. This was the powerplant for the Fw 190; it was practical and reliable.

The two outer engines of the P.170 turned in opposing directions, all but eliminating torque on the aircraft. The aircraft had a traditional tail dragger configuration, except that its main landing gear consisted of three undercarriage legs. The P.170 was designed to carry 4,400 pounds of bombs on ordnance stations beneath its expansive wing.

This warplane was designed for speed, which is why it lacked defensive armament. It was the same kind of thinking that had gone into Britain's speedy De Havilland Mosquito, which Adolf Hitler considered such a pest. According to Hamburger Flugzeubau documents, the P.170 was expected to reach the extraordinary speed of 510 miles per hour at twenty-six thousand feet. This aircraft was larger than surviving illustrations suggest and would have weighed almost thirty thousand pounds when fully loaded for combat.

Not many company documents survived the Allied bombing of the Hamburg aircraft manufacturer. It appears Vogt's design team explored several variations on the design, including two- and three-crew versions for the *Schnellbomber* (fast bomber) and *Schlachtflugzeug* (ground attack aircraft).

Today, historians can only speculate as to why the Third Reich continued designing and developing a wide range of variations on aviation technology. Work on the P.170 may have continued long after men in Berlin knew they were losing the war. After all, the

Germans continued their efforts on a variety of war readiness proj-ects, including recruiting teenagers as fresh troops, right up until the final day of fighting.

What leaps out about the P.170 is that it would have been very, very difficult to taxi. The real question is not why Blohm und Voss didn't build it, but why it survived so long as a viable proposal. In a different universe, perhaps swarms of P.170s might have been avail-able in time to stymie the American daylight bombing campaign. In reality, with Germany's attention and resources spread thin, it didn't happen.

On the American side, the P-47 remained the most numerous and important fighter well into the fall and early winter of 1943.

Republic, the Farmingdale, New York, manufacturer of the Thunderbolt, was known as the Republic Iron Works and had a reputation for building fighters that were big, roomy, and brought airmen home. Pilots nicknamed the P-47 the "Jug" because of its corpulence and resemblance to a fat milk bottle. And, as pilot Valmore Beaudrault wrote, the P-47 was "sturdy and tough as a tin can." One P-47 returned to its English base with body parts from a German fighter pilot embedded in its engine cowling. Another landed safely riddled with 183 holes from bullets and shrapnel.

P-47s rolled out of American factories in greater numbers than any other U.S. fighter ever. There were 15,683 Thunderbolts, a total that compares to 15,486 P-51 Mustangs and 10,037 P-38 Lightnings. In the Jug, pilots and ground crews had a rugged, reliable fighter, perfect for the wet, corrosive English weather and the mud that sometimes clogged taxiways.

The P-47 was already flying when the United States entered the war. Built around the two thousand–horsepower Pratt & Whitney R-2800 Double Wasp eighteen-cylinder radial engine and the duct-ing for its turbo-supercharger, the brutish P-47 fuselage was wedded to a graceful pair of elliptical wings, mounting eight heavy .50-cal-iber machine guns. With full tanks, ammunition, and two 1,000-pound bombs, the P-47 weighed in at an astonishing 16,475 pounds to become the heaviest single-engine fighter of World War II. Yet its massive engine could push it to a speed of 420 miles per hour at thirty thousand feet, and the new Thunderbolt had a 200–mile combat radius, about 50 miles greater than the British Spitfire. Delayed by technical glitches after reaching England months earlier, the Jug entered combat in March 1943. The combat mission took place on March 10 and was simply a fighter sweep over France. The mission was plagued by radio malfunctions and achieved little.

"The 47s haven't any combat yet, but should soon," 2nd Lt. Grant Turley wrote in his diary on April 11, 1943. Turley was quite tall but otherwise was an exact double of a Hollywood actor who had not yet been born and whose life would not overlap with his own—Bill Murray. Turley had a slightly mischievous streak that sharpened his resemblance to the future actor.

Turley could be shy and inner-directed: he was made up of many parts, like all of the young citizen-soldiers from modest upbringings who squeezed into cockpits and went to war near the edge of the stratosphere. He was more withdrawn, more rural in his roots, perhaps a little less cocky than future P-51 Mustang pilot Clayton Kelly Gross, who underwent pilot training class a year before he did, or the decidedly urban, erudite B-17 Flying Fortress copilot Robert Des Lauriers, who took the pilot training course exactly a year later.

While these young pilots were in training, American bomber crews were going through their most difficult period of the war. The fighters and flak defending the Third Reich were taking a terrible toll. Eighth Air Force commander Lt. Gen. Ira C. Eaker, VIII Bomber Command boss Maj. Gen. Frederick L. Anderson, and 3rd Air Division commander Brig. Gen. Curtis E. LeMay were among leaders who were forging new tactics for a new kind of warfare. Initially, however, they were placing too much trust in the combat box formation that concentrated the defensive fire of a bomber's guns and not enough in the protection that could be provided by escort fighters. Bomber crews were fighting under unspeakably horrible conditions and sustaining almost unbearable numbers of killed, wounded, and captured. Yet Eaker, Anderson, and LeMay believed, correctly, that the bombing campaign was inflicting serious hurt on Hitler's war machine. The risks to crewmembers would decline, and the size of the hurt would increase, once escort fighters could form a buffer between the Luftwaffe and the bombers.

While the Thunderbolt was the best escort available, bomber crewmembers were already referring to escort fighters—any kind of escort fighters—as "little friends." But all too often, the "big friends" were still fending for themselves.

While Valmore Beaudrault, Grant Turley, and others were being introduced to the Jug, the Eighth Air Force's VIII Fighter Command in England was struggling to give the P-47 enough range to accompany bombers to their targets. Equipping P-47s with big, bulbous two hundred–U.S. gallon ferry tanks dangling from the fuselage centerline was a partial solution. The tanks were unpressurized, so they proved to be effective only at low altitudes. However, they could be carried half full, used during the long climb over the English Channel, and then dropped, adding seventy-five miles of radius. This method was awkward and apparently used only briefly. Moreover, carrying this type of center point drop tank on the outbound leg of an escort mission increased the reach of the P-47 only to 325 miles, which was nowhere near enough. The Luftwaffe readily understood when Jug escorts would have to turn back because of fuel restrictions and waited to intercept bombers just a few miles beyond the Thunderbolt's radius of action. The number of miles kept changing with the addition of larger tanks, but bombers kept traveling deeper into the Reich and no change to the Thunderbolt would enable it to keep up.

Eventually, under-wing shackles brought from the United States to England permitted several options for external fuel tanks for the Jug. By February 1944, the Thunderbolt could carry a single 150-gallon belly tank or, to travel even farther, two 108-gallon under-wing tanks, increasing the P-47's radius of action to four hundred to five hundred miles. Thunderbolts could now reach Frankfurt or Hamburg (with difficulty), but not more distant targets such as

Munich, Prague, and Berlin. By mid-1944, a P-51D Mustang with two 108-gallon tanks could travel anywhere American bombers might go, not merely to Berlin but as far as Prague. The Mustang's range was the key as bombers kept going deeper and deeper into Nazi-occupied Europe.

Major General William E. Kepner, who headed up VIII Fighter Command from August 29, 1943, onward, wrote: "If it can be said that if the P-38s struck the Luftwaffe in its vitals and the P-51s gave the coup de grace, it was the Thunderbolt that broke its back."

Lying in wait for the growing American air armada in East Anglia was a German fighter force that in 1942 and 1943 was experienced, robust, and aggressive—German officers constantly refreshing their tactics to defeat Allied fighters and attack four-engine bombers. In large measure, the air campaign was aimed at neutralizing the Luftwaffe fighter force. Early in the campaign, the Germans had the top hand. As the war progressed, the Allies overcame their air defenses not by shooting down their aircraft or bombing their production plants—although both actions inflicted horrendous harm— but by killing their pilots. As the air campaign in Europe progressed, the Luftwaffe would continue to have plenty of fighter planes, but its leadership, talent, and experience would become casualties of war.

Confronting the Americans were twin-engine, rocket-armed Messerschmitt Bf 110 and Me 210 fighters, joined later in the war by the Me 410 *Hornisse* (Hornet)—all of which would ultimately be defeated by single-engine Allied fighters. Later, the jet-propelled Messerschmitt Me 262 joined the mix. But in the early months of the campaign, the same months when only the P-38 Lightning and P-47 Thunderbolt were available as escorts, the German fighter force relied most heavily on its two iconic, single-engine fighters.

The Messerschmitt Bf 109 was a nimble, versatile, and reliable high-altitude fighter of light construction that crumpled easily when sustaining battle damage and was, as noted earlier, out of date. It was eclipsed by newer and better fighters in all air forces, including Germany's. It remained the mount of most Luftwaffe aces, remained in production, and was a potent adversary until the final day of the war. The Bf 109G, or "Gustav," version confronting the Eighth Air Force in 1943 was powered by a 1,475-horsepower DB 605A inverted V-12 liquid-cooled inline engine and armed with four nose- and wing-mounted machine guns and a hub-mounted cannon. A German pilot's manual listed a top speed of 579 kilometers per hour (360 miles per hour), although the speeds of all fighters varied according to weight, temperature, payload, and other factors.

A 1,700-horsepower BMW 801D fourteen-cylinder radial engine powered the Focke-Wulf Fw 190 *Wurger* (Butcher Bird). The powerplant initially caused overheating problems, high cockpit temperatures, and leaking gasses in the cockpit, but it overcame these teething troubles at an early stage when it was also being considered for the Blohm und Voss P.170.

The Focke Wulf had the fastest rate of roll of any fighter and featured an automatic system that operated the manifold pressure, revolutions per minute, and fuel mixture, relieving the pilot of these duties. The Butcher Bird lacked the leading edge automatic slats that sometimes caused gun-laying accuracy in the Bf 109, had better visibility, and had an unusually wide track main landing gear for easier takeoffs, landings, and ground handling. It was the only World War II fighter that had electrically operated flaps and landing gear. The Fw 190 had only a mediocre rate of climb and sometimes could not get to altitude quickly enough to be effective against American bombers.

Having attacked the center of the ball-bearing industry in force, the American bomber force hesitated to return. LeMay biographer Warren Kozak wrote:

[T]he Allies did not understand the impact of the mission on the other side, as ball bearing production dropped by 38 percent after the raid. Albert Speer said that Germany "barely escaped a catastrophic blow" and that the Allies were right to take aim at the ball bearing plants. But their crucial mistake was in spreading out their forces and not concentrating on Schweinfurt. It was not just the Allies who did not understand the impact of these attacks. When Speer spoke to Hitler after the attack on Schweinfurt, the German leader was in great spirits because "the countryside was strewn with downed American bombers." Although true, every plant in Schweinfurt had been hit and was on fire. "But what really saved us was the fact that from this time on, the enemy, to our astonishment, once again ceased his attacks on the ball bearing industry," Speer later revealed.

On September 13, 1943, pilot Turley arrived at Duxford, England, to become part of the 78th Fighter Group. Turley now had about 140 flying hours in the P-47. He flew his first routine mission on October 9. Unable to accompany the bombers all the way to their target, Turley wrote: "Had a long 'Fort' raid today, clear across Germany. Our group of 47s was supposed to give withdrawal support—meeting the bombers about 70 miles on the other side of Paris." But the 78th Fighter Group's portion of the mission was cancelled after Turley and his fellow pilots had warmed up and taxied out. "Orders came through to cut off the engines but remain in our planes," Turley wrote. "We waited for 45 minutes this way and then were told to taxi back to the dispersal area and get out of our planes." Though his part of the mission was scrubbed due to bad weather, Turley wrote that Messerschmitt Bf 110Gs and Me 210s intercepted the unescorted bombers firing air-to-air rockets and the Flying Fortress crews suffered terribly.

Turley may not have known the details, but the German twin-engine fighters each had four under-wing tubes firing spin-stabilized 248-pound Wurfgranate 210mm mortar rockets. This standoff method of air defense was decimating U.S. bomber formations. Twin-engine Messerschmitts could fire the rockets from almost a mile away, far beyond the reach of the bombers' machine guns. If a rocket detonated within fifty feet of a bomber, it was likely to go down. In a tight formation, a bomber thrown out of control by a rocket blast could plow through several more bombers before falling from the sky. The Achilles tendon of the rocket-launching scheme was the launch platform. If the right fighter could be found to go up against them while far from home in hostile sky, the twin-engine Messerschmitts would be unable to continue using their rockets to pick off bombers like ducks in a shooting gallery.

Turley was describing a mortar rocket attack introduced on a large scale during the *second* big mission to Schweinfurt, the one that unfolded when the Eighth Air Force belatedly decided, as Turley put it, "to hit the big time again." On "Second Schweinfurt" on October 14, "Black Thursday," 196 Thunderbolts from other fighter groups, although not Turley's, got into the air—but most were unable to find the bombers they were supposed to escort partway. The entire 4th Fighter Group, still equipped with P-47s, then had to be recalled after going astray in heavy clouds. The 352nd Fighter Group attached itself to a segment of the bomber stream that eventually abandoned the mission. Of the 291 bombers sent on the mission, 77 were lost. Despite the availability of P-38s and P-47s in vast numbers, despite the firepower of the bombers' own guns when they clung together in tight, combat-box formations, and despite the growing size and reach of the bomber force, German defenses were still more formidable than the American attackers.

It was a time of bad news and great danger for bomber crews. A study showed that a typical bomber crew stood only a fifty-fifty chance of completing the required combat tour of twenty-five missions. While the ink was still wet on the study, the required total was raised to thirty. It was a time of heavy casualties and—for some—low morale.

But there was good news. The bombing campaign against the Third Reich was becoming serious. By October 1943, a second front was opened in the great air war when the Fifteenth Air Force in Italy began dispatching B-17s and B-24s in significant numbers against Reich targets.

Turley wrote in his diary that he flew his first escort mission on October 24, 1943, briefly glimpsing a gaggle of Bf 109s and logging four eventless flight hours. In fact, no bombers were launched that day; Thunderbolts flew a fighter sweep. The fighters of VIII Fighter Command were now the property of the tough-hewn Kepner, born in 1893 and now approaching fifty, an extraordinary figure who had been a marine, cavalryman, infantryman, and balloonist before flying fighters on the eve of war. Kepner apparently lacked the right chemistry with Eighth Air Force boss Eaker, but that would change within a couple of short months when Eaker, too, would be gone.

October and November 1943 marked a time of optimism for the Americans and their unprecedented air campaign. Cracks were beginning to show in Third Reich defenses and more bombers were getting through—just as the brass had said, all along, they would. The Luftwaffe could mount a formidable defense against combat boxes of Flying Fortresses and Liberators, but its forces could no longer counter both the Eighth and Fifteenth Air Forces, which were hitting them from two directions. It was not unusual, now, for as many as five hundred heavy bombers to arrive over the Third Reich at once, and the Germans had to pick and choose where and when to mount a defense. The Eighth Air Force and its subordinate VIII Bomber Command and VII Fighter Command were continuing to grow. On November 4, 1943, the ground echelon of the 354th Fighter Group arrived in England, not yet accompanied by its aircraft but soon to be the first fighter group in Europe to operate the new, long-range P-51B Mustangs. The 354th was assigned to IX Fighter Command but was tapped to fly escort. More P-47 and P-51 fighter groups arrived before the end of November.

SIX

MUSTANG UNLEASHED

First Lieutenant Charles F. Gumm Jr. fidgeted in the cockpit of his factory-fresh fighter plane, peered into the distance, and watched for trouble.

Chuck was twenty-two years old and a distant relative of film star Judy Garland, whose real name was Frances Gumm. He was a gentle man, his wife, Toni, liked to say, unassuming and earnest. His handsome face often had a sheepish look accompanied by a faint smile, as if he couldn't quite believe he was here, doing this. He was so thin his buddies wondered, despite his constant good cheer, if he was healthy. And now Gumm was a P-51B Mustang fighter pilot escorting American bombers to Bremen on December 16, 1943.

With the Merlin engine of his sleek, pointy fighter turning over smoothly in front of him, Gumm peered upward toward a mercilessly bright sun in a region where the weather was usually gray and wet. He squinted. They were only small blemishes at first, but they were getting larger. He was looking at four Messerschmitt Bf 109 fighters jockeying into position to attack a box of bombers.

"Looks like we'll have to climb into them," said the voice in Gumm's earphones. That was 1st Lt. Gilbert F. "Deacon" Talbot. His olive-drab P-51B was glinting in the sun off Gumm's wing. The two men could look at each other, but not see the other's facial expressions because of their helmets and oxygen masks. Gumm flicked a switch to arm his plane's four .50-caliber M2 machine guns and knew Talbot was doing the same.

The Messerschmitts were lining up to attack the B-17 Flying Fortress heavy bombers from behind, a hint that the Luftwaffe pilots might not be skilled enough for a frontal attack from a few degrees above the centerline—the position the Americans called twelve o'clock high. A frontal attack was difficult to pull off, but it gave German fighter pilots their best chance to kill the Americans in the B-17 cockpits.

"Talbot and I climbed after them, and when within four hundred yards range, two of the enemy aircraft saw us and broke left and straight down," Gumm later said in a report. "We closed on the other two and I dropped back a little to cover Lieutenant Talbot's tail, but the enemy saw him and broke left and down.

"By then I was almost in a position to fire on my 109, which was still flying straight for the bombers. Lieutenant Talbot pulled up and to the right to cover my tail while I closed to about one hundred yards and fired a two-second burst, noticing no effects. I then closed to about fifty yards and fired a three-second burst, noticing a thin trail of smoke coming from the right side of the engine. I fired again at very close range and was showered with smoke and oil and pieces, which I pulled up through and glanced back to see the fighter going down to the left with a large plume of smoke coming from the right side of the engine. Then I looked for Lieutenant Talbot again, and saw him chasing an Fw 190 [Focke-Wulf Fw 190 fighter], with another 109 closing on him. I went down after the latter fighter and they both broke down and away, so we went back to the bombers."

November 1943

They were new, young, eager, aggressive, and overconfident, trickling in to an airfield called Boxted, construction of which had just been completed. They were new men who had unexpectedly been given new airplanes—P-51 Mustangs that no one else in the U.S. military had.

Their leader was Col. Kenneth R. Martin, a "hardass" one of the pilots called him, a twenty-seven-year-old colonel who often seemed uncompromising and inflexible. Another pilot called Martin "a straitlaced, 'go by the book' kind of guy." He was commander of the 354th Fighter Group, the outfit that was, for now, the first and only but would soon become the first of many Mustang combat groups arrayed against the German air force, the Luftwaffe.

Martin showed mixed reactions when seasoned combat veteran Donald Blakeslee was "seconded" to the 354th to lend a hand on early missions, prompting some to wonder who was in charge. Martin may have disliked Blakeslee for being too much like himself, only more so—forceful, non-nonsense, more interested in results than being well liked.

Tension between Martin and Blakeslee was at a high pitch when Martin's 354th group shuffled into the briefing room on the morning of December 1, 1943, and settled into stiff metal chairs, staring up at a map, about to hear about the first American Mustang mission to the European continent. Martin was off to one side but standing in front of them; unknown to most in the room was Blakeslee.

Although just twenty-seven years old, the forceful, no-nonsense Blakeslee had maturity no one else in the room possessed. His eyes were cold. His face was hard. He was on his way to flying more fighter missions than any other American in the war but was no candidate for a popularity contest. He'd flown a civilian Piper Cub before the war and joined the Royal Canadian Air Force to become part of the Eagle Squadrons serving with the British. He'd transferred to the U.S. forces and commanded a squadron in the 4th Fighter Group. An air ace, Blakeslee was not a good shot (He "couldn't hit the broad side of a barn," historian Thomas McKelvey Cleaver wrote), but was a master of the principles involved in air fighting tactics. He was a gifted leader without being particularly well liked—a stern disciplinarian and harsh taskmaster. In December 1943, Blakeslee was a lieutenant colonel.

One of the shavetail lieutenants in the 354th group, 2nd Lt. Clayton Kelly Gross, wrote: "I remember in Don Blakeslee's first briefing before he led our first combat mission he said, 'Whoever breaks first in a head-on pass situation is at a disadvantage. We don't break first. Make the other guy do that.' We wondered at the time what happens when the 'other guy' gets the same lecture? Martin agreed—'That's the way we'll do it!' " It may or may not have been the right advice for young, eager pilots heading into a dogfight, but it was to become a harbinger for Martin.

Gross belonged to the group's 355th squadron, the Bulldogs, alias the "Pugnacious Pups," commanded by Maj. George R. Bickell, a veteran who had flown at Midway in the Pacific after the great battle there. Gross reveled in the camaraderie of the young lieutenants around him, but felt constant tension with Bickell, with whom he'd had a run-in while the group was training in the states. Gross and his wife, Gwen, had been in the front seat of their car, Bickell in the back, when Gross narrowly averted killing all of them when accelerating across a railroad track with a speeding train rushing straight at them. Bickell, a small and stern man who would later command the entire group, "rarely spoke a civil word to me in the next two years" following the railroad incident, Gross wrote.

Gross, hardly impartial, later said Bickell was "small of stature and made up for it with a kind of 'Little Caesar' attitude in my estimation."

Bickell would eventually replace Martin as commander of the 354th Fighter Group. Blakeslee, never a fan of the P-47 Thunderbolt with which his own 4th Fighter Group was equipped, realized that Martin's Mustang men had a better airplane than his Thunderbolt pilots did—at least a better plane for the crucial job of escorting bombers. "I made up my mind this was the airplane we needed and we had to get them, too," Blakeslee said later.

The Mustang men of Martin's 354th Fighter Group were going into battle against a tough and determined enemy. Plenty was at stake. Unless losses of heavy bombers could be reduced, the aerial campaign against Hitler's Third Reich would not be able to continue. Unless the formidable pilots and aircraft of the German air arm, the Luftwaffe, could be countered, the Allies might have to delay their longstanding plans to invade Europe a few months ahead in the summer of 1944. Whether the P-51 Mustang and its pilots could make a difference would be determined by Gumm, Talbot, Martin, Gross, Bickell, and many more like them. For the diminutive, ever-intent Bickell, taking on Adolf Hitler was not what he originally had in mind. As 1st Lt. Donald F. Snow wrote:

> When he was given the assignment of organizing and train-ing fighter-pilots and men for combat, the nucleus of the 355th Fighter Squadron, at Hamilton Field, California, Capt. George R. Bickell was looking toward the Land of the Rising Sun. He hoped that through his leadership, his pilots would make a name for themselves in smashing back at the Jap. This month of November 1942 was less than a year after the Pearl Harbor disaster [and] Bickell had seen that holocaust and had flown P-40 aircraft off Navy carriers during the Battle of Midway. But there was another Big League shaping up in the skies of Europe in which he was to play a major role.

By December 1943, Bickell was at the other end of the world in Boxted, England. "He was a small man, confident, not very talkative, not always the most likeable, and for some reason that eludes me they called him Uncle George," said Sgt. Nathan Serenko, a crew chief with the pioneer P-51 Mustang fighter group. With Martin as group commander and Bickell in command of one squadron, the men in the group looked across the English Channel (figuratively speak-ing), saw the German air force waiting for them, and were ready to go. The Ninth Air Force took ownership of Boxted airfield, but the 354th group and its 353rd, 355th, and 356th Fighter Squadrons were placed under the operational control of the VIII Fighter Command, a component of the Eighth Air Force—the growing military forma-tion that would eventually inhabit no fewer than 122 airfields along the eastern rim of the British Isles known as East Anglia.

Until now, American fighter pilots in Europe had followed the air tactical school edict to closely escort bombers. The eager young pilots of VIII Fighter Command, especially those gifted with the new P-51, were clamoring to attack German warplanes when they were forming up, long before they reached the bombers.

Technically, the 354th Fighter Group and its commander Ken Martin didn't exactly belong to Doolittle or Kepner. As part of the Ninth Air Force even while assigned to Doolittle's Eighth, they belonged for administrative purposes to the rather lackluster Maj. Gen. Lewis H. Brereton and Brereton's dynamic IX Fighter Command boss, Brig. Gen. Elwood R. "Pete" Quesada. Martin may have seemed stiff to some—others regarded him as amiable—but he had brought these men together stateside, had brought them across the Atlantic on a scow of a troopship, and was going to take them into battle.

While they were still looking at their new Mustangs for the first time, Quesada asked Martin, "Exactly how much time do you need to make the group combat ready?" Quesada was thinking in terms of months, so he added a caution: "Before you answer, be sure. When I say 'ready,' I mean precisely that. Now, how long?"

Martin had already put a lot of thought into the answer he had ready.

"Two weeks, general."

Quesada later said that placing his confidence in Martin was a gamble. Quesada could be ruthless in overseeing fighter group com-manders and, if necessary, in firing them. But Martin performed exactly as promised. That was the way they'd taught him during flight training in Flying Class 38-A (the two digits in a class num-ber referred to a year, e.g. 1938), and it was reinforced in the minds of the men by Martin's constant presence, looking into a spare-parts problem here, checking out an intelligence report there, questioning but not meddling, always at hand to help if asked—"looking over the shoulders of others without appearing to be looking over their shoulders," as Gross put it.

Chuck Gumm's first aerial victory at the controls of a P-51 Mustang, and the first for any by an American pilot—over a respected adversary flying a formidable warplane—might never have happened if the top brass in Washington had decided how the war in Europe was going to go. Air staff officers in the newly opened Pentagon building disliked the P-51 and allowed it to reach squadrons in England only with reluctance. Not for many more months— until spring 1944—would the P-51 appear in sufficient numbers to test whether it could fill that role. At the beginning, even the need for such a warplane received no recognition. It was understood only that there was a need for "pursuit" planes, as they were then called. It was not until U.S. bomber losses in Europe became overwhelming that top air generals saw that the Luftwaffe had to be defeated.

December 13, 1943

The twin-engine, prop-driven German fighters that had been a menace to bomber formations were a menace no longer by December 1943. The Bf 110 had been one of these planes.

Before the arrival of the 354th Fighter Group had a chance to make its mark with the new and unproven P-51 Mustang, bomber crews dreaded the twin-engine Messerschmitt Bf 110 Zerstörer (Destroyer). It seemed invulnerable as it traveled freely to within its own firing range of American formations—while staying well beyond the range of the bombers' defensive .50-caliber machine guns.

Each Bf 110 typically carried four spin-stabilized 248-pound Wurfgranate 210mm rocket projectiles. Although not very accurate, the rocket's 80-pound warhead made it extremely effective, even without proximity fuses. The warheads were time fused to detonate at 600 to 1,200 yards from the launch aircraft. To tear a bomber apart, the rocket needed only to explode within fifty feet. Often an exploding B-17 in a tight formation caused enough damage to adjacent planes to damage or bring down more B-17s. And even when the rocket missed, one large explosion inside a formation tended to make the formation spread out, making it vulnerable to attack by the Germans' more nimble single-engine fighters. The Bf 110 was a mighty weapon of war, and it was to be the first against which the Mustang and the Mustang men would be tested.

On December 13, 1943, the target was Kiel. Later that spring and summer, the Mustang men would change everything about the way the war was going. One of the young men in Mustangs in the 354th Fighter Group was shavetail Felix M. "Mike" Rogers. This was his first mission. He was itching to get into the fight. He had been told that German fighter pilots were the best.

"I had two and one-half hours in the Mustang," said Rogers. "None of us understood why they'd given this new fighter to our group, which had no combat experience in another aircraft. Our mechanics and ground crew had been issued tools for the P-47 Thunderbolt, which we had expected to fly. We had never flown above fifteen thousand and now we were going to Kiel at thirty-two thousand, on oxygen." To Rogers, the new P-51B/C Mustangs were far from perfect. "We had a lot of problems with armament, oxygen, spark plugs, and coolant," he said. The temperature over Kiel was minus twenty-eight degrees Fahrenheit.

Forty-one Mustangs were escorting 710 bombers. Rogers was "tail end Charlie," as he put it, or number four in the flight led by 1st Lt. Donald M. Beerbower. "I was spooked by the size of the sun and by the old adage 'Beware the Hun in the sun!' "

In one of the B-17 Flying Fortress bombers being escorted by Mustangs, tail gunner Staff Sgt. John Gabay watched forty Junkers Ju 88 twin-engine German fighters appear out of nowhere. "They came in close, one at a time," Gabay remembered. "The flame from the cannons, tracers from their machine guns, and rockets from under their wings made the situation a bit hairy. All I could do, besides being scared, was to spray each one as they came in and call for evasive action. I hit the second one and he rolled over and burned. I saw my tracers slam into the cockpit of the third. I may have hit the pilot, as the ship started to go out of control. I poured more into it, knocking off the canopy under the nose. It looked like a leg hung out of the ship for an instant, then fell out."

Altogether, about 1,500 American aircraft were in the region of Kiel that day. It appears the number of German fighters confronting them was fairly small. Everybody on both sides saw the Mustangs. Everybody on both sides looked at them and decided they were Messerschmitt Bf 109s. That included many of the gunners aboard the Fortresses who, unlike Gabay, reported engaging single-engine fighters.

Rogers flew into battle in proper wing position on his element leader John Mattie. Rogers was chafing at the bit to engage the vaunted German fighter pilots. "They were the first team. We knew they were the first team and we wanted to test ourselves against them," Rogers said. There were reports the Germans were developing even newer and better fighters using new technology—all the more reason to want to confront them.

In the cold, high blue sky over Kiel, Rogers saw two or three Ju 88s in the distance. In another direction were other twin-engine German fighters, including a few examples of the Messerschmitt Bf 110, the twin-engine fighter that was so lethal against the bombers. Rogers doubts there were forty twin-engine fighters as Gabay wrote. He was measuring the threat, calculating a way to engage, when he looked down and saw a top turret of a B-17 rotating its guns toward him. There were muzzle flashes and the streaked gray of bullets flying through the air.

It sounded like rain when the bullets pattered against right wing of his Mustang. Looking out, Rogers noticed the metal was pointed up around a number of bullet hole punctures in his right wing tank. He had also taken hits in the right wing root. He called a break and followed his flight leader.

Beerbower, a future American ace who had been born in Canada, later wrote in his diary that a twin-engine German fighter "put a hole in Rogers' wing." Thinking he was fighting for his life, Rogers was very certain where the bullets had come from.

He was neither the first nor the last American fighter pilot to be hit by gunfire from an American bomber. It was a case of mistaken identity, a case of someone deciding his P-51 was a Bf 109. Frank Birtciel, who began the war in the P-38 Lightning, a plane with a distinctive twin-boom design that could not be mistaken for any other, said that American pilots and crewmembers simply didn't know about the P-51. "We had very thorough intelligence briefings," said Birtciel. "They showed us charts. They showed us airplane recognition models. They taught us about our planes and the Germans.

"But," he added, "they didn't teach us about the P-51.

"The people who made the charts, the people who made the recognition models, they had never heard of it. Most of us never knew anything about the P-51 until the first time we saw one," he added.

After breaking and accelerating out of harm's way, Rogers discovered that he wasn't fighting for his life after all. His Mustang was responding normally to his touch—or, at least, as far as he could tell with only about twenty-five hours in the cockpit.

His Mustang was the first aircraft Rogers had ever piloted that had self-sealing fuel tanks. "That's what got me home that day. We were very skeptical that they would work. But the self-sealing fuel tanks did work and they got me to safety," he said.

Only when the P-38 and P-47 had both failed as escorts in Europe did the Army Air Forces, the AAF, turn to the P-51, the plane that even American aircraft recognition experts hadn't heard of and that the Pentagon didn't want.

The P-51 was never written into any AAF specifications. North American Aviation designed it for the British, and the British came up with the idea of replacing its Allison engine with the Rolls-Royce Merlin. The Merlin was built in the United States by Packard and was superior to the Allison, which never overcame all of its flaws. With its half-British heritage, the AAF had strong institutional biases against the P-51, and the top brass showed little interest in the early Mustangs and even tried to kill off the plane.

The P-51 finally emerged as the dominant fighter because North American engineers rapidly made the field modifications needed to make it work as a long-range escort fighter—well before any of its competitors could be perfected. The replacement of its Allison engine with the Merlin was the first and most important idea adopted from the field, and ironically it happened only because the P-51 was not originally an AAF airplane. The final key modification was the addition of a large internal fuselage fuel tank to extend the range of the P-51B, a change proposed by the chief of the AAF's fighter branch, Col. Mark Bradley. The P-51 was thus successfully flying and fighting well before the AAF was able to get one of its other more favored planes to function as a long-range escort fighter.

Why did the first Mustangs go to Ken Martin's inexperienced 354th Fighter Group rather than the battle-hardened 4th or 56th groups? Documents from the era suggest that no one in the AAF, from boss Gen. Henry H. "Hap" Arnold on down, had much confidence in—or even interest in—the North American fighter. At the end of 1943, only a few dozen were in service in East Anglia as part of a battle force that still relied too heavily on P-38s and P-47s.

January 1, 1944

The Luftwaffe had eight hundred to one thousand fighters arrayed along the western front to confront the Eighth Air Force's heavy bombers. The Germans were beginning to experience some attrition of their best pilots, but they still had a full force of very experienced veterans who'd fought in the Battle of Britain and on the eastern front. The Americans were being told that German air defenses were expanding and would soon have even better warplanes. It's unclear whether U.S. intelligence knew about a November 26, 1943, display of the *Wunderwaffen*, or "wonder weapons" held at Insterburg for Adolf Hitler. However, the U.S. side did know that the Messerschmitt Me 262 jet fighter was coming.

On January 1, 1944, Col. Donald Blakeslee took command of the 4th Fighter Group at Debden. In his first speech to his outfit—now,

the third American combat group equipped with the P-51 Mustang—
Blakeslee uttered a now widely quoted speech: "The Fourth Fighter
Group is going to be the top fighter group in the Eighth Air Force.
We are here to fight. To those who don't believe me I would suggest
transferring to another group. I'm going to fly the ass off each one
of you. Those who keep up with me, good; those who don't, I don't
want them anyway."

Wrote historian Thomas McKelvey Cleaver: "Most fighter pilots
played to the crowd, crushing their hats in the '50 mission look,' putting their girl's name on the nose of their plane beneath their scores.
Blakeslee did none of this. His hat was 'G.I.,' and so were his airplanes, none of which ever wore a personal name or carried a 'victory' cross under the cockpit." Blakeslee may have been the only
fighter pilot who hated publicity and shunned would-be biographers.

RED TAILS

Many miles from Blakeslee, New Year's Day 1944 marked a
buildup of a formidable fighter force in the Mediterranean Theater
of Operations, where the Fifteenth Air Force was carrying the
torch. Three new squadrons bolstered a single squadron of black
Americans, the Tuskegee Airmen. In time, all were amalgamated
into the 332nd Fighter Group under Col. Benjamin O. Davis Jr.
After wasting months on dubious dive-bombing and strafing
missions, the Italy-based 332nd fliers were given the crucial job
of escorting Fifteenth Air Force heavy bombers on missions into
the Reich. Theirs was one of seven fighter escort groups in the
Mediterranean Theater, and they wanted to stand out: when they
received Mustangs, they applied a distinctive coat of red paint
on the rear of each aircraft, and the pilots of the 332nd became
known as the Red Tails. Among them were pilots Roscoe Brown
and Earl Lane, who would find themselves fighting Hitler's jets on
March 24, 1945.

In July 1944, the 332nd escorted bombers on a mission against
railyards and Capt. Joseph Elsberry shot down three Fw-190s,

becoming the first black pilot to achieve this feat. On July 13, they flew thier first mission on the oil refineries at Ploesti, Romania. Three days later, they met Italian Macchi fighters (Italy had surrendered on June 11, but followers of strongman Benito Mussolini maintained a rump state in the north, the Italian Social Republic) and they downed two of them. Two days later, July 18, Lt. Clarence "Lucky" Lester destroyed three German airplanes, and the 332nd group claimed eleven kills.

January 6, 1944

From July to October 1944, the Red Tails flew countless missions, usually bomber escorts. Sometimes they shot down German aircraft, and they began to build a respectable group tally. Less often, they lost one of their own.

On January 6, 1944, Lt. Gen. James H. Doolittle, the new Eighth Air Force commander, ordered his fighter boss, Maj. Gen. William Kepner, to turn these young men loose. "Your priority is to take the offensive," Doolittle told Kepner.

Historian Dik A. Daso described a change that many regarded as dramatic: "Prominently hung on Kepner's office wall was a sign that read, 'The first duty of the Eighth Fighter Command is to bring the bombers back alive.' Kepner had argued against being strictly tied to the bombers for many months, but Eaker and even Spaatz had insisted upon such a philosophy. Doolittle ordered Kepner to remove 'that damned sign' and replace it with one that said, 'The first duty of the Eighth Air Force fighters is to destroy German fighters.' " Kepner was thankful.

Under Doolittle's liberating order, American fighters were to converge in mass groups all along the bomber path into Germany, to engage the intercepting German fighters wherever they found them. Now, American fighters would be able to catch the foe on the ground, inflicting mortal damage. No German aircraft, no German airfield, was safe now. Every German pilot was now at risk, everywhere, and they could not be replaced.

While the Mustang men were getting their first taste of war, Detroit-born 2nd Lt. Urban L. Drew was getting a foul taste from being an instructor in Bartow, Florida. Drew had an outgoing, aggressive personality and being part of a schoolhouse wasn't what he wanted. It was in Bartow that he acquired the nickname Ben, by which most people would know him thereafter. It was in Bartow that Drew and a wingman named Kemp, flying P-51s, buzzed an air show at very low level, upsetting a lot of important people. Drew would claim afterward that it happened more or less by accident, but the buzzing incident resulted in being placed in the military equivalent of house arrest.

"I was certain they would give me the ultimate punishment and make me a stateside instructor for the rest of my life," said Drew. Their commander spoke vaguely to Drew and wingman Kemp, of judge, jury, and execution. As R. R. Powell later wrote, the boss promised: "You two screw-ups will be the longest serving lieutenants in the history of this man's Air Force." The boss also told Drew that he was "sorely tempted to let you go to court-martial."

This was the lowest moment of Ben Drew's life—until the commander continued: "However, you two are probably the best instructors we have ever had in this unit, and that includes some of the combat veterans. Both of you could be superb fighter pilots. Drew, three of your students are already aces and, Kemp, one of yours also."

Still, not happy at all and seething with rage, the commander ordered Drew and his wingman reassigned: "Send them over to the Eighth Air Force." And then: "I want them off this base within twenty-four hours."

"He called me a screw-up," said Drew. "He had no idea he was giving me exactly what I wanted."

TASTE OF DEFEAT

"They are kicking our asses," a pilot said to Clayton Kelly Gross after one of the very first Mustang missions against the Luftwaffe. Gross looked around at Boxted and saw fatigue and frustration on the faces of fellow Mustang pilots, who were starting to say, more openly now, that they were being defeated by the supremely experienced and very able men in Messerschmitts and Focke-Wulfs.

In those early days, was there ever a time when Gross thought, "We aren't winning this"? When he wondered if the learning curve was too steep, the odds too great, the foe too formidable? Did Gross himself ever sense that the odds were too great, that the Mustang Men would not be able to prevail?

"The answer is no," Gross said. "Our government was very good to me in giving me one full year in fighters before leaving for the combat zone.

"I was good. I developed confidence in my abilities that lasted throughout my career. Before arriving in England and being introduced to the Mustang, we were stationed in the San Francisco Bay area and had daily fights with navy fighters. I stated, 'I can whip anything the navy has with my P-39 Airacobra.' Admittedly, I started slowly in combat, but I think the weather and getting shot at by antiaircraft fire, plus learning the capabilities of the new aircraft, had a lot to do with that.

"The 354th was a great group. We had a great esprit de corps from the start. New pilots joined, and very quickly the winning attitude caught on with them. I never heard a pilot say he was scared or show evidence of that. We felt as if we had an advantage even if their numbers were greater than ours. I actually heard Glen Eagleston radio on one mission, 'Hey guys. I'm alone at the back of this bomber formation and I have twenty of the bastards cornered.' He may have exaggerated a little."

BITTERSWEET BEGINNING

Early successes by the Mustang men were tarnished by tragedy: eight Mustangs lost, most due to technical problems. On the day of Chuck Gumm's first aerial victory, the group lost Maj. Owen M. Seaman, commander of the 353rd squadron, who vanished over the North Sea.

The group's pilots were adjusting to what amounted to a new kind of warfare. Now, the Mustang pilots were facing four- to five-hour missions. This kind of flying imposed new demands on the pilot, creating all kinds of discomfort, but it was even worse on the airplane. The Mustang was prone to coolant loss at high altitude, where engines overheated and eventually seized. Coolant, oil, and oxygen problems needed to be resolved.

MOSQUITO MISSION

The P-38, P-47, and P-51 were key players, but the Americans high over the Reich were also flying Hitler's least favorite flying machine, the De Havilland Mosquito. Pilot 1st Lt. Richard Geary and navigator 1st Lt. Floyd Mann of the 25th Bombardment Group (Recon) were high over a snow-covered Reich on a weather reconnaissance flight, supporting a mission to the Politz Oil Refinery at Stettin in German-occupied Poland, when they came under attack. Four Mustangs from the 20th Fighter Group escorted them, which gave Geary plenty of confidence, although communication with the P-51s was not always good. The date was January 21, 1945. That month, Eighth Air Force pilots, all flying Mustangs, claimed six Me 262s—but not on this mission.

An Me 262 appeared head-on, maneuvered into position to chase Geary, and followed him in a high-speed dive. Author and researcher Norman Malayney quoted Geary on what happened next:

> I was doing close to 400 mph in a left breaking dive, a customary maneuver. What else was there to do? I had no chance to look back. In a flurry of desperation, I slammed on opposite rudder and aileron. The Mosquito cartwheeled 180 degrees across the sky in the opposite direction. I don't know what kind of maneuver this was, and it is a miracle the aircraft did not disintegrate. God must have been on my side. I didn't even have my lap belt on. Dust flew up from the floor, emergency maps came off the wall, and loose material floated in the cockpit. The Me 262 hurtled directly

over me, seemingly a few feet from my cockpit canopy. There was just one big flash of silver chrome as the uncamouflaged jet shot by. He had me in his sights, but my unexpected action put us on a collision course. Instead of shooting at me, the jet pilot had to use all his talents to avoid a midair collision. That both the German pilot and I lived through the encounter, I credit to his reflexes.

The German pilot was seemingly too preoccupied with survival to open fire. Geary maneuvered out of the situation and lost contact with both the jet and the escorting Mustangs. The Mosquito recovered at twenty-seven thousand feet, east of Berlin, when *four* Me 262s rushed past him within fifty yards. Soon, four more appeared. This time, there was no close-quarters engagement: Geary and Mann fought their way out of an intended trap and made it safely home.

BIG WEEK

Between February 20 and 25, 1944, the Allied bomber force launched Operation Argument, a series of missions against the Third Reich that became known as Big Week. The object was to lure the Luftwaffe into a decisive battle by sustaining persistent attacks on the German aircraft industry. By defeating the Luftwaffe, the Allies would achieve air superiority and the invasion of Europe could proceed.

The Americans flew heavily escorted missions against airframe manufacturing and assembly plants and other targets in numerous German cities. As the week-long air campaign unfolded on February 21, 1944, Chuck Gumm became the first air ace of the 354th Fighter Group by downing a Bf 110 over Brunswick.

In six days, the Eighth Air Force flew three thousand sorties and the Fifteenth Air Force based in Italy flew more than five hundred. Together they dropped roughly ten thousand tons of bombs.

During Big Week, the Eighth Air Force lost ninety-seven B-17s, forty B-24s, and another twenty were scrapped due to damage. The Fifteenth Air Force in Italy lost ninety aircraft, and American fighter losses stood at twenty-eight. Although these numbers are high in absolute terms, the numbers of bombers involved in the missions were much higher than in previous missions, and the losses represented a much smaller percentage of the attacking force. U.S. air crews claimed more than five hundred German fighters destroyed, though the numbers were massively exaggerated.

Luftwaffe losses were high amongst their twin-engine *Zerstörer* units, and the Bf 110 and Me 410 groups were decimated. More worrying for the Germans was the loss of 17 percent of their pilots: nearly one hundred were killed. In contrast to the raids of the previous year, the U.S. losses were entirely replaceable and being made good as their industrial might ramped up, while the Germans were already hard pressed due to the war in the East. Although not fatal, the Big Week was an extremely worrying development for the Germans.

Big Week demonstrated that the Luftwaffe's best antibomber weapons, twin-engine *Zerstörer* designs such as the Me 410 *Hornisse*, were appallingly vulnerable against Allied fighters. The planes were removed from service in the West, passing the role of defense primarily to the higher performance single-engine designs. Due to the effective protection offered by Allied fighters, a change of tactics was introduced: German fighters formed up well in front of the bombers, took a single head-on pass through the stream, and then left. This gave the defending fighters little time to react, and a few shells into the cockpit area could destroy a bomber in one pass.

LOSS OF A PILOT

Not long after Big Week, the first pilot to score an aerial victory in an American P-51, air ace Chuck Gumm, took off from Boxted on March 1, 1944. He wasn't going into harm's way. He was merely checking out some maintenance work on a P-51B. His aircraft wasn't the plane he usually flew, named *Toni* after his wife.

Could he have been a little too relaxed that morning? After all, he was the top American Mustang pilot in the war, credited with seven and a half aerial victories, and today was going to be an easy day. "We all wore seat belts and shoulder harnesses," said another P-51B pilot, reflecting on Gumm's fate that day. "In the beginning they were fastened separately, then we got a ring that locked both seat and shoulder belts." It was exactly the same cockpit arrangement as on German fighters, from the Messerschmitt Bf 109 to the Me 262.

Could Gumm have forgotten to strap in?

He'd barely lifted off the runway when he encountered engine trouble. He may have had an exchange of words with the tower at Boxted. No one seems to know. Heading out from the airfield, the problem got worse and Gumm was suddenly struggling to control his Mustang.

Gumm realized he was over the town of Nayland. If he bailed out to save himself, his plane would crash in the English town and claim innocent lives. He decided to stay with his plane. Gumm struggled to find his way down, searching for a spot for an emergency landing. He neared an open field but was too low and the wing caught a tree. The Mustang cartwheeled, throwing Gumm from the cockpit to his death. He was twenty-three years old.

A Nayland resident was later quoted in *Nostalgia* magazine about the incident: "We were astonished that he didn't jump out. Instead, he wove the plane above our streets to avoid the chimneys. Clearly, Mr. Gumm was concerned for our lives."

In St. James Church in Nayland, where the community has congregated since the 1400s, a plaque honors Chuck Gumm. He was briefly interred at an American cemetery in Cambridge, England, where a poster reminds visitors of him and men like him. It reads: "Time will not dim the glory of their deeds." Gumm's remains were later repatriated, and today he is buried at Greenwood Memorial Terrace in his hometown, Spokane, Washington. Gumm's father escorted Toni Gumm down the aisle when she remarried, to Duke Shearin, another pilot in the 354th Fighter Group.

William Marshall, a historian of the 354th, said in a telephone interview that by the time of Gumm's death, Mustang pilots had begun a process "that would virtually eliminate German twin-engine day fighter units and chewed up most of the single-engine units as well." Marshall said this made it possible for U.S. bombers to "go deep with acceptable losses and destroy Germany's oil and chemical industry" and "effectively destroyed Luftwaffe fighter capability to oppose the invasion before D-Day."

According to Marshall, the losses inflicted on the Luftwaffe from February through April 1944 killed about one thousand skilled pilots and destroyed more than 2,500 aircraft.

Chuck Gumm was there at the beginning.

SEVEN

ROCKET SCIENCE

American heavy bombers mounted the first-ever, full-scale day-light attack on Berlin on March 6, 1944. Planners in the Eighth Air Force knew the Germans were developing jet fighters. They'd studied intelligence reports about the Messerschmitt Me 163 *Komet* and Me 262 *Schwalbe* (Swallow). They weren't sure the jets were ready yet, but they knew the defense of the Reich was in the hands of capable pilots. And although the P-51 Mustang was thinning the Luftwaffe's ranks, attacking the capital of the Reich would be no piece of cake.

The mission came only after two failed attempts. "We tried twice to get to Berlin, the third and the fourth of March, and were recalled," said former Capt. Charles R. Bennett, a bombardier in the 390th Bombardment Group. Some bombers did make it to the German capital on March 4, 1944, but only a few.

Reaching Berlin was a symbolic milestone in the relentless building up of the Eighth Air Force and its bombing capabilities, and it would have been impossible without escort fighters to accom-pany the B-17 Flying Fortresses and B-24 Liberators. But striking Berlin remained a difficult task that meant terrible loss of life on the

American side—the highest number of aircraft lost in any mission mounted by the Eighth Air Force—as crewmembers fought every inch of the way to their objective. "As we went toward Berlin, you could just about navigate by the planes that had gone down ahead of us," said Bennett. "Every hundred miles or so, you'd see a burning plane on the ground." Many airmen on both sides saw the first Berlin mission not as an achievement for the Americans but as a debacle, and indeed as a victory for the Germans.

The first Berlin mission included 504 B-17 Flying Fortresses and 226 B-24s. The escort force included 86 P-38 Lightnings, 615 P-47 Thunderbolts, and 100 of the magnificent new P-51D Mustangs that were the only fighters with the range to go all the way.

One of the escort pilots, P-47 Thunderbolt airman 2nd Lt. Grant Turley, said to a buddy as they rode to the flight line: "This is the big one." The same thought had to be on the minds of P-51D Mustang pilots such as Col. Donald Blakeslee and Lt. Col. Tommy L. Hayes, who'd been chaffing to go all the way to the city that symbolized the foe. Perhaps unaware that the Führer spent little time in the capital, Hayes allowed as how it wouldn't be a bad idea to bring the war personally to Adolf Hitler.

Berlin was the first large-scale mission for the final wartime model of the Flying Fortress, the B-17G, which boasted a chin nose turret with two .50-caliber guns. Turbo-supercharged Pratt & Whitney R-1820-97 Cyclone engines powered the G model, which raised the service ceiling to thirty-five thousand feet.

The running air-ground battle raged along hundreds of miles of invisible highway in the sky. The bomber stream stretched ninety-four miles from the very first Pathfinder to the final "tail end Charlie."

For bomber crews, the mission began with a wakeup shortly after midnight. Briefing, warmup, takeoff, form-up, and ingress all entailed work and risks. The fighting began around 11:00 a.m., when the first Focke-Wulf Fw 190s engaged Flying Fortresses over Holland. The first casualty may have been the Fortress piloted by 2nd Lt. Brent Evertson of the 322nd Bombardment Squadron, 91st

Bombardment Group, which was riddled by gunfire from fighters near Magdeburg. Evertson's crew bailed out and the Flying Fortress smashed to the ground at Wilmersdorf near Bernau, northeast of Berlin. Evertson's ten-man crew became prisoners, but others were not so lucky. At least three bombers were rammed by German fighters, one by a twin-engine Messerschmitt Me 410. Although combat box formation of the bombers enabled them to concentrate defensive gunfire, more bombers took hits and fell away. Sometimes there was no smoke. Sometimes there were no parachutes.

Contrary to the expectations of some, German jets were not in the air during the first big Berlin mission. Thunderbolt pilot Turley, like Mustang pilot Gumm, became an ace and made a mark in shaping the force that would soon be fighting Hitler's jets, but neither ever got the chance.

Dale VanBlair, a B-24 Liberator gunner with the 448th Bombardment Group, remembered how it felt to have Berlin as his destination that day. "I participated in the first mass daylight raid on Berlin," said VanBlair. "A few of those 'other planes' [B-17s] had briefly hit the outskirts of the city on March 3 and 4 after ignoring a recall, but this was the first true mission to the capital. Although I normally flew in the tail turret, I was drafted to occupy the nose turret with another crew for this one. I knew the enlisted men of this crew but not the officers, and when I looked ahead at the flak barrage we were approaching, my main concern was whether the navigator or bombardier on this crew would take the time to let a stranger out of the nose turret if we had to bail out. I always left the doors of my tail turret open, thus didn't have to depend on anyone to let me out. I couldn't do that, of course, in the nose turret. Fortunately, we made it through without any major damage. After that, I was ready to go back to my tail turret where I didn't have to worry about the flak that I saw, since by the time I saw it, we were leaving it: 'Out of sight, out of mind.' "

Jerry Wolf was an engineer gunner in the top turret of a B-17 who flew no fewer than four missions over Berlin, something few airmen accomplished. Wolf belonged to the 390th Bombardment Group. "We would get bulletins on mimeograph paper telling us about new events. I assumed they came from Eighth Air Force headquarters. In one of them, they told us the Germans were building something called a jet. That was the word. Jet. Nobody had ever used it before. I didn't know what it was. When we heard that they had jets, it just put a shiver through you."

Wolf did not see a jet on March 6, 1944, but he did later.

Blakeslee's 4th Fighter Group had worked hard to integrate the P-51 Mustang into air operations. Still, the Mustang that traveled to Berlin on that first mission was a work in progress. The P-51B model of March 6, 1944, was not fully developed and was plagued by reliability issues. The Mustang's four (later, six) Browning M2 .50-caliber machine guns were mounted in the wing at an acute angle, which made them susceptible to jamming during high-G maneuvers. Sometimes, a pilot was reduced to only one gun within moments of opening fire. Moreover, the extreme cold at high altitude froze the oil in the guns. The U.S.-produced Packard V-1650 version of the famous Merlin engine had problems operating with the poor-quality British aviation gasoline until U.S. airmen scrounged up British spark plugs. The big, four-bladed Hamilton Standard paddle propeller was flexible and reliable, but could run hot, bleeding off some of the "push" that was supposed to propel the Mustang through the air. As late as two months after that first journey to Berlin, more Mustangs were being lost to mechanical failure than to enemy action.

The P-47 Thunderbolt lacked the Mustang's teething problems but still could not travel all the way to Berlin, a city whose rooftops 2nd Lt. Grant Turley never saw.

Over Germany but still many miles from the capital, apparently near the point where they would have to turn back, Focke-Wulf Fw 190s intercepted Turley's 78th Fighter Group. "We were escorting American bombers in Germany when suddenly some Germans appeared," group commander Col. James Stone later wrote. "They were going to attack the bombers, but before they could, Grant and a few other pilots intercepted them and a dogfight started. In the general confusion of the dogfight, everyone became separated and Grant was last seen chasing a German fighter that was headed for the ground."

"This all took place at a very high altitude," continued Stone, "so that Grant disappeared below before anyone could go after him to help. Grant probably chased this German and shot him down. Then he was probably alone, and may have been attacked by a superior number of German fighters while close to the ground. We will never know what happened. Grant, by his will to do all he could for his fellow flyers and his country, was responsible for saving the lives of many of the bombers and their crews."

Major Richard Hewitt, commander of the group's 82nd Fighter Squadron, wrote that after Grant Turley chased an Fw 190 toward the ground, "three other 190s were seen to bounce Grant's flight. Grant's wingman fought with one of them and Grant got on the tail of the one of the others and shot him down. The third 190 positioned himself behind Grant and several hits were seen on his ship. It is believed that he crashed. This story was told by Grant's wingman and he is the only one who saw the fight."

Turley became a first lieutenant, just as he'd predicted in a letter he'd sent home—but the promotion was posthumous.

April 1944

The Messerschmitt Me 262 jet fighter became operational in April 1944 with Erprobungskommando 262, or EKd 262 (Testing Command) based at Lechfeld. Here, Messerschmitt test pilots provided indoctrination in the new aircraft to Luftwaffe line pilots who were to fly the jet in combat. This test unit flew operational sorties and may have come within eyesight, at least, of Allied warplanes.

Separately, the buglike, rocket-propelled Messerschmitt Me 163 *Komet* fighter was being tweaked up to operational status in Erprobungskommando 16, or EKd 16, located at Peenemünde-

West—not far from the development site for the V-2 rocket—and commanded by Maj. Wolfgang Späte. After an initial round of flying in the Me 163, EKd 16 moved to Bad Zwischenahn, also in the far north of Germany and throughout the remainder of the war the largest airfield in the Reich.

Of the two Messerschmitt fighters that went into production without being pulled by propellers, the Me 163 arrived first. The Arado Ar 234 twin-jet reconnaissance aircraft and bomber was roughly between them in the development process, but at least one Ar 234 was operational on the morning of what Generalfeldmarschall (Field Marshal) Erwin Rommel called "the longest day."

June 6, 1944

The German warplanes and pilots committed to the defense of the Reich did their best to blunt the Allied air campaign and to forestall an Allied invasion of occupied Western Europe. To some extent, they can be credited with succeeding because some Allied leaders had hoped landings could take place much earlier.

The D-Day landing was a remarkable achievement of logistics, planning, and synchronized military action. On June 6, 1944, no fewer than 176,475 men, 3,000 guns, 1,500 tanks, and 15,000 other assorted vehicles landed in German-held Normandy across the five assault beaches or by glider and parachute in the fields of France.

Omaha was the code name for the second beach from the right of the five landing areas of the Normandy invasion. It ran for six miles, with a one hundred–foot cliff at its western extreme. "Bloody Omaha," assigned to the U.S. V Corps commanded by Maj. Gen. Leonard T. Gerow, was also the beach where everything went wrong.

"None of the plans were able to survive initial contact with the enemy," said author and analyst Tim Kilvert-Jones. "The Germans were highly effective soldiers, sited in well-prepared defensive positions on a naturally fortified escarpment overlooking the landing beach."

Kilvert-Jones also is a defense consultant and instructs U.S. Army units in lessons learned from past battles. Omaha Beach is a metaphor for the larger Normandy battle and was the day's greatest challenge to American troops.

The 16th Regiment of the 1st Infantry Division ("The Big Red One") and the 116th Regiment of the 29th Infantry Division made the initial assault at Omaha. The 16th Regiment landed at Omaha's Easy Red and Fox Green sectors at 6:30 a.m. The sectors drew their names from the military phonetic alphabet.

Soaked, cold, and overloaded with equipment, the men of the 16th Regiment encountered so much German resistance that, hours after the landing, they believed they had failed.

Amphibious Sherman tanks fitted with flotation screens that were supposed to support the 116th Regiment sank in the choppy waters of the English Channel after being offloaded too far from shore. Nearly every man in those tanks drowned. Only two of the twenty-nine Shermans made it to the beach. Except for one rifle company, no element of the 116th came ashore where it was planned.

The 16th Regiment bogged down and fought for its life on the Easy Red sector of Omaha Beach near Colleville-sur-Mer. For two hours, soldiers huddled behind the seawall. The beach was so congested with dead and dying there was no room to land reinforcements. Colonel George Taylor, regiment commander, told his men, "Two kinds of people are staying on this beach. The dead and those who are going to die! Now let's get the hell out of here!" The troops moved inland.

Rangers at Dog Green sector of Omaha Beach—re-created half a century later in the Steven Spielberg film *Saving Private Ryan*—had to improvise without any of the air and armor support they'd been promised.

Farther west, approaching in tricky coastal waters after being delayed by a navigational error, Rangers under Col. James E. Rudder had to come ashore on a bullet-raked shingle shelf under the face of a one hundred–foot cliff, scale the cliff, and attack German coastal artillery batteries. The location was Pointe du Hoc, on the extreme western end of Omaha Beach. Rudder hadn't believed the magnitude of the task at first. "The first time I heard about it," he told a superior officer, "I thought you were trying to scare me."

At Omaha, heavy bombers of the Eighth Air Force dropped bombs three miles from their intended targets, missing fortified German bunkers.

General Dwight D. Eisenhower prepared a statement of regret he would issue if the Germans pushed his troops into the sea. He never had to read it. The issue was never in doubt at Juno, Gold, and Sword Beaches, taken by British and Canadian troops, or at Utah Beach, taken by American forces. At Omaha, thanks largely to junior U.S. officers and noncommissioned officers—by tradition, exercising greater initiative than their counterparts in other armies—Gerow's V Corps overcame horrendous difficulties and seized the beach.

In the air over the beaches was a massive armada of Allied warplanes that included light and medium bomber units of the Ninth Air Force. "The Ninth rarely gets the mention it deserves," said retired Maj. Gen. John O. Moench.

Moench flew over the invasion beaches in an aircraft that would later spend much of its time fighting Hitler's jets: the B-26 Marauder medium bomber. Accounts of the D-Day battle rarely pay tribute to the heroism of the A-20 Havoc light bomber and or Moench's B-26.

"I was a member of the 454th Bombardment Squadron, 323rd Bombardment Group, stationed at Earl's Colne, England. On June 6, I was a second lieutenant who had been around for about two months. I was one of the early replacements in the unit and was getting experience pretty fast," Moench said

At the controls of his B-26, Moench was responsible for a seven-man crew consisting of a pilot, copilot, bombardier, navigator, radio operator, engineer (who was also a gunner at the top turret), and tail gunner. Some B-26s had had their copilot seats removed and were flown by a single pilot.

What was it like, flying over the largest invasion in history?

"The water was just loaded with ships out there. The fields of France were cluttered with gliders and parachutes. You're looking down at all this and thinking, 'Holy mackerel, look at all that stuff!' "

Moench knew that bombing near the invasion beaches to support ground troops would be no piece of cake. "The only thing that got me really uptight was when they said we would have go in at any altitude. That meant we'd have to fly very low if the situation demanded it, and we had lost a lot of airplanes the last time we did that," he said.

"In fact, the weather was such that we were able to go in at four thousand or five thousand feet where you got light antiaircraft fire. It was the first time I encountered tracer fire from the ground," he added. "The damn things come up at you, and you swear, 'Every one of those is going to hit me!'

"Some crews were assigned to drop bombs in the water. Guys coming ashore looked at that and said, 'Why are those damned aircraft dumping their bombs in the water?' But it was done on purpose. The intention was to set off underwater German mines. Otherwise, those mines were a threat to our troops. There was some success with this."

A fortnight after D-Day, as Allied armies battled to expand their foothold on Europe, Eisenhower took his newly commissioned son, John, on a tour of the invasion beaches. Second Lieutenant John Eisenhower was astonished to see vehicles moving to the front bumper-to-bumper, violating the textbook doctrine that called for dispersal to protect from air attack. "You would never get away with this if you didn't have air supremacy," John said to his father. The older Eisenhower retorted: "If I didn't have air supremacy, I wouldn't be here!"

It's true that the Allies dominated the skies, but on August 2, 1944, an Arado Ar 234 *Blitz* (Lightning) twin jet reconnaissance aircraft whizzed right past the Americans, British, and Canadians without any of them firing a shot at it or, perhaps, even batting an eye at it.

The Ar 234—the history of which will be related in chapter 13—was still very much an experiment taking shape, but the number seven aircraft was equipped to fly a mission and did. Despite the problems, the Ar 234 V7 prototype became the first jet aircraft ever to fly a reconnaissance mission. On August 2, 1944, Leutnant (2nd Lt.) Erich Sommer whizzed over the Normandy beachheads at about 460 miles per hour and used two Rb 50/30 cameras to take one set of photos every eleven seconds. Although the Allies supposedly had air superiority over the beaches, as Dwight D. Eisenhower famously said, Sommer's warplane returned with its fuel, unscathed.

The Messerschmitt Me 163 *Komet* was a weird and wonderful flying apparition that became the only rocket-powered fighter ever to fly in combat. Like so many of Adolf Hitler's *Wunderwaffen*, the Me 163 incorporated revolutionary technology, yet it was also a simple machine made largely of wood and could be a fiery deathtrap for its pilot. Some associated with it called it not the *Komet* but the *Kraftei* (Power Egg) or the flea. This mix of bright promise coupled with serious flaws makes a good metaphor for Adolf Hitler's mood and Nazi Germany's prospects at the start of a foreboding new year.

As with so many aircraft that emerged from the Messerschmitt works at Augsberg, the Me 163 was not the work of Willy Messerschmitt. In fact, the plane maker was lukewarm toward the concept and had tense relations with the rocket plane's designer, Alexander Lippisch. The lean, gaunt Lippisch, who rarely failed to remind others of his genius and was not easy to get along with in any event, had been hooked on aviation since at age fourteen he observed a flight demonstration by Orville Wright at Berlin's Tempelhof Airport in 1909.

It's widely believed that Wright influenced many of the German aviation figures who were approaching middle age during the war years. Wright and his sister Kate sailed from New York aboard the ocean liner SS *Kronprinzessin Cecilie* and arrived in London on August 16, 1909, and in Berlin on August 19. Between August 30 and October 15, Orville made nineteen flights and set world records for altitude and duration of flight, including flight with a passenger, in front of crowds of two hundred thousand people. He even took the crown prince up for a flight. Small wonder Lippisch was impressed.

Lippisch was an aerial observer during the Great War and designed a tailless glider in 1921. After initially working on a future rocket plane at the Heinkel works and transferring to Messerschmitt to see the Me 163 through its design and early development, Lippisch transferred to the Luftfahrtforschungsanstalt Wien (Vienna Aeronautical Research Institute) to concentrate on the problems of high-speed flight.

Lippisch seems to have been impervious to the other "wonder weapon" developments taking place around him. Some of these developments were enjoying more traction than others. The Reich had never had much of an atomic weapons program and it did not have much of one now. The V-1 robot bomb and V-2 rocket were terrorizing London but not slowing the advance of Allied troops. In later years, those who love conspiracy theories would claim that Nazi scientists were developing everything from antigravity propulsion to a time machine—a device called Die Glocke (the Bell) was said to be the latter—but much of it was fancy. The Messerschmitt Me 262 *Schwalbe* (Swallow) jet fighter was making itself felt in the air war, but too often that was happening precisely because hundreds of Allied bombers were overhead.

If someone should have been terrified of the Me 163, it was not the Americans pressing toward Berlin in the air, not men such as Val Beaudrault or Clayton Kelly Gross. It was a German Rudolf "Rudy" Opitz, who was thirty-four years old when the year 1945 began and who once said he struggled with the Me 163 "just when looking at it." He didn't know it himself, but Opitz had just the right mix of youthful daring and steadfast maturity to survive in the cockpit of a fragile wooden machine with a fire-breathing exhaust that looked like a bullet and wobbled like a drunken sailor. The small, gaunt, rather plain-looking Opitz, who'd had an unsatisfying encounter with Hermann Göring at Insterburg fourteen months earlier, went into 1944 as the settled, steady mentor for the young men who were going to take the 163 into combat.

Opitz's experience with the rocket-propelled Me 163 dated back to the beginning of the war in Europe. When he first saw plans for the Me 163, he couldn't believe it. The aircraft was incredibly small, lacked a tail, and required its pilot to sit between aluminum fuel tanks containing extremely volatile fuels. At least one pilot was killed when caustic propellants leaked into the cockpit. Opitz entered 1945 as commander of the Second Group of Jagdgeschwader 400 (JG 400), the only squadron to operate the Me 163 in combat.

In order to strap himself into the Me 163, attempt to fly in it, and even attempt to fight in it, a pilot needed the courage to recognize that only inches behind his back was raw heat igniting a series of recurring explosions—and at any time, a larger blast could envelop the entire aircraft. In its original incarnation as the Me 163A version, the rocket engine could not even be controlled by a throttle. The rocket motor's fuel of hydrazine hydrate, methanol, and an oxidizer was exceedingly toxic, in addition to being explosive.

Major Wolfgang Späte was an award-winning prewar glider pilot, thirty-three years of age in 1944, and was remarkably self-effacing. He was said to be unhappy when ground crews painted his Me 163 in a red color scheme patterned after the Fokker Dr-1 piloted by Manfred von Richthofen in the Great War. He quietly ordered a more subdued paint design.

He seems to have earned the distinction of being the first pilot of a "wonder weapon" to engage the Americans. On May 13, 1944—the day Allied naval forces in the Atlantic Ocean sank a submarine transporting plans for the Me 163 from Germany to Japan—Späte took off from Bad Zwischenahn and was vectored to intercept a pair of P-47 Thunderbolts operating at twenty-thousand feet over the Reich.

Späte got a visual fix on the Thunderbolts and was closing in when his rocket engine quit. This happened often in testing and was to be a recurring problem with the Me 163. Späte worked his way through a cumbersome restart procedure, got the engine working, and made a second attempt to close in on the P-47s.

The Thunderbolt pilots apparently never knew he was on their tail. Späte was squinting into his crude, ring-type gunsight, drawing within shooting distance when abruptly the left wing of his *Komet* dipped and he began to lose control. Späte groped around in the cockpit, managed to get the *Komet* under control, and looked up to see the Thunderbolts disappearing in the distance.

July 29, 1943

wrong year

The first encounter between Americans and the Me 163 happened on July 29, 1943, when B-17 Flying Fortress heavy bombers were making one of their repetitive attacks on Merseburg, a city so heavily defended airmen called it Merciless Merseburg. Arkansas native Capt. Arthur F. Jeffrey of the 479th Fighter Group went partway to the target at the controls of a P-38 Lightning named *Boomerang*— and almost certainly freezing in the big, twin-prop fighter whose cockpit heater never worked. Jeffrey went to help the beleaguered crew of a straggling Fortress of the 100th Bombardment Group near Wessermunde.

An Me 163 appeared in the vicinity of the bomber. Jeffrey later said it was weaving around. Jeffrey turned into the *Komet* and lined it up in his gunsight. Like all P-38s, *Boomerang* had a control wheel rather than a stick (on late P-38s like Jeffrey's, it was actually two conventional stick grips mounted on cross braces), and triggers on both side operated the guns. Jeffrey started shooting and saw his rounds striking the small, odd-looking German aircraft. A rush of fire came back from the rocket exhaust, and the Me 163 abruptly vaulted from Jeffrey's altitude of eleven thousand feet to fifteen thousand.

Jeffrey chased the Me 163 up to sixteen thousand feet when it executed a hard left turn and began to bleed off precious airspeed. Jeffrey closed in on the rocket plane and opened fire again at three hundred yards. Again, he saw his rounds hitting home, again and again. The *Komet* dove hard for the cloud deck below and vanished at three hundred feet at more than 550 miles per hour. The Me 163's flight envelope indicates that a pullout would have been impossible given its ninety-degree dive angle, speed, and low altitude. Jeffrey claimed and was credited with the kill. Many years later, when records from the German side became available, it appeared the Luftwaffe did not lose an Me 163 that day, which would mean that the official first kill of an advanced German warplane wasn't really a kill after all. Two other P-38 pilots flying with Jeffrey came across a second Me 163 while Jeffrey was busy with the first. The rocket-plane pilot took advantage of his strong suit—speed—and raced away from the P-38s, unharmed.

EIGHT

THE JET PLANE BOOGIE

Belatedly, in July 1944, the Messerschmitt Me 262 went into front-line service in its first operational unit.

The unit evolved from Erprobungskommando 262, or EKdo 262. Its first commander, the accomplished ace Hauptman (Capt.) Werner Thierfelder, twenty-eight, lost his life on July 18, 1944, when his Me 262 crashed for reasons that are unclear but remind us that Me 262 operations were hampered by parts and supply shortages, irregular availability of fuel, and overall reliability issues. At one juncture, the Reich would lose ten Me 262s in six weeks to noncombat causes.

Austria-born, 258-kill air ace Walter Nowotny, twenty-three, replaced Thierfelder. Nowotny was well liked by fellow pilots but few others. He was full of himself. He was better at shooting than at leading. A seasoned Bf 109 and Fw 190 veteran of fighting on the Eastern Front, he had no credentials for leadership or organization, but to his credit, he formed the unit, later to be named after him as Kommando Nowotny, while continuing to fly operational missions and claiming three aerial victories in the newfangled jet.

Essentially a trial-and-development unit, Kommando Nowotny holds the distinction of having mounted the world's first jet fighter operations. Trials continued slowly, with initial operational missions against the Allies in August 1944 allegedly downing nineteen Allied aircraft for six Me 262s lost. However, these claims can't be verified by cross-checking with Army Air Forces records and the Royal Air Force Museum holds no intelligence reports of RAF aircraft engaging in combat with Me 262s in August, although there is a report of an unarmed encounter between an Me 262 and a Mosquito.

The unit took shape at a succession of airfields near Osnabrück, suffered painful attrition rates, and never resolved the Me 262's teething troubles. Nowotny was a genuine pioneer in testing and developing tactics to employ the Me 262 in combat, but he was also difficult and, to some, strange. He appears to have totally ignored orders to remain on the ground while introducing a new form of warfare to the skies. He was an intensely superstitious young man and always wore a particular pair of trousers that had served him well in an earlier action—his "victory pants," as he called them.

Nowotny was said to have become cockier after being summoned to a personal audience with Adolf Hitler and being awarded the Ritterkreuz des Eisernen Kreuzes mit Eichenlaub, Schwertern und Brillanten (Knight's Cross of the Iron Cross with Oak Leaves, Swords, and Diamonds), making him the eighth of twenty-seven men to be so honored. Superstitious, a perfectionist, confident, and arrogant, Nowotny never ceased showing himself to be a better pilot than a leader: his fledgling unit with newly delivered Me 262s was being so poorly administered that pilots complained outside the chain of command. Generalleutnant (Maj. Gen.) Adolf "Dolfo" Galland, on a visit to Nowotny's unit (described in greater detail in the next chapter), was bombarded with complaints that the Me 262 was not ready for battle.

It may have been like a homesick angel when it tucked in its wheels, broke free from the airfield pattern, and vaulted to medium or high altitudes where it performed best, but the Me 262 was hindered by more than logistical issues and the all-too-familiar reliability problems with jet engines. Although the existence of the Me 262 quickly became well known throughout the Reich and outside it, the rules dictating secrecy were an additional hindrance. Some supply and support contractors were physically prevented from doing their jobs by the guards who maintained things and by loose—but at times, pervasive—security around jet bases.

Although the Me 262 was a straightforward design operating from relatively primitive airfields, Nowotny, in particular, stressed to pilots the importance of secrecy, a tradition he passed on to his successors. Hans Busch, the youngster from Lübeck who had flown gliders in the Hitlerjungen, the Hitler Youth, took the proscription most seriously. Wrote Busch:

> We were sternly instructed to never, ever talk to anyone, military or civilian, about this aircraft. Secrecy was enforced! We used to take pictures of us sitting in all sorts of aircraft or standing in front of one, but with the Me 262 that was an absolute NO! NO! That's why relatively speaking so few pictures of the Me 262 are available today. Together with expert pilots with lots of flying experience and many combat missions under their belts, we ten [new pilots] formed a flight training group and maintained rigid secrecy.

Nowotny, Busch, and the others were being asked to go into battle in an aircraft that performed beautifully at altitude and was remarkably quiet inside the cockpit. "No aircraft we had flown or seen so far looked as sleek or as streamlined," wrote Busch. But the aircraft had plenty of problems when taxying or operating in the airfield pattern. Busch was constantly having problems with the brakes and with the nose wheel. He wrote:

> The nose wheel was a weak part of the aircraft. We were careful not to put too much stress on it. It was not steerable; in other words it was freewheeling. At one time when I turned the aircraft at the end of the runway into takeoff position I made a mistake

and stepped on the right brake just a little too hard. The aircraft promptly swung around, but then it would not move forward any more. The nosewheel had flipped into a crossway position.

Busch was stuck with no choice but to "idle the engines, unbuckle the seat belt, unbuckle the parachute, disconnect the radio, open the cockpit, jump to the ground and kick the nose wheel very hard with my foot until it was in an about 45-degree position," he wrote.

With very limited information, U.S. intelligence experts searched for a flaw in the Me 262. Over time, they would conclude that the jet fighter relied on poor structural workmanship and that its flight duration could vary from forty-five to ninety minutes. The intelligence officers were many months away from actually getting their hands on a real Me 262, but they were already deciding that if U.S. fighters were going to defeat the Me 262, the place to do it would be close to the ground, in the airfield pattern.

July 26, 1944

On July 26, 1944, Leutnant (Lieutenant) Alfred "Bubi" Schreiber intercepted and attacked a De Havilland Mosquito PR XVI, a photoreconnaissance aircraft from No. 544 Squadron of the Royal Air Force, while piloting a Messerschmitt Me 262A-1a.

Schreiber did several things that had never been done before. One was to mount a serious challenge to the Mosquito, the all-wood, twin-engine British warplane that until now had sailed over the Reich on a daily basis with almost total impunity. Adolf Hitler called the Mosquito "imprudent" and shook his head in contempt when he added, "and it's made of wood!" The Führer personally regarded the Mosquito as a thorn in his side. His "wonder weapons," he hoped, would finally enable his pilots to counter the aircraft he considered both a threat and a pest.

The all-wood Mosquito was in some ways the most useful Allied aircraft of World War II. It flew fast and high, and Hitler and Göring looked up and could do nothing about it. They would essentially be defenseless until they could put a wonder weapon up to confront the plane the Brits called the "wooden wonder."

When De Havilland proposed the Mosquito, nobody was interested. A twin-engine, two-man bomber with no defensive armament was an ideal that some RAF officers called laughable. But the Mosquito was fast and nimble, and it performed well in an attack on Gestapo headquarters in Oslo, which was thwarted by dud bombs. High-speed, precision air strikes became the stock in trade for the Mosquito, which also adapted quickly to other missions.

A typical Mosquito was pulled through the air by two 1,480-horsepower Rolls-Royce Merlin 21/21 or 23/23 liquid-cooled V-12 engines, the same powerplant that would eventually enable the P-51 Mustang to prevail over the Luftwaffe. The two-man, tail-dragger Mosquito had a wingspan of fifty-four feet two inches (almost thirteen feet greater than the Me 262) and a maximum takeoff weight of 18,649 pounds (compared to 15,720 pounds for a typical Me 262).

When the Mosquito entered production in 1941, it was one of the fastest operational aircraft in the world. Entering widespread service in 1942, the Mosquito first operated as a high-speed, high-altitude photo reconnaissance aircraft, and it continued in this role throughout the war. From mid-1942 to mid-1943 Mosquito bombers were used in high-speed, medium-, or low-altitude missions, attacking factories, railways, and other pinpoint targets within Germany and German-occupied Europe. From late 1943, Mosquito bomber units were formed into the Light Night Strike Force and used as pathfinders for Royal Air Force Bomber Command's heavy-bomber raids. They were also used as nuisance bombers, often dropping four thousand–pound "cookies" (bombs) in high-altitude, high-speed raids that German night fighters were almost powerless to intercept.

Almost four dozen versions of the Mosquito carried out every wartime duty, from whisking spies behind the lines to photo mapping enemy territory. Precision bombing of special targets—Amiens prison, Gestapo headquarters in the Hague, V-1 "buzz bomb" launching sites—persisted throughout the war. Each time, the Mosquito demonstrated its unique ability to strike fast, hit hard, and get away clean.

Small wonder "Bubi" Schreiber regarded his target very seriously when he locked onto a Mosquito and launched the first air-to-air encounter in history involving a jet aircraft. He didn't know, at first, that he was going to have the encounter. It was a beautiful day for flying, and Schreiber, who loved to fly, was simply very glad to be in the air.

Author James Neal Harvey wrote, "It was a warm, sunny day, and there had been no reports of an impending attack by American bombers. This would be a routine training flight, although the magazines of the aircraft's four Mk-108 cannons were fully loaded. Schreiber enjoyed flying the jet and was proud of having been selected to join Ekdo 262 [his jet unit]. Because he'd logged many hours in [Messerschmitt] Bf 110s, he found the transition to the new [aircraft] relatively easy."

He didn't know a Mosquito was coming. The first Allied pilot to fight Hitler's jets, arriving over the Reich at a combat speed of about 430 miles per hour, was Flight Lt. Albert E. "Bertie" Wall. He was at the controls of the Mosquito approaching Schreiber and could not have known about the impending encounter either. Wall and his navigator Albert Sinclair "Jock" Lobban had every reason to believe they would make it safely home today.

As he cruised over the German countryside, Schreiber had to be happy that he'd made a smooth takeoff, despite the unreliability of his jet engines and the weak construction of the Me 262's nose wheel. Once away from the airfield pattern, where he could be vulnerable to marauding American fighters, Schreiber was at the controls of what he later called "a super ship to fly," smoothly responsive to his hand on the controls and free of torque or vibration. Instead of the clattering of pistons and propeller, Schreiber could detect only a faint whisper from his engines. Decent weather was rare in northern Europe, and Schreiber was going to make the most of what was intended as a short check flight.

Not that anyone ever made a long flight in the 262. Schreiber and his fellow pilots were under a restriction that required them to land after fifty minutes since the "wonder weapon" jet was good for only about an hour in the air.

Schreiber spotted the Mosquito, poured on the power, and engaged. For possibly the first time ever, a Mosquito was under attack from an aircraft that was faster than it was. Wall apparently thought at first that he was going to outrun his attacker, just as he'd outrun Bf 109s and Fw 190s in the past. He pushed his throttles to full power, looked back over his shoulder, and saw Schreiber's Me 262 pass him by and pull up to the right above him.

But Wall believed his aircraft was more maneuverable. He was right: the Mosquito had a wing loading of forty-eight pounds per square foot while the figure for the Me 262 was sixty-five pounds. At just the moment Schreiber spotted the Mosquito and banked to attack it, Lobban saw the German jet and shouted a warning over the intercom. Just as Schreiber's gloved thumb came down on the trigger for his four MK-108 cannons, Wall made a sharp, tight turn to the left and turned inside the Me 262.

Cannon shells ripped through the air. Three times, Schreiber repeated his maneuver, and each time Wall broke and turned inside the attacker. Schreiber thought he saw his rounds striking the Mosquito. He saw a piece of the aircraft fall off. He knew he had a kill. In German records, he would receive credit for the first air-to-air victory by a jet fighter.

When Wall and Lobban heard a muffled explosion, they, too, thought they'd been hit and perhaps mortally damaged. Wall ordered Lobban to open the emergency hatch in preparation for bailing out. When he did so, Lobban learned that the explosion had been the outer hatch blowing off due to the intensity of their maneuver. That was the piece Schreiber had seen.

Schreiber and his fellow pilots later looked at gun camera footage from his Me 262. It showed the Mosquito taking hits and a piece of the aircraft flying loose while the Mosquito itself plummeted downward. They celebrated the kill. They had no way to know that Wall nursed the Mosquito over the Austrian Alps and landed at Fermo, Italy. Schreiber apparently was luckier a few days later when he engaged a Spitfire and shot it down.

August 28, 1944

Major General William Kepner, the tough-as-nails boss of XIII Fighter Command—the air-to-air component of the Eighth Air Force—had been briefed on German jets and knew about the Me 163 and Me 262. Once the long-awaited Allied invasion of Nazi-occupied Europe was underway (observed from overhead by an Arado Ar 234 jet reconnaissance aircraft), Kepner began getting more intelligence on Adolf Hitler's "wonder weapons" and ideas to combat them. Kepner had already freed up his new P-51 Mustangs—the first U.S. fighter easily able to escort bombers all the way to targets deep inside the Reich—so that Mustang pilots could roam ahead of the bomber formations and, where appropriate, attack airfields. Now, Kepner realized that even the vaunted Me 262 could become meat on the table when operating in its airfield pattern.

On August 28, 1944, Kepner's men came up against Oberfeldwebel (First Sergeant) Hieronymus "Rony" Lauer, a straightforward, clean-cut young man who exuded quiet confidence and seemed incapable of being afraid.

He'd been living on the edge longer than any of the Americans who were fighting Hitler's jets. Lauer joined the Luftwaffe in 1937 and was in pilot training at the start of the war, in those early days when the Luftwaffe could afford the time for the same kind of rigorous training program that was typical of the Americans. That luxury would vanish, though, and Lauer would eventually find himself fighting alongside men with relatively little experience.

With an initial assignment similar to that of his fellow pilot Hans Busch, Lauer flew the twin-prop Junkers Ju 88 in the Mediterranean theater. In 1944, he was transferred to unit 1/KG51 for training on the Me 262 and flew in combat a few months later. He appeared to have a natural feel for the jet aircraft and to be stoic about its flaws. Lauer was to achieve several "firsts" as a jet pilot and one was becoming the first Me 262 pilot claimed as an aerial victory by the Allies.

It happened when Maj. Joseph Myers led the Surtax Blue Flight of P-47 Thunderbolts of the 82nd Fighter Squadron, 78th Fighter Group, on a fighter sweep at eleven thousand feet near Termonde, Belgium. At 7:15 p.m., Myers saw what he thought was a B-26 Marauder going south very fast and very low. He dove at forty-five degrees registering 450 miles per hour and got right above the aircraft at five thousand feet, observing that it was painted slate blue with no markings. The plane began doing ninety-degree-wide evasive turns, apparently demonstrating in the process what many pilots would conclude later—that it could not turn inside a P-47. Myers cut him off and closed in to within eight hundred yards. That's when Myers remembered that intelligence officers had shown him recognition plats of a new aircraft called the Me 262. The pilot: Rony Lauer.

Lauer's guns weren't even loaded. He was ferrying the Me 262 on a transfer from Juvincourt, near Reims, France, to Chievres, Belgium.

Myers and 2nd Lt. Manford O. Croy Jr. latched on and chased Lauer. As Myers held his thumb over the firing switch, Lauer slowed down and crashed in a plowed field. Myers started shooting as the M2 262 touched the ground and continued pumping bursts into it at close quarters, getting hits in the cockpit and both engines. The Me 262 skidded across a field, on fire. Lauer leaped out and ran. By then Croy was opening up with his eight .50-caliber guns, and the after-action report indicated that Croy hit the pilot as he ran from the jet. In fact, Lauer was never touched. Myers and Croy are each credited with one-half of an air-to-air victory, officially the first American kill of a jet.

Lauer wasn't finished being shot down—it would happen again—but at the very time Allied armies were making a breakout in France, there was a lull in engagements.

October 2, 1944

He was a big guy in a big plane. The good-natured giant from Milford, New Hampshire, Val Beaudrault, had been "the guy who always did the blocking on end-around plats, who usually got hit by three opposing linemen on trick formation," remembered Sgt. Bill Davidson. When he had been a machinist, "he was the one who had to wrestle the heavy equipment all over the floor," Davidson said. Now Beaudrault was wrestling with the heaviest single-engine American fighter of the war, the brute P-47 Thunderbolt. He was on his fourth P-47, named *Miss Pussy IV* after his girlfriend, Priscilla Pero. This war was tough on airplanes, and plenty of pilots lasted longer than their planes did.

It was late afternoon, October 2, 1944. Beaudrault's 386th Fighter Squadron, 365th Fighter Group, the "Hell Hawks," was on patrol southwest of Münster.

A muscular man at the controls of a muscular aircraft, one in which he had complete confidence even though it required constant monitoring, Beaudrault coaxed his P-47 along in a cold sky of good visibility with 7/10 multilayer cloud cover. Suitably for a fighter leader, he had grown an impressive moustache. His hair was brown with a reddish tinge, but the "cookie doctor," as he called it, was flaming red, a fitting adornment for an air warrior who would have looked good with a red flying scarf if he'd had one.

He was leading Plastic Blue Flight, a brace of four of the seven-ton Thunderbolts. Val Beaudrault had never heard of a man named Rony Lauer but was about to try to kill him.

"My God!" shouted 1st Lt. Robert Teeter, the number three pilot in the flight. "What is that?"

"Let's see what that sonofabitch is," Beaudrault said. He went into an abrupt climb, mindful that the cloud cover around him was tricky. His two-plane element, consisting of Beaudrault and 1st Lt. William F. "Pete" Peters, lost the rest of the squadron in the overcast. They were alone.

They went down below the clouds again and then Beaudrault spotted the same adversary.

"I sighted a bogie at 10 o'clock slightly low and in a shallow drive," Beaudrault wrote in his after-action report. A *bogie* was an unidentified aircraft, but a later *Stars & Stripes* story about the next few minutes would put Beaudrault in the middle of an aerial boogie—a dance. If a strong, fast beat was part of it, maybe the faux term wasn't so out of place after all. Val Beaudrault was flying into a jet plane boogie.

"I dropped my belly tank and led Plastic Blue Flight in a dive after him. The enemy aircraft turned toward us and steepened his dive to approximately 40 degrees, passing low and approximately 150 yards in front of me," Beaudrault added in his report.

The bogie was playing around. It seemed to slow down and let them come within range. And then it whipped around and passed within 150 yards.

"It's got wings like a C-47," said Beaudrault.

"No C-47 ever traveled along at five hundred miles an hour," said Peters.

"It's got a tail like a P-51."

"You never saw a P-51 with a paint job like that." Peters was a relatively new replacement pilot from Cold Spring, Minnesota, who may not have attended briefings about the remarkable new flying machines the Germans were building.

"He did a sharp, 360-degree turn," Beaudrault wrote. "However, I had no trouble turning inside of him with my P-47. During these maneuvers I failed to definitely identify the aircraft, so consequently held my fire. The aircraft then rolled out of the turn and applied full throttle and started to pull away, even though I was using full throttle and water injection.

"It seemed, however, to take a few seconds for the jet [engines] to take effect. At this time I took a few pictures with my gun camera. The aircraft flew straight, taking evasive action for approximately one minute. At this time I saw a second similar aircraft come in from the right and pull up sharply into a very steep climb at about 45 degrees. I saw my wingman Lt. Peters pull up after him. However, [Peters] could not climb as fast and fell behind. I then saw the aircraft I was chasing suddenly lose power."

The fast, nimble Me 262, which flew so very well once freed from the bonds of the airfield pattern, was always vulnerable to power issues and Beaudrault was now ready to seize the advantage. At the controls of the fleeing jet in front of Val Beaudrault was Oberfeldwebel (First Sergeant) Hieronymus "Rony" Lauer, a straightforward, clean-cut young man who exuded quiet confidence. If the name seems familiar it's because of Lauer's dubious distinction as the first Me 262 pilot to be shot down, sort of, by Maj. Joseph Myers and 2nd Lt. Manford O. Croy Jr. of Surtax Blue Flight five weeks earlier. Another pilot described Lauer as fearless, which was the right trait at the right time. After all, he had been living on the edge for a long time and now his aircraft was faltering and Beaudrault was closing in behind him, hand on trigger.

This should have been Lauer's day to die.

Possibly his long history in the Luftwaffe dating to 1937 gave Lauer just enough additional experience to evade the inevitable. He knew he could not turn inside a P-47, not with sixty-five pounds per square foot of wing load pressing down on his Me 262 while the Thunderbolt bore just forty-five. He knew he should have outrun his foe, but that he had missed his chance by allowing Beaudrault to get into firing position.

Lauer struggled with his controls and pondered the best way to go in the only possible direction—down.

In an official account, white puffs of smoke sputtered from the Me 262 and then stopped. "The German was out of fuel. Now it was Beaudrault's turn," the report read. "The German, in a 300-mile-an-hour glide, tried to take evasive action by slipping from side to side. Beaudrault moved in close for the final burst. The German slipped sideways a bit too much and hit the ground."

The account continued: "There was a tremendous explosion. Beaudrault made a pass over the field, but there was nothing left but a fearfully burning fire and shining pieces of aluminum scattered over three acres."

It's unclear where the explosion or the burning field came from, but both would undoubtedly be a surprise to Rony Lauer, who had survived being shot down in an Me 262 a second time. Beaudrault's after-action report cites no explosion or fire. Beaudrault wrote: "After I saw him strike the ground I immediately pulled up sharply to assist my wingman [Peters]. Consequently, I had no opportunity to photograph the crash. When I reached my wingman, he was chasing the other [Me 262] around in a circle and as I approached the aircraft went into a 10 to 15 degree dive and disappeared into clouds."

The P-47 Thunderbolt was back in the air against the Me 262 on October 7, 1944, when the busy 78th Fighter Group was on the prowl in the Osnabrück area. Major Richard E. Conner peered from his Thunderbolt at twenty-four thousand feet and, far below, saw two blurred objects in high-speed motion climbing toward the bombers he was escorting. Conner used hand signals to two P-47 pilots alongside and the trio went into a rapid dive. It appeared to Conner that the unidentified aircraft below were moving faster.

Author William N. Hess wrote:

> The P-47s' pursuit paid off when the Me 262s ran short of fuel and began to circle an airfield. As Conner closed on one of the aircraft, it came back toward him in a head-on pass. The Thunderbolt pilot easily turned inside the pass and fired a ninety-degree deflection burst. The 262 then headed for the airdrome, and Conner closed rapidly when the jet lowered its landing gear. The P-47 pilot let fly with a long burst that scored many strikes on the enemy aircraft. As Conner overran the 262, his wingmen watched as it crashed on the airfield. The downed Me 262 was from Kampfgeschwader 51, or KG 51 (Bomber Group 51) "Edelweiss," and, although the Americans did not report it, the German pilot is said to have bailed out.

On the day of Conner's aerial victory, P-51 Mustang pilots 1st Lt. Elmer T. Taylor and 1st Lt. Willard G. Erfkamp of the 364th Fighter Group encountered one of the pesky Me 163 *Komet* rocket planes and teamed up to shoot it down. Its pilot, with the surname Husser, survived. But despite the volatility and flaws that came hand in hand with the Me 163, rocket pilots claimed credit for two B-17 Flying Fortress heavy bombers shot down that day. Fortress bombardier 2nd Lt. Stuart W. Jakku of the 457th Bombardment Group had been married for just four weeks when his bomber went down and his crew perished.

October 7, 1944

The day wore on. October 7, 1944, was a long day over Europe for American bomber crews and fighter pilots, including 1st Lt. Urban L. "Ben" Drew of the 361st Fighter Group—one-time moviegoer and former instructor and sometime screw-up from Detroit—who was at the controls of a sleek new P-51 Mustang.

Leading his squadron that day, Drew was taking his P-51 pilots home after escorting B-17s to a target in Brux, Czechoslovakia. As testimony to the range of the P-51, Drew still had fuel in his external tanks. He called and received radio permission to swoop down on a pair of Me 262s of Kommando Nowotny, based at Achmer and that someone had spotted while the jets were on the ground.

Drew wrote: "I watched them for a while and saw one of them start to taxi. The lead ship was in takeoff position for a formation takeoff. I waited until they were both airborne and then I rolled over from 15,000 feet and headed for the attack with my flight behind me." The German jets were impressive, but the sight of four factory-fresh Mustangs in a near-vertical dive, glinting in the sun while rushing downward at high speed, had to be remarkable.

With Capt. Bruce Rowlett and 2nd Lt. Robert K. McCandliss close behind him, Drew watched the pair of Me 262s grow in his gunsight. A protective screen of Focke-Wulf Fw 190s (the long-nosed Fw 190D-9 or "Dora" version) was supposed to be protecting the airfield, but for reasons unknown they were nowhere to be seen. Leutnant (2nd Lt.) Gerhard Kobert and Oberfeldwebel (First Sgt.) Heinz Arnold were in a position where no Me 262 pilot wanted to find himself—vulnerable in the airfield pattern.

Drew wrote that he "caught up with one Me 262 when he was 1,000 feet off the ground. I was indicating 450 miles per hour. The Me 262 couldn't have been going more than 200 miles per hour. I started firing from approximately 400 yards, 30 degrees defection, and as I closed, I saw hits all over the wings and fuselage. Just as I passed him [Kobert], I saw a sheet of flame come out from near the right wing root and as I glanced back I saw gigantic explosions and a sheet of red flame over an area of 1,000 feet."

McCandliss was hoping to bag an Me 262. "I've got a shot," Drew heard McCandliss say. "Long range, but I have a shot."

Drew was surprised when the second Me 262 tried to climb away. Had the jet been moving at high speed at the beginning of the encounter, it would have gotten away. However, while the Me 262 was faster than a P-51, it did not accelerate faster. Drew turned inside the jet and closed in. He opened fire and saw hits striking the Me 262's tail section.

Wrote Drew: "Just then, the canopy flew off in two sections and the plane rolled over and went into a flat spin. The aircraft hit the ground on its back at about a sixty-degree angle. I did not see the pilot bail out, and the enemy aircraft exploded violently. As I looked back at the two wrecks, I saw two mounting columns of black smoke."

Instead of bagging his own Me 262, McCandliss found himself eyeball-to-eyeball with a flak battery. Drew last saw McCandliss when McCandliss's P-51 went into a veering steep turn, spraying pieces of debris in its wake.

When Drew returned to base, he found that not only had his wingman failed to return after being hit by flak following Drew's victories, but the gun camera also failed. The only eyewitness to Drew's extraordinary boldness over Ahmer during the war—McCandliss—was in the process of becoming a prisoner of war at a Stalag. Only after the war did Drew learn his wingman had survived. That's when McCandliss described his Me 262 encounter as "like trying to catch a motorcycle while on a bicycle." Drew was the first and only Allied pilot to shoot down two German jet aircraft in one aerial combat, the first operational losses of Kommando Novotny, but recognition did not come until long after the war (on May 12, 1983), when he was belatedly awarded the Air Force Cross.

On a subsequent mission, Drew and two wingmen destroyed the only Luftwaffe six-engine flying boat at Schlaalsee seaplane base in northern Germany. This six-engine aircraft was later acknowledged to be a Blohm und Voss BV 238 V1, a new very long-range, flying-boat bomber that had just finished its operational tests and with which Adolf Hitler had hoped to attack New York and Washington. It was also an aircraft Hitler aide Martin Bormann wanted available in case Hitler and other Reich leaders needed a means of escape from embattled Berlin.

The BV 238 was the heaviest aircraft ever flown when it made its initial flight on March 11, 1944. It was the largest flying boat and the largest Axis aircraft.

Some historical accounts say the BV 238 survived Drew's attack and was later destroyed by British Hawker Typhoons or Tempests. Either way, with the prototype sunk, the BV 238 program was abandoned and the aircraft was no longer a candidate to bomb the U.S. East Coast or to carry Adolf Hitler to safety in Antarctica, or Argentina—or somewhere.

Drew believed he had destroyed a Blohm und Voss BV 222 *Wiking* (Viking), the four-engine flying boat that was nearly as large, far more reliable, and equally a perfect candidate for both long-range bombing and leadership evacuation missions. Long after the war, researchers contacted Drew and told him their research indicated he'd wrecked the sole BV 238, the largest aircraft to be destroyed during the war.

During the war, a German newspaper reported that one of the thirteen BV 222s built flew via the North Pole to Sakhalin Island, the southern half of which was then part of the Japanese Empire (the northern half being Russian), prior to April 1944. The news story accurately reflected a capability that fascinated Bormann—the only Reich official who devoted a lot of time and attention to anticipating the need for a postwar escape by the Nazi leadership—but the flight to Japan apparently never took place.

October 12, 1944

Drew and other Eighth Air Force pilots were now able to use personal experience to inform and prepare others. Intelligence officers were now able to pore over maps of German airfields—nothing is more difficult to hide than a paved runway—and to discern when and where Me 163s and Me 262s would be most vulnerable. Having been freed up to roam away from the bomber formations, having learned that they could easily turn inside the jets once a maneuvering contest began, and having experienced how vulnerable the jets were in the airfield pattern, the P-51 pilots were becoming more and more confident.

On October 12, 1944, officer Robert W. "Bob" Cole in a British Hawker Tempest V fighter of No. 3 Squadron, Royal Air Force, shot down an Me 262 of KG 51. It was the first jet kill by a Tempest. Cole's air speed indicator was reading 480 miles per hour, yet the jet was pulling away. For reasons unclear, the Me 262 slowed down, Cole started shooting, and the jet fell in Allied territory, badly wrecked but a treasure for intelligence experts. A Cole's adversary, Unteroffizier (Corporal) Edmond Delatowski, bailed out, landed behind German lines, and emerged from the encounter with minor wounds. About a dozen other encounters in October resulted in Me 262s shooting down at least two British fighters and half a dozen bombers. One Me 262 pilot lost his life in a strike with a flock of birds.

The month of October 1944 was marked by a lull in encounters between German jets and American fighters. Official U.S. records do not support the widely reported sharing of an Me 262 aerial victory by Col. Hubert "Hub" Zemke and 1st Lt. Norman Benoit on October 7. Moreover, German records confirm that the Zemke-Benoit duo actually bagged a propeller-driven Messerschmitt Bf 109. The first American kill of the month occurred on October 15, when 1st Lt. Hugh O. Foster damaged an Me 262 and 2nd Lt. Huie H. Lamb Jr.

shot one down. Foster and Lamb were P-47 Thunderbolt pilots of the 78th Fighter Group, and Lamb's adversary was Feldwebel (Sgt.) Edgar Junghans.

Leutnant (Lieutenant) Alfred "Bubi" Schreiber, previously renowned for his duel with a speeding Mosquito, was credited with shooting down a Lockheed Lightning—a P-38 fighter or an F-5 photo ship—on October 29. It marked the end of a busy month.

November 1, 1944

On November 1, 1944, Me 262s from Kommando Nowotny tangled with Thunderbolts of the 56th Fighter Group and Mustangs of the 20th and 352nd Fighter Groups. Two of the P-47 pilots, 1st Lt. Walter R. Groce and 2nd Lt. William T. Gerbe Jr., shared an aerial victory credit.

The following day, after a period of down time spent reorganizing, the buglike Messerschmitt Me 163 *Komet* rocket fighter was back in action. Jagdgeschwader 400 (Fighter Group 400), or JG 400, commanded by the busy Maj. Wolfgang Späte, sent about a dozen Me 163s into the air from their base at Brandis. The *Komets* were going to use their limited fuel time of about nine minutes to confront American bomber formations boring toward petroleum targets in the Reich.

High over central Germany east of Leipzig, Capt. Fred Glover—called Freddie, from Ashville, North Carolina, and already an ace—was leading the 4th Fighter Group at the controls of a P-51 Mustang. He was minding a formation of four-engine bombers churning along at twenty-five thousand feet and was searching the sky alertly when he saw a blemish in motion. An Me 163 appeared in front of the bombers and dived toward them. Glover called in the sighting, dropped his external fuel tanks, and accelerated straight on toward the Me 163. Other pilots in Glover's formation were distracted by a gaggle of Bf 109s and sent two of them falling to earth. What the American Mustang men failed to see was that other Me 163s shot down two bombers, while gunners from those bombers bagged a pair of Me 163s, killing both German pilots, Oberfeldwebel (First Sgt.) Horst Rolly and Oberfeldwebel (First Sgt.) Herbert Straznicky.

Glover overshot the Me 163 and turned to approach it from behind. He unleashed his Mustang's six .50-caliber guns and saw hits on the tail, wings, and fuselage of the Me 163. He was drawing closer to fire again when the underside of the rocket plane erupted in an orange torrent of fire. Glover swept past, saw that the Me 163's tail was shot off, its canopy remained affixed, and Oberfeldwebel (First Sgt.) Gunther Andreas was struggling to get out.

Andreas told author Stephen Ransom, "I . . . attempted to jettison the canopy in case I had to bail out should the aircraft start to burn. At 600 [kilometers per hour], the canopy would not budge—it had probably been jammed by the enemy's fire."

Andreas slowed down, was able to jettison the canopy, and wriggled out of the *Komet* while it was in a dive. He was able to hit the silk and was seen dangling beneath a parachute. While Glover and Andreas were testing each other, another 4th group Mustang ace, Capt. Louis H. Norley, saw an Me 163 moving into position behind him. Norley made his first-ever use of a device that was being newly installed on Mustangs, the K-14 gyroscopic lead-computing gunsight.

With his air speed indicator at 450 miles per hour, Norley got off a burst, saw his rounds hit the tail of the Me 163, and closed in. He actually had to retard his throttle to remain in a tight turn behind the *Komet*. It wasn't good enough. Norley lost his adversary momentarily, maneuvered into firing position again, and fired again. The German pilot, Jacob Bollenrath, ignited the rocket engine briefly, but lost control as more .50-caliber rounds poured into the *Komet*. The Me 163 went down and exploded. Bollenrath was killed. His was the last Me 163 to be downed by Eighth Air Force Mustang pilots.

Air industry figure Willy
Messerschmitt had little
to do with the design of
the Messerschmitt Me
262 jet fighter, but he
did have a pivotal role
in a November 26, 1943,
discussion with Adolf
Hitler about how the
aircraft would be used.
Messerschmitt may have
been hasty in assuring the
Führer that the jet fighter
could carry bombs.
Colin Heaton collection

Adolf Hitler in an atypical
pose. The swastika dates
the photo to shortly before
September 1, 1939. After the
war began, Hitler wore only
military uniforms, which
did not have the Nazi Party
armband. *National Archives*

Hans Busch began flying gliders as a teenager in the Hitler Youth. He logged hundreds of hours in twin-engine, propeller-driven fighters like the Messerschmitt Bf 110 before advancing to the cockpit of the Messerschmitt Me 262 *Schwalbe* (Swallow) jet fighter. *Eleanor Garner*

The Messerschmitt Bf 110 was a twin-engine *Zerstörer* (Destroyer), or heavy fighter, but it was neither as fast nor as maneuverable as the American P-38 Lightning. These Bf 110C-2s are preparing to take off from an unpaved strip in occupied France on May 12, 1940. Hans Guido Mutke and Hans Busch piloted the Bf 110 but were aware that their aircraft was vulnerable in a dogfight with Allied fighters. *Robert F. Dorr collection*

L.TO R.: LT. VINING (PILOT) LT. SIKORA (CO-PILOT)
LT. HACKU (BOMB.-NAV.) CPL. YATES (ENG.-GUNNER)
CPL. ARMSTRONG (RADIO-GUNNER) Sgt. WINGER (ARM.-GUNNER)
(331) AAF G1760) (2 AUG 44) BARKSDALE FIELD, LA.

Just a kid when he learned about Pearl Harbor, nineteen-year-old bomber commander 2nd Lt. (later, Capt.) James L. Vining (left) stands with his B-26 Marauder at Barksdale Army Air Field near Bossierville, Louisiana, on August 2, 1944. The co-pilot and bombardier shown (second and third from left) were not on the crew's April 20, 1945, encounter with Me 262 jets. The others are Cpl. Henry C. Yates, engineer/gunner; Cpl. Newton C. Armstrong, radioman/gunner; and Sgt. William "Bill" Winger, gunner. Winger was killed during the jet encounter. *Vining family*

Edward Giller flew the P-38 Lightning and the P-51 Mustang. Among his aerial victories was a German twin-engine fighter that was either a Messerschmitt Bf 110 or an Me 410. He is also one of the Americans who found himself fighting Hitler's jets, scoring an air-to-air kill of an Me 262. *U.S. Air Force*

Second Lieutenant Grant Turley sits in his P-47 Thunderbolt, *Kitty*, of the 78th Fighter Group. Sitting in front of the cockpit is crew chief Staff Sgt. Albert Costelnik. On the wing at left is armorer Staff Sgt. James W. Sterner. Also on the wing is assistant crew chief Sgt. Albert J. Turrow. Symbolic of all the aces who flew the P-47, Turley never had the chance to confront German jets; he lost his life on a March 1944 mission to Berlin before his twenty-third birthday. *Turley family*

Clayton Kelly Gross began World War II by taking his girlfriend to a movie about flying and ended the war having done it all. He was a P-51 Mustang fighter pilot, an ace, and the victor of an air-to-air duel with Adolf Hitler's vaunted Messerschmitt Me 262 *Schwalbe* (Swallow). Called "Kelly" by friends—or "Doc" because of his postwar career in dentistry— Gross said he and his fellow Mustang pilots never lacked confidence when they learned they would be facing jets. *Robert F. Dorr collection*

The North American P-51 Mustang was one of the principal adversaries of the German jets. It wasn't as fast as a Messerschmitt Me 262, but under the right circumstances it could win a battle against the speedier jet. *Robert F. Dorr collection*

First Lieutenant Charles F. "Chuck" Gumm Jr. was the first pilot to shoot down an aircraft while flying an American-operated P-51 Mustang. In front of his P-51B Mustang (43-6320/CQ-V), *Toni*, Gumm (second from left) poses with his ground crew, from left: Bob Seger, Marv Lippoff, and Paul Leonard. *Robert F. Dorr collection*

Surrounded by the P-80 Shooting Star jet fighters that almost made it into World War II in American colors, this is the Messerschmitt Me 163B Komet rocket aircraft (werke number 191301, U.S. serial T-2-500/FE-500). Although an archivist wrote that this photo was taken at Homestead Field, Florida, the location is thought to be Freeman Field, Indiana, at the time of the Air Force Fair on October 13, 1945. *Lloyd Fergus*

The Messerschmitt ME 163 *Komet* rocket was extremely fast but had a short fuel burn and could become unstable in flight. *Robert F. Dorr Collection*

First Lieutenant William F. "Pete" Peters was the wingman to Capt. Valmore Beaudrault during the October 2, 1944, battle between American P-47 Thunderbolts and German Messerschmitt Me 262s. *Craig Meyer*

Captain Valmore "Val" Beaudrault, who prevailed in his October 2, 1944, "jet plane boogie" against the Messerschmitt Me 262, poses with his P-47D Thunderbolt, *Miss Pussy IV*, named for his future wife, Priscilla Pero. *Priscilla Beaudrault*

Similar to the 457th Bombardment Group aircraft that were shot down by Messerschmitt Me 163 *Komets* on October 7, 1944, this is a Vega-built B-17G-20-VE Flying Fortress (42-97587/U-T) of the 750th Bombardment Squadron, 457th Bombardment Group. *Robert A. Hadley*

Captured by the U.S. intelligence team known as Watson's Whizzers and brought to U.S. soil, this is a Heinkel He 162A-2 *Volksjäger* (People's Fighter) on display at Freeman Army Air Field, Indiana, in 1946. *U. S. Air Force*

Almost overlooked by historians are the four American YP-80A Shooting Star jet fighters that reached Europe during World War II, two in England and two in Italy. They were identical in appearance to this P-80A (Army serial number 44-85000, Navy bureau number 29667) seen in this previously unpublished portrait during tests at Naval Air Station Patuxent River, Maryland, in 1945. *Jim Hawkins*

This is one of two YP-80A Shooting Star fighters (44-83029) that went to Italy in 1945 in Project Extraversion, seen shortly after its return. Piloted by Maj. Steve Pisanos, the aircraft made an emergency landing in a bean field. It was repaired and was about to take off from the road. The location of this picture does not appear to have been recorded; the aircraft was flying from a U.S. port of entry to Wright Field, Ohio. *Bob Esposito*

The Bachem 349 *Natter*, perhaps one of the weirdest of Nazi *Wunderwaffen*, or "wonder weapons," on display at Wright Field, Ohio, during the Air Force Fair on October 13, 1945. *Paul Shoemacher*

Similar to the one engaged by Don Bryan, this is an Arado Ar 234 jet bomber with a bomb slung under the fuselage at a German airfield. *U.S. Army*

Don Bryan was a P-51 Mustang ace before he engaged an Arado Ar 234 near the bridge at Remagen. *U.S. Army*

Given the name *Jane I* by the Americans who captured it, Arado Ar 234B-2 Blitz (bureau number 121445) appears to be in derelict condition at Naval Air Station Patuxent River, Maryland, circa 1946. The Navy had it but never flew it. *Jim Hawkins*

Pictured are Tuskegee airmen (left to right) 1st Lt. Roscoe C. Brown, 1st Lt. Marcellus G. Smith, and Col. Benjamin O. Davis in Ramitelli, Italy, March 1945. On the March 24, Brown (left) became one of three members of the 332nd Fighter Group to be credited with shooting down a Messerschmitt Me 262 jet fighter. *U.S. Army*

In one of the last air-to-air engagements of the war, 1st Lt. William B. "Brad" Hoelscher shot at a Messerschmitt Me 262 near Prague, Czechoslovakia, on April 25, 1945. Hoelscher and his wingman were certain he shot down the Me 262, but he did not receive credit for an aerial victory. *Hollis Barnhart*

First Lieutenant Urban L. "Ben" Drew is credited with shooting down two Me 262s on October 15, 1944. Drew (left) talks at Royal Air Force Bottisham with William Kemp and Leonard Wood. All are members of the 375th Fighter Squadron, 361st Fighter Group. *U.S. Air Force*

Tuskegee airmen 1st Lt. Marcellus G. Smith, left, and 1st Lt. Roscoe C. Brown working on a P-51 Mustang in Ramitelli, Italy, in March 1945. *U.S. Army*

The Martin B-26 Marauder became a favorite target of Me 262 jet pilots in the final weeks of the war—but it could fight back. This B-26 belonged to the 394th Bombardment Group and was on a mission over Europe. *Warren E. "Buzz" Buhler*

Hans Guido Mutke believed he flew faster than sound in the Me 262 on April 9, 1945. Most observers seem to think he didn't exceed the speed of sound. Or did he? *Walter J. Boyne*

Jim Vining was the youngest B-26 Marauder medium bomber pilot in the Army Air Forces. He battled an Me 262 and was shot down on Adolf Hitler's birthday, April 20, in 1945. *Vining family*

Could Adolf Hitler have escaped from Berlin in one of these? This is the Junkers Ju 290A-7 that was one of the largest aircraft built by Nazi Germany during the war, seen here as it appeared at an American air show at Freeman Field, Indiana, in 1946. *Robert F. Dorr collection*

One aircraft the Führer never saw was the Blohm und Voss P.170, a bizarre design that reached an advanced stage on the drawing board but was never built or flown. With three engines on the forward wing, a tail wheel, and the pilot located far to the rear, this aircraft would have been difficult to taxi. Timothy Barb made this scale model of the P.170 from a 1:72 scale kit from the Czech model company Planet. Mike Fleckenstein took the portrait. *Mike Fleckenstein*

This is a front view of a Messerschmitt Me 262A-2 *Schwalbe* (werke number 111711), which was delivered to the Allies on March 30, 1945, by Luftwaffe pilot Hans Fay. After appearing at the October 1945 air show at Freeman Field, this aircraft crashed on August 20, 1946, at Xenia, Ohio, and pilot 1st Lt. Walter J. McAuley bailed out. *U.S. Air Force*

Is this a metaphor for the Reich and its wonder weapons? Derelict outside the main gate of the Naval Laboratory in Washington, D.C., on January 27, 1957, this Messerschmitt Me 262A-1a *Schwalbe* would be considered a priceless artifact today. This Me 262 was assigned the U.S. Navy bureau number 121444. The Japanese Kawanishi N1K1 Shiden fighter, *George,* beside the jet was saved, but the Me 262's final disposition is unknown. *Robert F. Dorr collection*

Messerschmitt Me 163 rocket fighters at the "Air Force Fair" at Wright Field, Ohio, on October 13, 1945. This was a display of war prizes captured by U.S. intelligence officers. *Paul Schoemacher*

A captured Me 262 two-seater. *Jim Hawkins*

NINE

MUSTANG MEN

At the start of November 1944, no fewer than seven P-47 Thunderbolt pilots had achieved success against Me 262s: Joseph Myers and Manford Croy on August 28; Richard Conner and Ben Drew on October 1; Huie Lamb on October 25; and Walter Groce and William Gerbe on November 1. The newly arrived P-51 Mustang was marking its mark in profound ways, but had not yet bagged a jet.

This would be no easy task for the Mustang men. In early 1944, German defenses were formidable. Under the command of Gen. Gunter Korten, the Luftwaffe pulled back many of its far-flung fighter squadrons to defend the Reich. The Eighth Air Force's primary targets, German centers of production and operation, were ringed by hundreds of deadly 88mm antiaircraft guns. The morale of the German citizenry on the ground was high.

On November 6, 1944, some P-47s were still in the air—one piloted by 1st Lt. William J. Quinn who was the next Thunderbolt pilot to be credited with a kill of an Me 262. But most of the action took place when four combat groups of the newly arrived P-51 Mustangs escorted B-24 Liberator heavy bombers near Minden,

Germany. Although one Mustang was lost near Minden, it was not in air-to-air combat. Major Robert Foy of the 357th Fighter Group, "The Yoxford Boys," was leading the Mustang formation. When the Me 262s arrived in force, the Mustang men were ready for them. Foy tangled with them inconclusively.

Air ace Capt. Charles E. "Chuck" Yeager of the 357th Fighter Group—who had been previously shot down, evaded capture, and returned to combat—became the first P-51 Mustang pilot to chalk up a score. In his after-action report, Yeager wrote: "I was leading 'Cement White Flight' when north of Osnabrück we spotted three Me 262s going 280 degrees to us at about two o'clock, low. We were at 10,000 feet. I and my flight turned to the right and headed the last man off. I got a hit or two on him before he pulled away. They were flying a loose V-formation and they did not take any evasive action, but seemed to depend on their superior speed. They pulled out of range in the haze.

"We were flying along in overcast, which was very thin and the edge of it was over to the right, altitude about 5,000 feet. I went under it and flew along for a minute or two and I met them head-on again only they were now flying at about 2,000 feet. I split-S'ed on the leader and they all separated. I fired a high deflection burst from above on the leader, got behind him and was pulling 75 inches of mercury and indicating 430 miles per hour. I fired two or three bursts and got hits on the fuselage and wings from 300 yards, then he pulled away and went into the haze where I lost him.

"In this engagement I lost the rest of the flight and found myself alone. I climbed to 8,000 feet and headed north. I found a large airfield with black runways about 6,000 feet long and started flying around it. [He was referring to the base at Achmer.] I got a few bursts of flak, but it was very inaccurate.

"I spotted a lone 262 approaching the field from the south at 500 feet. Flak started coming up very thick and accurate. I fired a short burst at him from about 400 yards and got hits on the wings. I had to break off at 300 yards because the flak was getting too close. I broke straight up, looked back, and saw the enemy jet aircraft crash-land about 400 yards short of the field in a wooded area. A wing flew off outside the right jet, but the plane did not burn."

Yeager's opponent appears to have been one Oberfeldwebel (First Sgt.) Freutzer, whose first name is lost to history, although Fruetzer survived the encounter and walked away from his wrecked jet.

Yeager, of course, would go on to serve as a postwar test pilot flying dozens of aircraft types that were strongly influenced by wartime German designs. Yeager's October 14, 1947, flight at Muroc, California, in the Bell XS-1 rocket plane is the first recorded supersonic flight, although an Me 262 pilot named Hans Guido Mutke, whom we will meet soon, did not think so. Yeager's success against an Me 262 in the airfield pattern brought a visit to Achmer the next day—November 7, 1944—by the ubiquitous and often angry Generalleutnant (Maj. Gen.) Adolf "Dolfo" Galland. The German fighter leader had cordial talks with Maj. Walter "Nowi" Nowotny, whom he'd hand-picked to lead history's first fighter jet unit, but was annoyed that Kommando Nowotny hadn't followed the practice of keeping a patrol of Focke-Wulf Fw 190s in the air to protect the Me 262s during their vulnerable period when taking off and landing. For various reasons, the long-nosed Fw 190D-9 "Dora" fighters never seemed to be in the right place at the right time. Galland believed that many in the fledgling Me 262 force were unaware of how big a target they'd become, or how important the Fw 190 support mission was.

The FW 190D-9s were stationed at Achmer and nearby Hesepe. The idea was that the Focke-Wulfs would prowl above the airfields and form a shield between marauding Mustangs, Tempests, and Typhoons, and the Me 262s when taking off and landing. But the Fw 190D-9 pilots were in a separate unit and underestimated their adversary. Nowotny and others initially believed they needed as few as six Fw 190D-9s in the air to provide adequate protection and that the Focke-Wulfs could achieve their purpose flying very short sorties. In one air battle shortly before Galland's arrival, P-51 pilots of the 78th Fighter Group, who outnumbered the Focke-Wulfs forty to six, shot down several of the "Doras," and damaged others. The plan wasn't working. Galland made it clear he wanted larger numbers of the Focke-Wulfs in the air for longer periods to coincide with jet operations in the airfield pattern.

Over coffee in Nowotny's hut, Galland expressed his concern that the Allies had identified Me 262 bases and were singling them out for attention. Galland also had to tell his handpicked wing commander that he could do little or nothing about a serious shortage of J-2 jet aviation fuel. The bombing campaign was disrupting the flow of all fuel, everywhere, and the jet force would continue to be directly impacted.

Both sides were making a maximum effort in the air battles over Europe on November 8, 1944. To the German side it was part of what the Luftwaffe called "The Big Blow," a maximum effort to put as many as one thousand fighters into the sky to confront oncoming American bombers. Galland followed the action from the radio shack at Achmer. Oberleutnant (1st Lt.) Franz Schäll engaged 1st Lt. Warren Corwin and mixed it up in a close-quarters maneuvering contest. Corwin made the mistake of pulling a sharp turn in front of the Me 262, and his Mustang was torn apart by shells from Schäll's guns. Some of his wingmen heard Corwin cry out, "This jet job got me!" First Lieutenant James W. Kenney, nearby, should have heard the transmission but didn't. Neither Corwin nor the wreckage of his Mustang has ever been found.

Kenney shot down an Me 262 with short bursts and photographed its pilot dangling from a yellow parachute. Second Lieutenant Anthony Maurice also shot down an Me 262 while 1st Lt. Ernest C. "Feeb" Fiebelkorn Jr. and 1st Lt. Edward "Buddy" Haydon combined their skills to shoot down another. But it was left for 1st Lt. Richard W. Stevens of the 364th Fighter Group to rack up the most important tally of the day. While Galland listened on the radio, Nowotny talked of being under attack by a Mustang—it was Stevens—and of his left engine being damaged. "My god, I'm burning!" were the last four words ever spoken by Maj. Walter Nowotny. Galland burst out of the radio shack in time to see Nowotny's jet crash. Galland and others rushed to the scene in a car, but it was too late. It was the only sortie on which Nowotny was not wearing his storied "victory pants." On his death, Galland promoted Hauptmann (Capt.) Georg-Pete Eder to command the unit, but Kommando Nowotny never reached its potential: it claimed twenty-two Allied aircraft shot down in exchange for twenty-six Me 262s before the Kommando was withdrawn for further training and a revision of combat tactics to optimize the Me 262's strengths. The unit was broken up with most of its pilots going to Jagdgeschwader 7, or JG 7, the first jet line unit. Kommando Nowotny essentially became part of JG 7.

While the evidence is strong that Stevens got Nowotny, some sources credit the kill to Haydon and Fiebelkorn, while British pilots believed for years that Nowotny was bagged by a Typhoon. The credit to Stevens appears to be the best case that historians can make, however.

December 1944

December 1944, a young, earnest, and impressionable Oberfaehnrich (Senior Officer Candidate) Hans Busch was ready for a new assignment with KG 51 at Neuburg an der Donau, commanded by Maj. Wolfgang Schenck.

"I wanted a fighter unit but was ordered to Bomber Group 51," said Busch. "This was meant to be fighter-bomber duty." Elements of the wing converted to the Messerschmitt Me 262 and flew fighter-bomber and bomber-intercept missions against Allied bomber streams from June 1944 through the end of the war.

Before Busch and his buddy Horst Netzeband could fulfill their aspiration to strap into a jet cockpit, they were required to undergo single-seat training at München Riem.

Busch was experienced in aircraft that had a crew, like the Heinkel He 111 bomber. However, like other newcomers to the jet world of KG 51, he had little aptitude for single-seat flying. Although a two-seat version of the Me 262 existed, none would be available to KG 51 in time to help Busch and his buddies learn the aircraft.

While doing classroom work on the Jumo 004 jet engine, Busch was assigned to log single-seat time in the Fw 190 at München Riem.

Busch felt himself gaining confidence as he flung the highly maneuverable Fw 190 around the sky. He hoped to run up against American warplanes while at the controls of an Fw 190, but did not. "I was mystified that during my Fw training I never saw an American aircraft or heard of one being overhead," he said. Actually, he said, on second thought, he did see a small group of four-engine Allied plans overhead once, but "they didn't hit anything of importance." Although the Reich no longer had the luxury of taking a long time to train a pilot, as the Americans still did, the Fw 190 flights were designed and scheduled for training only at times when Allied aircraft were not operating nearby.

The Fw 190 was a low-cost way of teaching pilots who'd previously worked with a crew that "you had to start your own engine," said Busch. "Some of the old experienced hands were a little nervous about that and made mistakes. If you're going to fly a single-seat aircraft, especially a complex aircraft with two jets engines, you need to have practice being the only one who turns on the radio, lowers the flaps, lowers the landing gear, and so on."

Some pilots say no one ever wants to witness or experience a disaster, but according to Busch, most airmen keep inside a dark curiosity about what it looks like when things go wrong. A disaster of his own lay in the near future, but in the meanwhile Busch observed a seriously bad event that happened to someone else and illustrated the need for single-seat training.

On possibly the only day of the year when the sun was shining brightly and the sky was almost cloudless, Busch and Netzeband were watching planes take off and land. A mottled gray Fw 190 was turning at the runway's end, beautiful and sleek in "clean" flying condition. Busch watched the fighter descend. "He doesn't have his wheels down," Busch said.

"He's not going to land," said Netzeband. "He's just practicing."

"I'm not so sure."

The screech of metal against pavement reverberated across the airfield. As if grabbed by a giant hand, the Fw 190 rotated 180 degrees and came hurtling down the runway sideways, throwing off sparks and debris. The distinctive sound of the propeller beating itself to death against a hard surface was louder than the complaint of the battered engine. Busch watched as the pilot, a fellow cadet, pushed back the canopy and climbed out. The pilot then slammed a gloved fist against the windshield bow.

Does bellying in a perfectly good Fw 190 disqualify a hopeful officer candidate from ever strapping into the cockpit of an Me 262? The only certain fact is that the upset cadet did not receive grips and grins from his commander. Unfortunately, history does not record what happened to this particular pilot after he ranged a plane, lost his temper, and hurt a hand.

"He was a mature guy," Busch said, "just like several of us. He had a lot of flying hours. But like several of us, he was used to a copilot being in the right seat at his side. Yes, we had checklists and safety practices, but the fact remains, he was used to a different person reaching for the handle and putting down the retractable undercarriage. He ripped open the guts of an Fw 190 by scraping it on pavement because he forgot to put down the landing gear."

One reason the transition was difficult: unlike almost every other air force in the world, the Luftwaffe did not use checklists. "They relied instead on a pilot's really knowing the aircraft handbooks," writer-researcher Walter J. Boyne said in an interview for this book. "This was complicated by the way the Germans broadly allowed pilots to fly different aircraft. The onus was on the pilot to know. Checklists were not used, even in the later stages of the war when courses were hurried and not a lot of time was available for studying manuals." That the Luftwaffe did not follow the American practice of using checklists "seems incredible," Boyne said, "considering the complexity of starting an Me 262 or a twin-engine Heinkel."

Busch vowed never to make a similar mistake. In late December 1944, after Ben Drew and other P-51 pilots had begun sprinkling Me 262s over the German landscape—and while Me 262s were batting American bombers out of the sky, right and left—Busch was ready for his first flight at the controls of the jet.

He arrived at Neuburg from München Riem disappointed that it was a bomber unit, but excited that he would now fly jets. Busch's cadet status made him less than an officer but higher in rank than the sergeant pilots of KG 51, some of whom had considerable combat experience. He and his buddies, he said, were known for wild behavior when circumstances permitted. Busch himself said he had no mechanical aptitude and had to hope that a sense for operating the Me 262 would come naturally. Together with his best buddy Horst Netzeband, Busch found that his first look at the Me 262 was an unforgettable experience.

Busch wrote: "We walked up to this mysterious airplane that we had never seen a picture of and heard that it was *Geheime Kommandosache* [top secret]. What an excitement! We were allowed to touch this bird that looked like it had just dropped in from the future or from another planet. No aircraft we had flown or seen so far looked as streamlined as the Me 262. We were allowed to sit in the cockpit but that was all." Before the new pilots could fly the jet, "there was a lot of learning and familiarization necessary," he added.

Men who fly and fight together often form close bonds, and Busch felt his friendship with Netzeband was closer than most. The two German pilots were very different: Busch pliable and humorless, Netzeband witty and something of a prankster in a good way. They learned the Me 262 together and shared free time, snacks, and jokes.

"Here I sat in the cockpit, parachute strapped on, flight helmet secured, radio-telephone hooked up, throat mike buttoned down, and shoulder and belly straps tightly secured," Busch said. Wearing gloves as required, and under the watchful eye of a crew chief standing on his wing, Busch made certain he could grasp every knob or lever in front of him. "The instruments and controls were not exactly

How about see captain? Did Arthur come out alive? How many Bombers + Aircraft

designed with my comfort in mind, but they were not uncomfortable to reach either."

fighters did the Jets get? Were they

The Jumo 004B turbojet engines came with their own starters, Reidel motorcycle motors situated in the intake section of the turbines and connected with a claw clutch to the front end of the turbine shaft. Although earlier versions were cranked by hand, lawn mower style, the Reidels came with electric starters. Busch ran them up to one thousand revolutions per minute and then depressed the button on the throttle handle that turned on the fuel pump.

a success overall? what how the

The Me 262 was not easy to taxi, nor to steer, as Busch noted earlier. Its landing gear had a bit of a stalky feel, but the aircraft was robust enough to taxi well and to respond well as he went into his takeoff roll. After that it was . . . "well, it was a miracle," he said.

comparison airplanes?

With wheels up and throttles on full power, the Me 262 climbed like the swallow after which it was named. If Busch needed anything to increase his fascination with this airplane, his first flight did it. He was truly hooked.

Combat + flying me-262 probably start of book, but this is not the book. what is new in this? the book who gets a kill?

Interview?

He 280 discussed but no pic.

TEN

THE UNDERGROUND AIRPLANE

When Robert Bush saw a Heinkel He 162 *Volksjäger* (People's Fighter) while flying a combat mission, he thought it was some sort of mysterious bomb or missile. The words *aerial torpedo* sprang into his mind.

"We'd been briefed on German jets and had a recognition chart showing what a Messerschmitt Me 262 jet fighter looked like. There were rumors the Germans were working on other strange and new gadgets. But nothing in our briefing covered a short, stub-winged jet that looked a little like an arrow shot from a quiver. No one had told us anything about this," he said.

Early 1945

Bush was in a P-51 Mustang with a broken heater at twenty-eight thousand feet over Germany. He was cold. He'd never felt so cold. Below him, cloud banks interrupted the sky at intervals of altitude. The He 162 was at about sixteen thousand feet moving in a straight line. Bush saw puffs escaping from the back of the aircraft.

"I uncaged my K-14 gunsight, said something to my wingman, rolled over, and went after him," Bush said. His wingman followed and two silvery Mustangs went into a forty-five-degree dive behind the He 162.

"My flight leader was pissed off and said something on the radio about flight discipline. That's when I realized that my plan to get up close to this 'thing' wasn't working. It continued to give off spurts of exhaust and to pull away from me," Bush said.

Bush said he returned to formation, made his way home, and got an "ass chewing" for being curious about a flying object that was too far away, and too fast, to catch. He still didn't know what it was. Rumors about mysterious and even magical German weapons were making the rounds, but no one seemed to have heard of this one. Bush sat down with a pair of flinty intelligence officers—not by choice, he was ordered to—and made sketches while giving his account. "They didn't thank me, but about three weeks later, in the very final days of the war, we finally got a briefing and we all knew what it was," Bush said.

The Heinkel He 162 *Volksjäger*, built under a program called Salamander, was a shoulder-wing monoplane of mostly wooden construction with retractable tricycle landing gear and a tailplane with twin fins astride an upwardly canted horizontal stabilizer. This design allowed its single turbojet to be positioned in an easy maintenance position atop the fuselage with the exhaust blowing straight back. It was supposed to be the aircraft any youngster could fly. It was also called the Emergency Fighter—a rushed attempt by the Reich's battered armaments industry to provide a mass-produced fighter that would stem the Allied bombing offensive on Germany. In a perfect world, it would be incredibly cheap, anyone could fly it, and it could be disposed of easily if it suffered damage. It might have helped had there existed a ground simulator to train fledgling pilots, but the concept of a simulator still lay in the future.

Mustang pilot Bush, the ex–Boy Scout from Washington, D.C., came as close to shooting down a He 162 as any American in World

War II. "I learned only years later that it was a very interesting and very formidable aircraft. I learned that I probably would never have caught it because it was so damned fast. Apparently, nobody ever came any closer to a He 162 than I did," he said.

September 8, 1944

Minus Ernst Heinkel himself, the company bearing his name wanted a second chance—following its near success with the Heinkel He 280—to get an operational jet into service. The company submitted its design as part of an overall program called Salamander to fulfill a September 8, 1944, requirement for a simple, lightweight jet fighter that even a novice could operate—specifically, a teenage member of the Hitlerjugend (Hitler Youth).

The requirement amounted to an invitation to the German aircraft industry, which was in the process of vexing the Allies by continuing to develop and produce aircraft even while being bombed. Industry was happy to respond. At first glance, it appeared to be an opportunity to manufacture an enormous number of aircraft, possibly several thousands, paid for from the coffers of the Reich. The intended production goal was no fewer than four thousand airframes per month, to overwhelm the Allies with sheer numbers.

Focke-Wulf weighed in with a variation of designer Kurt Tank's previous, and never built, Ta 183, a jet design with high-swept wings and a T tail. The Ta 183 itself would later exert enormous influence on the Soviet Union's Mikoyan-Gurevich design bureau, with a curious and unforeseen result: in the 1950s, a fake photo of the Ta 183 emblazoned with red stars would appear everywhere in American fan magazines labeled as the MiG-19. In reality, no version of the Ta 183, even one with a MiG prefix, was ever built, although the design influenced the MiG-15 of Korean War fame.

Blohm und Voss, already well known for weird and wonderful aircraft designs, weighed in with a very sensible design for a fighter for the common man, but the Heinkel design team had too much of a head start. Since the designation of P.1073, Heinkel had been mulling small, single-engine jet fighter designs for years and had a solution ready on the drawing board. The Heinkel firm was given an order on September 15, 1944, only a week after the requirement was enunciated.*

Of course, the idea of a jet fighter for the common folk resulted from a motive stronger than egalitarianism. The Reich's leaders were worried about real and anticipated shortages of strategic materials, and the *Volksjäger* was constructed primarily of wood. This concern about aluminum, rubber, plastic, and other materials was reflected on both sides and was seen in a small, prop-driven American fighter, the Bell XP-77. In the case of both sides, it was essentially a false alarm since supplies remained abundant; Germany was still manufacturing aircraft at a respectable rate on the last day of the war.

A more realistic motive behind the simplicity of the He 162: it could be assembled on a crude assembly line in the field, far from any building that might be easily identified as an aircraft factory, using unskilled or semi-skilled labor. While Ernst Heinkel, unlike Willy Messerschmitt, never made use of slave laborers, the Heinkel company after his departure suffered no such compunction. The He 162 was, to put it bluntly, a throwaway fighter, one that could be lost along with its hapless pilot at relatively little expense to the Reich. For all of that, it was fundamentally a solid design and was not, as often described, flimsy. It offered excellent aerodynamic properties and, once away from the airfield pattern, was a stable and reliable platform.

*The idea of a simple, cheap "wonder weapon," a "people's fighter" that could be operated by just about anyone, must have been influenced by the Volkswagen, the "people's car" concept. In a country where few owned automobiles, Adolf Hitler wanted anybody to be able to own a car, and the Führer's wishes coincided with a proposal by car designer Ferdinand Porsche—although much of this design was inspired by the advanced Tatra cars of Hans Ledwinka. The concept dates to the 1920s, became a 1937 project by a German trade union, and produced several designs before evolving into the postwar Beetle. The Volkswagen may have evolved into a trendy personal get-about in the 1960s for American college girls who wouldn't give the time of day to the author of this book, but the Volkswagen began as the *Volksjäger* did, in a quest for simple construction, low cost, and wide availability.

Generalleutnant (Maj. Gen.) Adolf Galland, the seasoned ace in command of the Luftwaffe's fighter force, bitterly opposed the *Volksjäger* and the concept behind it since he felt it would divert resources from existing aircraft programs, particular the Messerschmitt Me 262 jet fighter. Galland objected with the support of Willy Messerschmitt and Focke-Wulf's Kurt Tank. But the *Volksjäger* was a concept dear to the Führer himself and backed by Göring and Speer, so the objections went nowhere.

The Heinkel company was instructed to have a full-scale mockup ready by October 1, a finished aircraft by December 10, and the beginning of production on an unspecified date in January 1945. It met all of these goals. Wind tunnel tests, also completed in January, demonstrated some instability at high speeds and other control issues but proved that this was a workable, high-speed combat aircraft. The wind tunnel effort did not begin until after the aircraft was flying. It demonstrated, as an American technical report later explained, an aerodynamic need for a slight downward displacement of the wing or by drawing down the trailing edge of the landing flaps.

1943 and 1944

Throughout the Reich—in Germany, Austria, and Czechoslovakia— the Germans continued to produce "Ottos" (propeller-driven planes), jets, and other "wonder weapons," despite Allied bombing because of a massive effort to move assembly plants underground. In August 1943, Hitler ordered assembly of the V-1 robot bomb and the V-2 rocket (the "V-weapons") moved underground.

A broader effort to put production capacity beneath the surface came much later, with a February 1944 general order to disperse the aircraft industry.

One of the best-known subterranean plants was Mittelwerk, at Thüringen near Nordhausen, where slave laborers assembled V-weapons and Messerschmitt Me 262 jet fighters inside tunnels carved deep within a mountain. They also manufactured Taifun antiaircraft missiles and, near the end of the war, the He 162.* Three colossal underground facilities in Czechoslovakia were dubbed the Rabštejn Underground Factory (dug out of sandstone rock in northern Bohemia), Underground Factory Richard (inside a hill near the city of Litoměřice), and Underground Complex Výpustek (dug out of karst in the south of the country). Five thousand prisoners from the Terazin concentration camp died in constructing Richard, which is a series of low-ceilinged caves where many kinds of weapons were built.

Two groups of woodworking/furniture manufacturing companies were established in Erfurt and Stuttgart for the difficult task of assembling and bonding the He 162's wooden tail section, wings, and other components. Metal fuselages and completed aircraft were to be produced at Aschersleben, Barth, Bernburg, Halberstadt, Leopodsall, Oranieburg, Pünitz, and Stassfurt, and in a former salt mine at Tarthun.

March and April 1945

Belatedly placed into operation in March 1945, the Tarthun underground facility (code name Maulwurf and also known as Egeln), near Magdeburg, occupied about two hundred thousand square feet in a salt mine. There, some 2,400 men performed subassembly work twelve hours a day, seven days a week, and final-assembled Focke-Wulf Fw 190s, Junkers Ju 88s, and especially the He 162. The workers lived in camps near the mine or in the adjacent town of Schönbeck.

Most of this remained unknown to the Allies, until soldiers of the U.S. Ninth Army arrived at Egeln. On April 14, 1945, the *New York Times* reported: "Two curious American soldiers today unlocked the secrecy surrounding Adolf Hitler's deadly jet-propelled plane by strolling through a salt mine and literally dropping into a vast underground factory."

Private First Class James Prenger and Warrant Officer Joseph Crocker descended into the mineshaft, dropping 950 feet in a small

---

*The underground camp at Oberammergau is discussed in chapter 16 and is where Willy Messerschmitt ended his war.

elevator, and discovered a factory winding through miles of subterranean corridors—most of it dismantled and wrecked by the Germans the previous day. The corridors were paved with concrete, and there were motor-driven carts for key employees and inspectors to travel through the plant. Like so many of the subterranean plants, Tarthun/Egeln was not only untouched by bombing, but it also was apparently never detected while fighting was under way.

In the He 162 program, engines were to be produced in a salt mine in Urseburg, to which the Berlin-Spandau and Basdorf-Zülsdorf engine plants had transferred. Pre-production He 162s were produced at Schwechat, which was phased into the mass production effort. Many 162 fuselage units, the only component of the aircraft using more than a token amount of metal, were assembled at Seegrotte, a former chalk mine at Hinterbrühl on the outskirts of Vienna, also known as the Langusta (Lobster) assembly plant. This was also the site of final assembly of most of the He 162s built.

Seegrotte was the site of the largest underground lake in Europe, and it became a subterranean aircraft factory. To permit installation of production equipment—including jigs and holding fixtures needed to integrate and install structural parts, ribs, longerons, stiffeners, and aircraft skin—water had to be pumped out of the mine every day and warm air had to be pumped in. Much of the underground work on He 162 fuselages at Seegrotte was performed by slave labor from the Hinterbrühl satellite camp of the Mauthausen Concentration Camp, and some by Allied prisoners of war.*

Hastily developed, the He 162 had structural problems related to its wooden construction. It was nearly all wood (except for for principal fuselage components, which were all metal). It made extensive use of an adhesive that turned out to be harmfully acidic, failed to bond properly, and caused technical problems. Some attribute the

---

*Soviet troops captured two He 162s at Seegrotte that were sent back to Moscow for testing. Today, a small museum-style display at Seegrotte preserves two He 162 instrument panels, a set of landing gear, and other bits and pieces of the aircraft.

Volksjäger's infamous fin and rudder problems—the tail routinely broke off and fell away during maneuvering, with fatal results—to problems with the glue, at least in part.

The He 162 was designed to use Tego film, a casein adhesive similar to the Aerolite used on the British De Havilland Mosquito. The only factory that produced Tego film was destroyed in an Allied bombing raid. The Heinkel firm then resorted to what was later called ersatz glue, developed by Dynamit AG of Leverkusen. This was a cold resin glue that was straightforwardly applied, unlike the planned Tego adhesive, which was placed on the wood and then heated while the sheets were in a press. The ersatz glue left an acidic residue after curing, which ate at the very wood it was supposed to be bonding. The problem was well known to those who were building and fielding the He 162. They made improvements in the curing process and other changes, but they never completely resolved the glue-wood bonding issue.

From an aerodynamic and engineering standpoint, the He 162 was a sound aircraft. Its small size made the He 162 difficult for an adversary to see, an early form of stealth. The pilot of the He 162 had superb visibility straight ahead and to the side. However, the engine location blocked visibility to the rear, making it necessary for the pilot to maneuver from side to side in order to "check six"—observe the six o'clock position behind the plane.

Engine reliability was always a concern for all of the German jets. In the case of the Me 262, a complete failure of one engine would leave a second engine still functioning. But the He 162 had just one jet engine. All of the available German turbojet engines were tried on the He 162, including the BMW 003A-1 *Sturm* (Storm) and the Junkers Jumo 004. All had slow throttle response. All had high rates of flameouts and other failures. But when the engine worked, and when the pilot didn't over-control the rudder, the He 162 had world-beating potential: some German officers envisioned swarms of He 162s engaging Allied fighters, freeing up the less nimble Me 262s to attack the bombers.

From nose to tail, the He 162 made economical use of all functions—lift, propulsion, yaw, roll, and bank. Its low weight, high-
thrust engine (when it worked properly), and the small size of the
aircraft combined with its sensibly sized wings and aerodynamically
clean design to give the He 162 high speed, a high rate of climb, and a
superb turn rate and roll characteristics. British test pilot Eric Brown,
who evaluated the He 162 after the war, called it a first class fighter,
fun, and a delight to fly. Brown was unique, having flown nearly all
of the jet aircraft of the era—American, British, and German. He
repeatedly said the He 162 was the easiest and most comfortable of
the lot.

But Brown also warned that the He 162 had too much rudder
response and that its twin fins could fall off if overhandled. This well-
known issue is probably overstated in literature about the Heinkel
jet: pilots tend to control fighter aircraft aggressively. The He 162 was
designed in an era when pilots used a lot of rudder. But in a jet, the
pilot doesn't need to use a lot of rudder, just enough to coordinate a
turn or correct for a crosswind when landing. The rudder handling
issue would have been resolved in time with training, practice, and
greater institutional knowledge. — reflects deep experience + knowledge on part

Reactions were different in France, where half a dozen test pilots
tested the He 162 in the postwar era. They found it pleasant to fly
but difficult to maneuver. When a He 162 landed with a landing gear
door torn partway off the aircraft, indicating that the He 162 could be
unpredictable, the French discontinued their test flights.

Only one version appeared in numbers before the war ended,
the He 162A. It had two variations: the He 162A-1 was armed with
two 30mm Rheinmetall MK108 cannons with one hundred rounds
per gun and with their short barrels entirely enclosed within the
fuselage; empty shell casings were extracted by the belts that fed the
gun, rendering an ejection port unnecessary on the A-1 model. The
He 162A-2 dispensed with these big guns and offered two lighter
high-velocity Mauser MG 151 20mm cannons with 120 rounds per
weapon and with their longer barrels protruding from the fuselage

and with portals for ejected shell casings below and beyond the nose wheel. Both the A-1 and A-2 variants were flown with all of the Reich's models of jet engines.

A distinguishing feature of the He 162 was the turbojet engine mounted in a housing atop the fuselage on the centerline. The oil tank and other supporting equipment were positioned atop the engine housing, giving it a distinct bulge. Just forward of the engine air intake was the hinged, bubble-type canopy.

Some features of the He 162 were remarkable. Together with the propeller-driven Dornier Do 335 *Pfeil* (Arrow) tandem tractor-pusher and Heinkel He 219 *Uhu* (Eagle-Owl) twin-engine night fighter—each a very advanced aircraft in its own right—the He 162 had an ejection seat similar to all that would be used on future jet aircraft for decades to come. The parachute was stored in the seat pan. An explosive cartridge fired the seat vertically up two rails. This made it different in kind from the compressed-air ejection seat of the Heinkel He 280 and more like the seats used on jet aircraft in postwar years. In a curious sidelight, ejection seats were tried on the Me 262 but were not used operationally.

December 6, 1944

Haste was the keynote with the He 162. Rushing the aircraft into production, the Heinkel firm relied on a landing gear design copied with minor variations from the Messerschmitt Bf 109. Officials at the company claimed that because their aircraft was so simple and light, it would achieve with one engine the same performance the Me 262 attained with two.

Rushed into production with less than one hundred days elapsing from production order to actual flight, the He 162 first took to the air on December 6, 1944. On its second flight, the leading edge of its unswept wing collapsed and the prototype broke up in the air. The crash was mysterious: it may have been caused by a phenomenon known later as inertia coupling. This is a potentially deadly phenomenon in high-speed flight in which the inertia of the heavier fuselage overpowers the aerodynamic stabilizing forces of the wing and tail section. The problem became apparent as single-engine jet fighter aircraft were developed with narrow wingspans that had relatively low roll inertia, relative to the pitch and yaw inertia dominated by the long slender high-density fuselage.

deep knowledge [handwritten margin note]

Intentionally flimsy in design, the He 162 turned out to be structurally too weak to accommodate the two 30mm cannons installed on the He 162A-1 variant. This was the reason for the shift in armament that resulted in two lighter and somewhat smaller 20mm cannons being substituted on the He 162A-2 version.

Some 116 He 162s were built. The aircraft came from the facilities named above, plus plants operated by Heinkel and separately by Junkers in Vienna. In January 1945, the Luftwaffe formed a special Erprobungskommando 162 He 162 test pilot evaluation group to which the first forty-six aircraft were delivered. The group was based at the Luftwaffe test center at Rechlin under the command of Heinz Bär. Bär, an experienced combat pilot credited with two hundred kills, familiarized himself and his group with the new airplanes.

February saw deliveries of the He 162 to its first operational unit, Jagdgeschwader 1 (No. 1 Fighter Wing). After JG 1, two additional units were slated to be equipped with the type, but the war ended before they could receive aircraft. The He-162A-2 was the main production variant. However, several prototypes of different versions were built with various engine types installed.

Only experienced line pilots flew the He 162. The dream of an aerial army of young Hitler Youth pilots was never realistic. The learning curve was too steep, and, as it turned out, time was too short. Although the He 162 had some qualities that would have made it user-friendly in the hands of a fledgling pilot with minimal training—it was almost impossible to mishandle on final approach and extremely gentle during a landing—potential Hitler Youth He 162 pilots never advanced beyond initial flight training using towed gliders.

April 19, 1945

With the He 162 belatedly in combat, on April 19, 1945, a British fighter pilot who had been captured told his German interrogators that he had been shot down by a jet fighter whose description was clearly that of a He 162. The Heinkel and its pilot were lost during the same fray, shot down by a Hawker Tempest fighter while returning to base.

The only American to claim a He 162 in combat was 2nd Lt. Guy F. Cary of the 15th Tactical Reconnaissance Squadron on March 18, 1945. But the U.S. aerial victories credits list does not identify the type of aircraft flown by the shooter or the type shot down, and evidence suggests that Cary actually shot down an Me 262.

Pilot Leutnant (2nd Lt.) Rudolf Schmitt had the only successful use of an ejection seat in a He 162 on April 20, 1945. Having lived to fight again, on May 4, 1945, Schmitt was credited with shooting down a Tempest. This may have been the Reich's last air-to-air victory because the war ended four days later. Schmitt was said to have been a relative novice, so his air-to-air victory is evidence of the He 162's mostly unrealized potential. The literature about Schmitt is confusing and contradictory, and one source asserts that while Schmitt claimed a He 162, the German side credited the kill to an antiaircraft battery.

Many planned versions of the *Volksjäger* never progressed beyond the drawing board. One version had swept-back wings (He 162C), another swept-forward wings (He 162D), and yet another (He 162E) a butterfly or V tail of the kind seen in postwar years on the Beech Bonanza. The BMW 109-003R turbojet propulsion unit with rocket boost was tested just once on an Me 262C-2b, but plans to fly an He 162E with this power unit didn't materialize before war's end.

Watson's Whizzers, the American team that evaluated captured German aircraft after the war, got their hands on a He 162. They spent several weeks wringing it out at Landsberg, Germany, in the summer of 1945 before taking it to the United States.

The Soviets also gathered up major parts of three unfinished Heinkel He 280s as well as two Me 262s found fully intact at a nearby airfield. Both the Americans and the Soviets conducted exhaustive postwar testing of their Nazi booty, including the He 162. Robert A. "Bob" Hoover, who spent sixteen months as a prisoner of war in German hands and was later a famous air show pilot, made a single flight in the He 162A-2 at Muroc, California (site of the future Edwards Air Force Base), in July 1946. Hoover commented that because the controls lacked any kind of power boost, he had to use both hands to put the Heinkel jet into a turn. Hoover called the aircraft "very risky" and reported, as any German pilot could have told him, that the landing speed of the He 162 was too high. This captured example apparently never flew again. Today, the aircraft Hoover flew is a display artifact in the Planes of Fame Museum in Chino, California, wearing authentic markings including the name *Nervenklau* (Nerve Stealer), the nickname of its last German pilot, Leutnant (2nd Lt.) Gerhard Hanf.

ELEVEN

NATTER

It's unclear whether Erich Bachem knew that Reichsführer-SS Heinrich Himmler had a temper, or that Himmler could have anyone killed on a whim. One of the most powerful men in the Reich, one of the primary architects of the Holocaust, even while not really a member of Adolf Hitler's inner circle, the deceptively bookish-looking Himmler was a man to be feared. You did not get an audience with Himmler easily and you did not want to make a mistake in his presence.

But Bachem was desperate. He had a military solution to what he saw as the Reich's military problems, and military men, including key leaders of the Luftwaffe, had rejected him.

Bachem's solution was a manned, vertical takeoff interceptor—today it might be called a surface-to-air missile with a cockpit—a semidisposable aircraft intended in its initial incarnation to wield a nose-mounted battery Henschel Hs 217 R4M 73mm rocket in its nose. It was the answer, Bachem believed, to those four-engine bombers that were increasingly plentiful in Germany's skies.

The idea of mounting an air-to-air defense using an aircraft carrying "dumb" or unguided rocket projectiles has recurred throughout air warfare history. Long after Bachem had the idea, the U.S. heartland was defended in the 1950s by fighter interceptors that carried only 2.75mm air-to-air rocket projectiles—24 in the case of the F-86D Sabre, no fewer than 104 in the F-89D Scorpion, and 48 in the F-94C Starfire. The difference was that the Sabre, Scorpion, and Starfire were costly, complicated warplanes designed to return safely from a mission and return to fight another day. The aircraft taking shape in Bachem's engineering drawings was cheap and expendable. The aircraft did not need to survive a mission, and it appears little concern was directed toward whether the pilot did either.

Thirty-four years old, credited with being a codesigner of the Feiesler Fi 156 *Storch* (Stork) light plane, Bachem was told Himmler would see him on a certain day in early 1944. Spurned by the Air Ministry and the Luftwaffe, Bachem had been led to believe that the SS chief would be receptive to becoming involved in military aviation.

It's easy to imagine Bachem presenting his proposal, in a meek and subservient way, explaining that his unique aircraft—eventually to be called the Bachem Ba 349 *Natter* (Adder)—would sweep the skies clear of American and British bombers. It's easy to imagine Himmler looking skeptical with a furrow in his brow, as he often did, and then lighting up. If Germany's air force wouldn't field this extraordinary aircraft, the SS would! It's even easy to imagine Himmler, perhaps, patting Bachem on the back.

Or not. Research for this book did not turn up a contemporaneous account of the meeting. All we know is that the *Natter*, which had been stalled, received a go-ahead, with Himmler becoming its champion.

In English, to "natter" is to talk casually, especially about unimportant matters. Spiro Agnew, a famous American vice president, dismissed his political opponents as "nattering nabobs of negativism." The Bachem aircraft certainly never lived up to its name in German, a language in which a *Natter* is a fearsome snake, but the *Natter* and other unsuccessful high-technological aircraft are anything but unimportant. All of the unsuccessful but advanced aircraft demonstrate how both sides made strides in aeronautical knowledge while experimenting with more aircraft types than they needed to win the war. Still, trying to build a bridge to the future with the *Natter* may have been a bridge too far.

"I can't imagine what the hell they were thinking," said American P-51 Mustang pilot Don Bryan, the California-born ace who bagged an Arado Ar 234 over the bridge at Remagen. Bryan was referring to two "wonder weapons" that appeared to him to be similarly weird, the rocket-propelled Messerschmitt Me 163 *Komet* and the rocket-booster Bachem Ba 349 *Natter*. "What if they had taken all the effort they put into those contraptions and used it to build an airplane something like ours?" He was referring to the P-51 Mustang.

Ironically, much later in life Bryan piloted a warplane whose makers dubbed it "the missile with the man in it." That was a Lockheed marketing pitch for the F-104 Starfighter. It would have been a perfect term for the Ba 349 *Natter* if only Himmler, or Bachem, or somebody had thought of it.

"I'm glad they didn't have more time to refine their experiments," said P-51 pilot Robert Bush, the Washington, D.C., youngster who got within eyesight of a Heinkel He 162 *Volksjäger*. "I don't know how far they might have gotten. They were willing to take extraordinary risks. I'm glad we were able to defeat them before most of their plans materialized." Bryan and Bush had both heard strange and bizarre rumors about Third Reich scientists in subterranean caverns developing advanced missiles, antigravity devices, and even a time machine. "They were nasty men with far-out ideas and I'm glad we beat them," Bush said.

Fighting the *Natter* would have been difficult for P-51 pilots such as Bryan and Bush, and near impossible for the gunners aboard American B-17 Flying Fortress and B-24 Liberator bombers. In fact, claims by gunners were hugely exaggerated: there is good reason to believe that a bomber would have been just as safe without them. Certainly they would have done more harm than good against Bachem's design. The *Natter* was designed to hit and run when sent up against bomber formations. With stubby little wings spanning less than a dozen feet, it was a very small target, and pushed through the sky by rocket power, it was an exceedingly fast one. Bachem's rocket-armed aircraft was in many respects more like an artillery shell than a fighter plane.

NASTY NATTER

Bachem's idea may have been a little too ambitious in the context of its era, but it seemed timely. The Reichsluftfahrtministerium, or RLM—the Air Ministry—had been looking at concepts for a point-defense interceptor that would be, in effect, a manned surface-to-air missile. This would be a weapon that could be deployed in massive swarms to engage approaching Allied bombers. The Heinkel P.1077 Julia, the most promising such design other than Bachem's, looked as if it had been designed by Rube Goldberg, the American cartoonist famous for drawing impossibly complex, eccentric gadgets to perform simple tasks in indirect, convoluted ways. The P.1077 was designed for the pilot to lie prone while at the controls, which would have placed him in an awkward standing-up position during vertical launch.

With some initial encouragement from a low-level factotum in the RLM, Bachem did his initial engineering work on the *Natter* in the sure belief that aviation authorities would eat up his revolutionary idea. He was well liked by bureaucrats in Berlin. They warmed to his enthusiasm. But Albert Speer, who had taken over the RLM, among other duties, from Erich Milch, was not interested, nor was Hermann Göring. It seemed no one in authority wanted to buy into Bachem's concept. Bachem received a little encouragement from the ubiquitous Generalleutnant (Maj. Gen.) Adolf "Dolfo" Galland, but not enough to overcome resistance.

It appears that after a Herculean effort, SS boss Himmler granted Bachem an interview and fully supported the project. In the middle of September 1944 the technical office of the Waffen-SS made an order for Bachem to develop and manufacture the *Natter* at his Waldsee factory. This decision is said to have been the only time the

SS significantly interfered with aircraft design and air fighting strat-
egy. Early in the project the RLM undertook an engineering assess-
ment of the *Natter*, which it reported on October 28, 1944. Various
stringent economies were imposed on an already frugal design.

The *Natter* concept had numerous strengths, including advantage of being cheap and simple. But no one seemed to see the beauty
of the idea—a sky full of *Natters*, blasting B-17 Flying Fortresses right
and left. Bachem came to the conclusion that he would never drum
up much support for his concept unless he sidestepped the established bureaucracy and went to Himmler. Even then, an enormous
gulf loomed between Bachem's expectations and anything like an
actual, realistic war weapon.

The concept was an accountant's dream in a nation worried
(and unduly so) about a shortage of strategic materials. The Bas
349 was a crude airframe, intended for ease of manufacture by
unskilled woodworkers.

The design of the wings was too simple for words: they were
plain rectangular slabs of wood devoid of ailerons, flaps, or control
devices. The control surfaces to make the Ba 349 roll, pitch, and yaw
were installed in its cruciform tail, made up of four fins and control surfaces. The four control surfaces in the tail connected to guide
vanes that augmented the control of aerodynamics.

The nearly cylindrical fuselage was wrapped around a Walter
109-509A-2 sustainer rocket capable of putting out thrust for seventy
seconds at full power and dependent upon volatile liquid fuel. The
aircraft was to be launched vertically by what would later be called
boosters, namely four Schmidding 109-533 solid-fuel rockets, two
on each side of the fuselage able to generate thrust for ten seconds. As
Allied bombers passed overhead, the *Natter* would be blasted vertically off the ground, climbing almost vertically on an internal rocket.
Nearing the bombers, the pilot would sight on one and fire his battery of rocket projectiles. He would then use his remaining kinetic
energy to climb higher than the bombers and swoop back for a ramming attack. Just before impact, the pilot was to trigger a mechanism

to separate his seat (or forward fuselage) and the rear portion with the rocket motor. The idea of a ramming attack was short-lived as planning for the *Natter* progressed, but the remainder of the scenario was unchanged: it would go straight up, attack, and recover.

The *Natter* had no landing gear, which saved weight, expense, and construction time. The pilot and the aircraft were both meant to be recovered safely—but separately. After intercepting bombers and discharging its weapons, the Ba 349 was to dive to a lower altitude and flatten out into level flight. The pilot would then open the cockpit canopy, the canopy would swing back, and the pilot would be thrown clear and would open his parachute. A separate parachute would deploy to bring the relatively lightweight *Natter* safely to the ground, ready to fight another day.

SS SCRUTINY

Lest there be any doubt of Himmler's influence, the SS openly took charge of *Natter* development and of unpowered, manned flights in which the *Natter* was effectively a glider. In December 1944 the project came largely under the control of the SS and Hans Kammler. Kammler was a longtime Himmler loyalist who razed the Warsaw Ghetto and later employed domestic prisoners to create an underground V-2 rocket assembly facility at Mittelwerk, making him responsible not just for the facility but for its attendant concentration camp complex, Mittelbau-Dora. Although he was a civil engineer, he apparently had neither education nor experience that qualified him to oversee the V-2—when it, too, came under SS control—or the *Natter*.

As a sidelight to the *Natter* story, it is not known how—or even whether—Kammler died. In recent years, Kammler's name has been linked to apocryphal Nazi "wonder weapons" such as Die Glocke (the Bell), which may have been an anti-gravity device or a time machine—or something. This link was suggested by author Nick Cook in *The Hunt for Zero Point*, which suggested that Kammler survived the war and was secretly whisked to the United States ahead of other German scientists as part of Operation Paperclip for the purpose of exploiting his knowledge of secret German projects.

But Kammler, who has since been a protagonist in half a dozen fantasy novels, had few qualifications that would have been useful to the Allies, and no solid evidence has ever surfaced that German leaders were brought to the United States secretly. There have been no Kammler sightings since the end of the war and Kammler never made it into pulp magazines such as the *Police Gazette* that repeatedly reported Hitler alive and thriving in Antarctica or Argentina—or somewhere.*

With or without much direct involvement by Kammler, the first of just fifteen *Natters* that were completed became available in October 1944 and was used for this series of four unpowered handling trials, towed aloft behind a Heinkel He 111 twin-engine bomber. Erich Klöckner piloted the *Natter*. Three times, it performed as predicted.

Something went wrong on the fourth flight. Klöckner abandoned the first Ba 349, known as aircraft M1 in mid-air and parachuted to safety.

To clear doubts about the *Natter* in the glider mode, Hans Zübert made a daring free flight in M8 on the February 14, and showed that once it was aloft and level, the *Natter* was a stable and comfortable aerodynamic platform. The problem, of course, was getting there.

The first vertical launch with booster and sustainer rockets firing, but without a pilot in the cockpit, took place on February 23, 1945. Bachem was now under pressure from authorities in Berlin who were telling him to achieve a manned vertical takeoff by the end of February.

March 1, 1945

In fact, it was March 1, 1945, when test pilot Lothar Sieber briefly—and fatally—became the bravest man in the world.

The location was Heuberg near Stetten am kalten Markt, Würtemberg, on an artificial plateau at a Truppenübungsplatz (military

*Kammler's name was implied but not used in the movie *Iron Sky* (2012) about a secret Nazi base on the dark side of the moon.

training area). Just short of his twenty-third birthday but a seasoned pilot, Sieber strapped into the fully fueled, camouflaged *Natter* vehicle for history's first manned vertical takeoff of a rocket. Designer Bachem comforted the pilot as they talked moments before what would later be called blastoff. If the *Natter* should veer off course, Bachem told Sieber, he should execute a half roll to stabilize the ship and attempt a recovery. Sieber's *Natter* was equipped with an FM transmitter for the purpose of transmitting flight data from various monitoring sensors in the machine. In addition, Sieber had a hard-wire interphone that connected him to engineers in the launch bunker.

The start worked as planned. On cue, the Walter main rocket motor built up to full thrust and Sieber depressed the switch to ignite the four rocket boosters. The sound was shattering. The *Natter* lifted aloft in a cloud of steam and rocket smoke and climbed rapidly to about five hundred feet, where it abruptly pitched back into a near upside-down attitude. Now, instead of climbing at ninety degrees it was climbing at thirty, but in an inverted curve. Onlookers thought they saw the four boosters detach and fall to earth as they were supposed to, but in fact one failed to break loose. No one knew this until 1998 when the crash site was excavated.

Sieber executed a roll maneuver but could not make the aircraft recover. Engineers on the ground saw the cockpit canopy fly loose at about 1,500 feet, suggesting that Sieber considered the aircraft out of control and had begun the escape sequence.

To the frustration of onwatchers, low-hanging stratus clouds swallowed up the *Natter*. The Walter motor was heard to cut out. The *Natter* soared to about five thousand feet and then came straight down. It blasted a fifteen-foot crater into the earth about five miles from the launch pad. Altogether, the *Natter* had been in the air for about fifty seconds.

Anxious onlookers searched the sky for Sieber to come descending out of the clouds beneath a parachute canopy. He did not. At the impact site, rescuers found a grisly assortment of body parts, including half of a left arm and half of a left leg. Before the main motor cut out, Sieber may have unintentionally become the first human to fly faster than sound (763 miles per hour at sea level), but only long after the departing canopy, with his headrest attached, snapped his head back and killed him.

Because an experienced test pilot lost his life struggling in vain to control the *Natter*—which, like the Heinkel He 162, was intended to be a "people's fighter" and be piloted by novice youngsters— Himmler's SS canceled the project. The cause was officially explained as a failure of the canopy, even though the evidence was overwhelming that Sieber had failed to fully close the canopy before launch. It can only be speculated that this seemingly minor error, not properly latching the canopy, led to disaster.

TWELVE

P-80

He was a pioneer like Hans von Ohain or Frank Whittle. He contributed more to aviation than Ernst Heinkel or Willy Messerschmitt. He was working on a design for a jet-propelled aircraft before the Heinkel He 280, the Messerschmitt Me 262, the XP-59A Airacomet, or the Gloster Meteor. He was without swagger or pretension. He was serious and studious and sometimes enthusiastic, but bragging wasn't in his nature and it wasn't his idea to call his enterprise the Skunk Works.

Clarence L. Johnson, called Kelly because he favored green neckties in spite of his Swedish ancestry, was the man behind the Lockheed P-80 Shooting Star, which, if the war went on long enough would end up fighting the Messerschmitt Me 262 in Europe's skies.

On June 18, 1943, Johnson took stairs two at a time, vaulting up to the office of Robert Gross, Lockheed's president, located at the company's headquarters in Burbank, California. In the office, Johnson found Gross and chief engineer Hal Hibbard.

"Wright Field wants us to submit a proposal for building a plane around a British jet engine," Kelly Johnson told the two corporate leaders. "I've worked out some figures. I think we can promise them 180-day delivery. What do you think?"

In fact, Johnson—who had pestered Hibbard to allow him to set up an experimental department where designers and artisans could work closely together—knew that the army had a requirement that the new aircraft be completed in 180 days, but committed himself a few days later to a first flight in 150. It was an extraordinary goal, similar to one Germany's Heinkel company would seek a year later with the Heinkel He 162 *Volksjäger*. Johnson was aware the Germans were on the verge of fielding jets, though he had few details.

ALMOST IMPOSSIBLE

Gross, Hibbard, and Johnson all knew that rosy legends about new aircraft being developed overnight are almost always the stuff of fiction. There were special circumstances when the NA-73X prototype went from blueprints to finished airframe in just four months and became the P-51 Mustang. In normal times, even in wartime, it was almost impossible to develop a new aircraft, especially when introducing a new kind of power—the turbo-jet engine—in any period that could be measured in days, weeks, or months.

In fact, at Johnson's behest, Lockheed apparently had established a goal of 180 days to first flight (changed to 150 as measured from June 23, 1943) when the company responded to a May 17, 1943, invitation from the Army Air Forces, the AAF, to propose a fighter using the de Havilland-built Halford H-1B engine. By then, the following other jet aircraft had already flown:

- Germany's Heinkel He 178 on August 27, 1939.
- Britain's Gloster E.28/39 test bed on May 15, 1941.
- Germany's Messerschmitt Me 262V3, under jet power for the first time, on July 18, 1942.
- The XP-59A Airacomet on October 1, 1942.
- Britain's Gloster Meteor on March 5, 1943.
- Britain's De Havilland Vampire on September 20, 1943.

Americans, who thought themselves leaders in world technology, had missed a chance offered to them earlier by Johnson.

Back in 1939, Johnson's design team—later to be dubbed the Skunk Works—had proposed a jet fighter. In a prewar environment when the P-39 Airacobra was becoming the standard AAF fighter, nothing but bureaucratic indifference greeted Lockheed's model L-133. Engineers drew up plans for several versions on the drawing board, culminating in the model L-133-02-01, a futuristic canard design that would have been powered not by a British import but by two company-designed L-1000 turbojet engines. The AAF simply had no interest. But the work on the never-to-be L-133 gave Lockheed's engineering team a wealth of experience when opportunity belatedly knocked.

In late 1943, Johnson and his staff put their new aircraft together ahead of the AAF's demanding schedule—not in 150 days but in 143!

Brigadier General Franklin O. Carroll, head of the AAF's engineering division, arranged for Kelly Johnson's design team to receive preliminary design studies undertaken by Bell for the unbuilt XP-59B of the Airacomet, as well as the specifications and drawings for the Halford engine. To proceed with engineering work on the L-140 as Lockheed initially named the XP-80, Johnson put together a team that never numbered more than 23 engineers and 105 assembly personnel, including designers W. P. Ralston and Don Palmer. Art Viereck, head of the engineering experimental department, supervised the shop group. Lieutenant Colonel Ralph Swofford was the original USAF project liaison on the XP-80.

Johnson's team concocted an aircraft that superficially appeared quite conventional, as if it might have been flyable with either a jet or a reciprocating engine in the nose. In fact, while the design was sensible and straightforward, it was anything but orthodox. Johnson stressed simplicity. The XP-80 was a clean design with straight wings, tail surfaces, and tricycle gear. To the extent it incorporated any unorthodox feature, the "gamble," as Johnson called it, was the wing. Departing from proven airfoil designs, Johnson picked what he called a wind tunnel wing—a low aspect ratio, laminar-flow surface never tested on a propeller-driven aircraft.

Air intakes positioned on the lower fuselage forward of the wing leading edge fed the De Havilland–built Halford H-1B Goblin centrifugal-flow turbojet, which occupied the rear of the main fuselage section. The aft fuselage, with engine and tail surfaces, was detachable for ready access to the powerplant. The cockpit was well forward and enclosed by a rearward-sliding bubble canopy. The absence of a propeller up front made it easy to install six forward-firing .50-caliber machine guns in the tear-shaped nose. After a full-scale mockup was evaluated on July 20 to 22, 1943, only exceedingly minor changes were recommended. Many years later, the final F-80 built looked little different from the first XP-80.

To make the powerplant installation accessible and easy to change, Lockheed designed the aft fuselage and tail assembly to be removed as a unit. Three bolts held the tail section in place. Control cables had quick disconnects as did the engine tailpipe, making it possible for maintenance crews to change engines in as little as twenty minutes.

PAPER PROTOTYPE

The XP-80 prototype was built without the team having an actual Halford engine. They had only blueprints. When Guy Bristow, the De Havilland engine expert, finally arrived with the H-1B powerplant seven days before completion of the airframe, minor changes had to be made that put the XP-80 6 pounds over the guaranteed contract weight of 8,600 pounds. Kelly Johnson's rule against working on Sunday—the design team's only day off—was broken to install the turbojet.

The Halford H-1B was to be produced by Allis-Chalmers as the J36. Before the XP-80's first flight, ground run-up tests inflicted damage requiring strengthening of the intake ducts, and the prototype eventually flew with the Halford engine. But the General Electric I-40 (later, the J33) was well advanced in the design stage in late 1943 and was chosen for subsequent airplanes in the series, designated

L-141 or XP-80A. Identical models designated YP-80A, with the "Y" indicating "service test," followed.

Milo Burcham took the spinach-green XP-80 up for its first flight on January 8, 1944. The XP-80 did much of the initial flying and then gave way to I-40-powered developmental airplanes.

The next aircraft was the first XP-80A model, dubbed *Gray Ghost* because of its painted, pearl gray exterior. The second XP-80A was dubbed *Silver Ghost* for its natural metal surface, which permitted comparison between this and the pearl gray finish. This aircraft was optimized as an engine test bed and was heavily instrumented with equipment for recording engine thrust, fuel consumption, intake ram pressure, exhaust temperatures, and other propulsion data. Lockheed installed a second seat behind the pilot's and this ship flew for the first time on August 1, 1944. It was considered an engine research vehicle and intended to carry an engineer on some flights.

On some flights, this aircraft carried Kelly Johnson. In due course, the second XP-80A flew against the P-51D Mustang in maneuverability trials at Wright Field, Ohio.

Late in its career, the *Silver Ghost* operated as a test bed for the three thousand–pound thrust Westinghouse J-34-WE-11 turbojet engine used on the Lockheed XF-90 penetration fighter and other jets of the postwar era. With this engine, it acquired a dorsal "spine" like that of the XF-90 and had a much-modified rear fuselage and exhaust area.

After the *Gray Ghost* made a significant contribution to the flight test effort, Lockheed modified it with reduced-size air intake ducts. In this configuration, the *Gray Ghost* suffered engine failure on March 20, 1945. Test pilot Tony LeVier—who had a reputation for flat-hatting around the airfield at speeds of 575 miles per hour—jettisoned the canopy after the airplane was ripped by what felt like an explosion. He bailed out successfully and wreckage was later found scattered over a wide area.

The YP-80A—like all succeeding versions, and called the L-080 in some company documents—was a service-test aircraft intended to pave the way for introduction of the Shooting Star into operational service.

The YP-80A aircraft were powered by the 3,850-pound thrust General Electric J33-GE-11 or Allison J33-A-9 turbojets also found on the production P-80A that followed—and both redesignations of the I-40—but for a time the engines were still hand-built and were highly unreliable. Until the proper metals, production techniques, maintenance procedures, and fuel controls were developed, engine failure was a frequent cause of accidents.

The first made a forty-five-minute first flight on September 13, 1944. Produced on an accelerated schedule, all thirteen aircraft were turned over to the army by December 31, 1944.

Sadly, by then the second ship had been lost on October 20, 1944. During takeoff at Lockheed's Burbank, California, terminal, landing gear and flaps appeared to retract slower than normal, a sign of engine failure. The aircraft got to a height of about three hundred feet and then plummeted. Unable to clear the rim of a crater off the runway's end, the aircraft came to the ground in a crackling, dry crash that killed the much-admired Milo Burcham. The test pilot, flying the YP-80A model for the first time, apparently had not been briefed on a modification that provided an emergency fuel system backup in the event of a main fuel pump failure.

The second of the thirteen YP-80A aircraft was modified to become a photo-reconnaissance aircraft with cameras in the nose and was redesignated F-14A. F-14 was the generic designation for this ship, which has been variously identified in published works as a YP-80A, XF-14, YF-14, or F-14A, although the "Y" for a service test prefix seems unlikely. The F-14A carried cameras in place of machine guns. A window for the camera was built into the hinged-forward, lower nose section in front of the nose wheel. This left the sides of the nose unblemished, unlike subsequent photo models of the P-80, which had camera windows on the side ahead of the air intakes. It is instructive to think of the sole F-14A as an integral part of the YP-80A flight test program during an early juncture in jet

He may be this [illegible handwritten note] droppy name

development, rather than as a precursor to the RF-80A photo ship that flew the first reconnaissance mission of the Korean War on June 28, 1950, with 1st Lt. Bryce Poe II at the controls.

The test pilot assigned to the F-14A, Lockheed's Perry E. "Ernie" Claypool Jr., was very much a pioneer jet flyer. Claypool was also one of many in industry who were intrigued by reports coming back from Europe about the Germans developing jet warplanes. The Lockheed team believed that their jet was superior and looked ahead to a time when it would prove itself in battle.

The test pilot and his bosses had heard that German jets left a readily visible, cometlike exhaust trail at night, making them readily visible to an adversary. It's unclear why they thought this, since the Luftwaffe had only a handful of Me 262 night fighters and opportunities to observe them would have been few. In any event, Claypool was sent aloft in the F-14A on December 6, 1944, to perform visual-recognition work with a Lockheed-owned B-25J Mitchell medium bomber being used as a chase and observation aircraft.

The American jet did not leave a highly visible exhaust trail, a fact that was tragically proven when the F-14A and the B-25J collided in mid-air near Boron, California, with the loss of all aboard. In addition to Claypool, those who died were Capt. Benjamin Van Doren Jr., 1st Lt. Henry L. Phillips, Tech Sgt. William P. Eckert, and civilian Robert C. Eickstaedt. Their names are part of the history of jet aviation, yet little is known about them. A news report in the *Bakersfield Californian* noted that Claypool was a former resident of Bakersfield, a truck driver for Union Oil Company, and a charter member of the Kern County Pilots Association before becoming a test pilot for Lockheed.

No number of aircraft losses was going to prevent the YP-80A from becoming operational. The AAF's commanding general, Gen. Henry H. "Hap" Arnold, was following jet developments in Germany and was eager to get YP-80As to Europe, where he hoped they would soon be fighting Hitler's jets.

Asked when he wanted the YP-80A in Europe, Arnold said, simply: "Now."

PROJECT EXTRAVERSION

On a trip to England, Arnold observed an early flight by the Gloster Meteor and was impressed. He was also thoroughly briefed on, but not overjoyed about, the XP-59A Airacomet, which he viewed as too slow and burdened by too many handling problems to serve in combat as a fighter. Arnold's key leaders overseas, Gen. Carl "Tooey" Spaatz and Lt. Gen. James H. "Jimmy" Doolittle, were telling him that the war in Europe would last until the end of 1945. Doolittle expressed his fear that by mid-1945 the Reich would have enough Me 262s and other jets to prevent American bombers from carrying out daylight missions. A change in targeting practices, which directed more bombers toward aircraft assembly plants, achieved little. Arnold was aware, however, that tests with the P-80 were proceeding relatively well and that production of P-80s would reach sixteen aircraft per month by the middle of the year.

Spaatz, as commander of U. S. Strategic Air Forces, saw the same reports on Arnold's desk that showed that in practical flying tests the P-80 could out-perform anything pulled by a propeller. Spaatz urged Arnold to conduct more realistic tests with the P-80, including tests in climate and weather conditions like those of northern Europe. Doolittle, who served under Spaatz and was commander of the Eighth Air Force, took the idea further by suggesting P-80s be deployed to the combat theater.

So, in a move that would later be almost unnoticed by historians, Arnold arranged for the P-80 to become operational in the combat theater before war's end. On November 13, 1944, Col. George E. Price received the go-ahead for Project Extraversion, in which four YP-80A service-test airplanes were earmarked to go to Europe—two to England in the European Theater of Operations (ETO) and two to Italy in the Mediterranean Theater of Operations (MTO). The word *extraversion* refers to a persistent personality trait that involves an outward mental orientation, meaning a person who is the opposite of an introvert. So perhaps this project was meant to symbolize reaching out. The four YP-80As were disassembled, put in boxes, and put aboard ships.

It's unclear whether Arnold, Price, and others expected these YP-80As to see combat. Clearly, one purpose of their journey was to build the morale of Eighth and Fifteenth Air Force heavy bomber crews, who were being pounded by German jets every day.

The pair for the ETO arrived in England on December 30, 1944. Ground crews assembled them at Burtonwood.

Their time in England, which might have yielded the stuff of high drama, turned out to be brief and tragic. Colonel Marcus Cooper and Maj. Fredrick Austin Borsodi, the Wright Field pilots assigned to the project, began flying in January 1945, with Cooper making the first flight of any P-80 outside the United States. Borsodi took a YP-80A into the air on January 28, 2013, but a failure in tension of the tail-pipe flange caused part of the hot gasses to vent inside the rear fuselage, expanding and burning through tail surfaces and causing the tail section to disintegrate. The aircraft crashed on a farm and Borsodi was killed.

The other YP-80A was available to be sent over the Reich if anyone wanted to use it to combat the Messerschmitt Me 262. It's unclear whether the YP-80A would have had sufficient range to reach Me 262 airfields, and it wouldn't have made much sense to send this single jet out on its own on a combat sortie. A later version, the F-80C, would later be credited with the first aerial victory in a jet-versus-jet battle (in Korea), but it was not destined to happen in 1945. Instead of fighting Hitler's jets, the sole YP-80A in England went off to Rolls-Royce, on loan for flight tests of with the Nene B.41 turbojet engine. It survived the war but was destroyed in a crash landing after an engine failure—oh so common in early jets—on November 14, 1945.

INTRO IN ITALY

Possibly by coincidence, the two YP-80As for Italy arrived in late January 1945, around the time Arado Ar 234B reconnaissance jets based at Udine, Northern Italy, began flying reconnaissance missions over Allied lines on the Italian front. It's clear the YP-80As weren't sent in *response* to Ar 234B operations, but it isn't clear whether, if events had unfolded differently, the Lockheed jets might have intercepted the Arado jets. The YP-80As were at Lesina airfield, which, with its single, pierced-steel planking runway, was part of the Foggia Airfield Complex, a series of World War II military airfields located within a twenty-five-mile radius of the city of Foggia.

Exact dates for the start of both YP-80A and Ar 234B operations in Italy are in dispute; dates for the latter appear variously as January, February, or March 1945 in various histories.

Almost everything we know about Project Extraversion in Italy comes from a draftee just past his twentieth birthday. Albert James "Jim" Bertoglio was the official photographer for the Italy-based 94th Fighter Squadron "Hat in the Ring," a part of the 1st Fighter Group, equipped with P-38 Lightnings and destined, later, to reequip with P-80 Shooting Stars in 1946. Bertoglio, who hailed from Medicine Lodge, Kansas, was widely interviewed after the war. He remembered that while both test and operational pilots flew the YP-80As, civilians maintained them. Bertoglio is widely quoted as seeing one YP-80A flying north of its base near Foggia, Italy, on some mysterious mission that was never explained.

Bob Esposito, an authority on the P-80 aircraft, says the two aircraft in Italy had fully functioning gunsights, machine guns, and ammunition.

After the war, a single P-80A was tested with a modified rotating nose, housing four machine-guns that could be elevated up to an angle of ninety degrees, and later with a second cockpit installed in the nose in which a pilot lay prone. The armament test was based on Germany's Schräge Musik, used on the Messerschmitt Bf 110 and other warplanes.

THIRTEEN

ARADO AR 234

When retired Lt. Col. Donald S. "Don" Bryan, 90, died on May 15, 2012, near his home in Adel, Georgia, shortly after being interviewed for this book, the United States lost an air ace who had fought in the skies of the Third Reich, was credited with shooting down more than thirteen German aircraft (including a jet), and received the Distinguished Service Cross, the nation's second highest award for valor.

Bryan loved the P-51 Mustang. It was, after all, the P-51, not the Me 262, that decided the air war in Europe.

Bryan's mount served him well on March 14, 1945, when he engaged and shot down an Arado Ar 234B-1 Blitz jet bomber high above the Ludendorff Bridge at Remagen. By that time, Bryan may have known more about the Ar 234 than any other American pilot. "It was my fourth encounter with one," he said. Others said the Arado aircraft was Bryan's nemesis.

In fact, it came very close to being an obsession. Bryan was too easygoing to be truly obsessed, but by the time of his fateful encounter, he'd thought about the Arado a lot.

Born in Hollister, California, in 1921, Bryan flew the P-47 Thunderbolt in combat before graduating to the Mustang. Bryan received a private pilot's license in college from the Civilian Pilot Training Program, learning on an Aeronca. He enlisted on January 6, 1943, and began his Army Air Forces training in PT-17 Kaydet biplanes at King City, California. He took his basic training at Moffett Field, California, and advanced training at Luke Field, Arizona. After earning pilot's wings and a commission, he was first stationed at Morris Field, South Carolina, in the 20th Fighter Group. He soloed in the P-40 Warhawk two days before he could legally buy a drink.

"Don was a fighter pilot's fighter pilot," Jay A. Stout, the author of *The Men Who Killed the Luftwaffe*, said in an interview for this book. "He was wry, fun-loving, and intelligent. When he climbed into the cockpit, he did it with no intent other than to win. He was in the war from July 1943 to May 1945. He played all four quarters."

No, the Ar 234 didn't obsess Bryan. But it came close.

December 1, 1944

In December 1944, Bryan became—he said—the first Allied pilot ever to see an Ar 234 in the air. He observed the twin jet just slightly too far away on the horizon. "If it had been a mile closer, I could have tried to get him," he said, even though the faster jet was pulling away on a parallel course.

Bryan wanted to get one.

He studied drawings of the jet in a group intelligence document. He looked for vulnerabilities and couldn't find any. He tried to compare it to the Me 262—which he never saw—and came up with few conclusions. "I scratched my head and wondered how many of these we would be seeing and whether they would threaten the advances our side was making in the war," he said.

Bryan spotted an Ar 234 on a second occasion later that month. "This time it wasn't even close," he said. "He was too far away and moving too fast."

During his third sighting on December 21, 1945, the Luftwaffe warplane crossed his flight path beneath him, flying from left to right. Bryan went after the Arado. He took a long shot, estimating deflection after the jet rushed by. He saw his rounds impact on one wing. Bryan was credited with an enemy aircraft damaged. "So at least I got a piece of him, but he pulled away. As I already knew by now, my P-51 was fast, but the Ar 234 was almost a hundred miles per hour faster," he said.

Able to reach a speed of 540 miles per hour, the Arado Ar 234 *Blitz* was the fastest combat aircraft in the world—slightly faster, even, than its cousin, the Messerschmitt Me 262 jet.

It was the world's first operational jet bomber, and in many ways the most advanced of the Reich's secret weapons. It was important enough that Hitler referred to it several times in staff meetings with his military leaders. The Führer often boasted to his staff that the jet Ar 234 was even faster than the prop-driven Mosquito.

The Ar 234 was a product of the German company Arado Flugzeugwerke. It was the Arado company's response to a 1940 German Air Ministry requirement for a fast reconnaissance aircraft. Walter Blume headed the Arado engineering team.

Blume had been an ace during the Great War with twenty-eight aerial victories and had been gravely wounded on a combat mission. Blume could appear absent-minded at times, prickly at others, but he'd studied aeronautical engineering for more than two decades and was up to date on the jet engines that some touted as the wave of the future. He was responsible for all of the key design features of the Ar 234, assisted by Hans Rebeski and others.

On their drawing boards, they conceived an aircraft that was extraordinarily clean. It had smooth, flush-riveted exterior skin. It had rakish lines and (eventually) tricycle landing gear. Where most planes needed a bulge or a step for the cockpit windshield, the Ar 234 had a completely smooth, glass-covered nose in the manner of the American B-29 Superfortress. The engine arrangement was similar to that of the better known Me 262, with long, deep-throated nacelles slung beneath the inboard portion of the wing.

Code-named the E370 while being designed, the new aircraft was built for a projected maximum speed of 485 miles per hour, which it eventually exceeded with ease. Its projected range of about two thousand miles was a little less than what the Air Ministry wanted, but officials in Berlin liked the design and ordered two prototypes, known as the Ar234 V1 and Ar 234 V2.

The success of the new plane would be dependent on the engine intended for it. The engine was the Jumo 004 axial-flow turbojet designed by a team headed by Dr. Anselm Franz of the Junkers aircraft company. It eventually became the world's first jet powerplant to enter production and become operational. But early jet engines being developed by the Germans and the British—with the Americans lagging a distant third in jet engine development—were cantankerous, unreliable, and trouble prone.

Design work on the Ar 234 airplane went smoothly. As related elsewhere in this narrative, the Junkers Jumo 004 turbojet engine was another matter. Tests that began in October 1940 were delayed by constant technical problems, including vibration of compressor blades. Steel blades had to be developed to replace the original alloy blades. Still, early versions of the engine sputtered, smoked, and died. One blew up on a test bench. When that didn't happen, the vibration problems continued until a second overhaul was made of the stator blade design. These and other problems delayed the engine, and that, in turn, delayed both the Messerschmitt Me 262 jet fighter and the Ar 234—for reasons unclear, the latter more than the former.

Once it became workable, the production version of the engine, the 004B-1, was rated at 1,980 pounds thrust, which was comparable to the turbojet Frank Whittle was developing for the British. Even then, the Jumo typically had a service life of only ten to twenty-five hours. Like all turbojets, it was sluggish in responding to the pilot's hand on the throttle.

The plane's landing gear was not part of the original design. Blume's design team was very much aware that the Luftwaffe wasn't fully satisfied with the plane's range and endurance. To increase internal fuel, they initially dispensed with wheels. Early Ar 234 versions took off using a three-wheeled trolley and landed by means of skids that worked well on a grassy surface. For increased thrust during takeoff, Ar 234s used Hellmuth Walter–designed, liquid-fueled rocket assisted takeoff (RATO) boosters, one mounted beneath each wing.

The Ar 234 was not as large as it looked. When Bryan first spotted one, he thought it was an American A-26 Invader. But the A-26 had a wingspan of seventy-one feet and was intended for a crew of three. In contrast, the Ar 234 had a wingspan of just over forty-six feet. Its crew consisted of just a single pilot who, as Bryan later said, "had to be a very busy and very lonely man."

The pilot got aboard by pulling down a retractable step on the left side, climbing up kick steps on the left side, and entering via the roof hatch. This hatch could be discarded, but there was no ejection seat and a pilot's prospects of getting out of the Arado under any circumstances were never good.

The pilot operated conventional throttle and rudder pedals and looked out with clear Plexiglas, giving him a superb view in all directions. Between the pilot's legs was the complex Lofte 7K tachometric bombsight. At the start of a bombing run, the pilot was expected to swing the control yoke out of his way and fly the aircraft using the bombsight control knobs, looking through the optical sight. Alternately, he could fly the aircraft using the yoke and a periscope sight (derived from the type used on German tanks), mounted on the cockpit roof and associated bombing computer to make a diving attack. Despite the very narrow landing gear that became standard after the skids were abandoned, the Ar 234 performed well when taxying, taking off, and landing, and it was not unduly vulnerable to crosswinds.

Although Arado began construction of the Ar 234 prototype at its factory in Warnemunde in spring 1941, almost two years elapsed before the plane maker received its first engines. No one seems to know why Willy Messerschmitt's aircraft company was able to get Jumo 004 engines for its Me 262 in June 1942, while Arado was forced to wait to receive its first engine until February 1943. For months, Blume and his engineers looked at the unfinished shell of the first plane, called the Ar 234 V1, and followed reports of Messerschmitt's aircraft undergoing flight tests.

June 15, 1943

The Ar 234 V1 prototype made its first flight on June 15, 1943, not at the factory, but at the company test facility at Rheine Airfield. At the controls was Arado chief test pilot Flugkapitän Selle, whose first name seems to be lost to history. By September, four prototypes were flying. The second prototype, the Arado Ar 234 V2, crashed October 2, 1943, at Rheine near Munster after suffering fire in the port wing, failure of both engines, and various instrumentation failure. The aircraft dived into the ground from four thousand feet, killing pilot Selle.

In flight tests, there were constant problems with the takeoff trolley and the landing skids. On one flight, the pilot correctly jettisoned the trolley at an altitude of two hundred feet, but its parachute failed to deploy and it was smashed. The skids often stayed in the extended position when they should have retracted, or collapsed when they should have been extended. At this rate, Arado experts and Luftwaffe officers agreed that during mass operations a typical airfield would become cluttered with disabled Ar 234s and following aircraft would be unable to land at all. Another drawback was that the Ar 234 could not taxi on the skids. It had to come to a halt and then be moved using a crane. Recognition of the need to change the landing arrangement prompted cancellation of a planned production version called the Ar 234A.

August 2, 1944

Despite the problems, the Ar 234 V7 prototype became the first jet aircraft ever to fly a reconnaissance mission. On August 2, 1944, Leutnant (Lt.) Erich Sommer whizzed over the Normandy beachheads at about 460 miles per hour and used two Rb 50/30 cameras to take one set of photos every eleven seconds. Although the Allies

Hitler escaped in a secret aircraft at the war's end. Where history and controversy collide with riveting narrative, *Fighting Hitler's Jets* furthers a repertoire that comprises some of the United States' most exceptional military writing.

ABOUT THE AUTHOR

Robert F. Dorr is an author (1955–), U.S. Air Force veteran (Korea, 1957–1960), and retired senior American diplomat (1964–1989). He is the author of the weekly "Back Talk" column in Air Force Times newspaper, the monthly "Washington Watch" feature in Aerospace America magazine (journal of the American Institute of Aeronautics and Astronautics), and numerous articles in major aviation and history magazines. He is both an analyst of present-day military events and a historian of past wars. He has published about seventy-five books and ten thousand articles. Dorr speaks to groups about aviation and military history and is often interviewed on history programs. He lives in Oakton, Virginia, with his family, which includes his Labrador retriever.

ABOUT ZENITH PRESS

Zenith Press publishes historical non-fiction in narrative, illustrated and graphic formats. Building on a core of 19th and 20th century military history in America, Zenith also publishes titles on the history of aviation, technology and science, and also in selected areas of cultural and social history - all with a distinctly American angle. From a narrative of a famed American WWII flying squadron to an illustrated celebration of NASA's famed Space Shuttle program to a cultural history of moonshine in the 19th and 20th centuries, Zenith books are engaging American stories with a firm historical foundation.

Author: Robert F. Dorr
Format: Hardcover, 304 Pages
Item: 200381
ISBN: 9780760343982
Publisher: Zenith Press
Illustrations: 20 b/w photos
Size: 6.25 x 9.25
Price: $30.00
Published: 10/15/2013

Media Contact: Nichole Schiele
Marketing Manager
612-344-8161
nschiele@quaysidepub.com

ZENITH PRESS

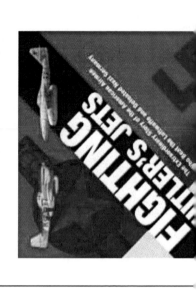

Fighting Hitler's Jets

The Extraordinary Story of the American Airmen Who Beat the Luftwaffe and Defeated Nazi Germany

By Robert F. Dorr

ABOUT THE BOOK

Fighting Hitler's Jets brings together in a single, character-driven narrative two groups of men at war: on one side, American fighter pilots and others who battled the secret "wonder weapons" with which Adolf Hitler hoped to turn the tide; on the other, the German scientists, engineers, and pilots who created and used these machines of war on the cutting edge of technology. Written by Robert F. Dorr, renowned author of Zenith Press titles Hell Hawks!, Mission to Berlin, and Mission to Tokyo, the story begins with a display of high-tech secret weapons arranged for Hitler at a time when Germany still had prospects of winning the war. It concludes with Berlin in rubble and the Allies seeking German technology in order to jumpstart their own jet-powered aviation programs. Along the way, Dorr supposedly had air superiority over the beaches, as Gen. Dwight D. Eisenhower famously said, Sommer's warplane returned with its fuel, unscathed.

The Ar 234B *Schnellbomber*, or "fast bomber" version introduced a widened fuselage that permitted conventional landing gear, albeit with a very narrow track. The B model—first flown March 10, 1944, piloted by civilian test pilot Joachim Carl, who replaced Selle—was slightly heavier than reconnaissance versions at 21,720 pounds. Because the Ar 234 was slender and entirely filled with fuel, it had no room for a bomb bay: its bombload had to be carried on external racks. The added weight and drag of a full bomb load reduced the speed, so on the B model two 20mm MG 151 cannons with two hundred rounds each were added in a remotely controlled tail mounting to give some measure of defense. Since the cockpit was directly in front of the fuselage, the pilot had no direct view to the rear, so the guns were aimed through the periscope. There exists no record of anyone ever hitting anything with these guns. Many pilots removed them to save weight.

It was not until June 1944 that twenty Ar 234Bs were produced and delivered. Some of these were diverted to the Luftwaffe test center at Rechlin. From October 1944, the German air unit known as KG 76 began to convert to the Ar 234B-2 bomber. The group began flying missions during heavy fighting in the Ardennes. In March 1945, coming in at low level and slinging bombs almost horizontally, after several attempts KG 76 finally succeeded in collapsing the Ludendorff Bridge at Remagen, but by then the loss of the bridge had little effect.

"I liked the Arado very much," said former Luftwaffe pilot Willi Kriessmann, who lives today in Burlingame, California. "It was a wonderful plane. I thought it was designed better than the Messerschmitt Me 262. It was a single-seater so we didn't have time to practice much, so we had some 'dry classes.' Landing and taking off was very different from a prop plane." Kriessmann noted that the RATO units often didn't work properly.

Two different configurations for a four-engine version of the Ar 234 were built and flown. The sixth and eighth planes in the series were powered by four BMW 003 jet engines instead of two Jumo 004s, the sixth (Ar 234 V6) having four engines housed in individual nacelles and the eighth (Ar 234 V8) flown with two pairs of BMW 003s installed within twinned nacelles underneath either wing. These were the world's first four-engine jets. They offered no performance advantage over the twin-engine version.

An improved Ar 234C was the final production version. This model introduced an improved pressurized cockpit and larger main wheels. A crescent-wing Ar 234—foretelling Britain's Handley Page Victor bomber of the 1950s—was under construction but never flown.

Kriessmann was assigned to ferry Ar 234s from the factory to different places where optical equipment and bombing equipment was installed. "I flew the first one on December 12, 1944, from Hamburg to Kampfgeschwader 76 and the last on May 1, 1945," he said. KG 76 flew the final Ar 234 sortie of the war against advancing Red Army troops near Berlin.

Plans existed for the manufacture of 2,500 Ar 234 *Blitz* bombers, but they were cut short by the war's end. Total production was 224 examples of all versions of the Ar 234.

March 14, 1945

"I'm not letting one get away from me again," Bryan thought out loud.

The usual soup over Germany had been transformed into brilliant sunshine on March 14. Eleven of the German jet bombers from flying unit KG 76 (Kampfgeschwader 76) were attacking the newly constructed floating engineer bridge south of the Ludendorff Bridge (which was the last traditional bridge standing on the Rhine when it was captured by soldiers of the U.S. 9th Armored Division on March 7, 1945).

Bryan, of the 352nd Fighter Group, "The Bluenosed Bastards of Bodney," was commander of the group's 328th squadron. He was leading a flight of four P-51D Mustangs escorting Ninth Air Force A-26 Invaders.

He saw the Arado pulling off the bridge and maneuvering into a tight turn to evade a formation of American P-47 Thunderbolts. This maneuver compromised the jet bomber's strongest asset—its superior speed—and Bryan was able to position himself so the German would have to fly toward him.

Bryan wrote in his encounter report: "I observed an Ar 234 cross in front of us headed for the Remagen bridgehead. I dropped tanks and started after the enemy aircraft. He was traveling about 50 miles per hour faster than we were, and crossed the Rhine south of the bridge going west and then turned north making a very shallow dive run on the bridge, but did not drop his bombs. I saw several P-47s to the northwest, so I headed in a northeasterly direction. I could not catch the enemy aircraft in a straight run, and thought he might turn east to avoid combat with the P-47s. When the enemy aircraft saw the P-47s, he turned east and had to pass directly under me. I turned east, and when he passed under me, I dove down on him and opened fire at about 250 yards."

Bryan rolled right into a dive to assure he would be on top of the jet as it passed. As the jet whooshed past, Bryan then rolled his wings—vertically left directly behind it— and prepared to fire. Said Bryan: "I probably knew as much about the Ar 234 as any American at this point, but I didn't know if it had forward-firing guns"—it didn't—"and I knew that if he was armed, he might be able to get the advantage on me. I got ahead of him and let him fly by me. I rolled in behind the 234 and fired when all g's were neutral."

"I hit him with the first burst and knocked his right jet out," Bryan said. "He made a shallow turn to the right and started very mild evasive maneuvers. They consisted of shallow turns and a few shallow dives and climbs."

Bryan saw none of the smoke-filled jet exhaust that was sometimes associated with the German jets. He banked the P-51 behind his adversary and fired long bursts, exhausting nearly all of his ammunition.

"I don't know what the hell was on his mind," Bryan said in an interview for this book, "but he should have gotten out of that airplane while he was high enough. I think he was afraid I would shoot at him in his parachute, which I would never do."

The Arado pilot, Hauptman (Capt.) Hans Hirshberger, waited too long to jettison his roof hatch and attempt to escape from his cockpit. He went down with the aircraft. It was his first and only combat mission.

Pilots are credited with a portion of an aerial victory when they share in a shootdown: Bryan's final score was 13.33 kills.

FOURTEEN

MARAUDER MAN

The girls always told him he had a special shine in his eyes. In fact, they still say that.

Jim Vining nowadays touches the throttle on his high-tech wheelchair and threads his way through people and furniture at Sunrise Senior Living in Oakton, Virginia. Look closely for that glint in his eyes. Look closely for a hint of how Vining used his deft touch on the throttle to fling an eighteen-ton Martin B-26 Marauder medium bomber all over the wartime sky.

"Adolf Hitler was pretty much an abstraction to us. His jets, we knew about. We had a briefing from a grim-faced intelligence guy who showed us silhouettes of the Messerschmitt Me 262. We also had information in a classified publication called *Impact*," Vining said. "Years later, someone told me that Hitler believed even in April 1945 that his miraculous jet fighters were going to turn the tide. His obsession, we knew about. He was a man obsessed."

Interviewed on July 20, 2012, Vining, eighty-seven, was spending his days in an assisted care facility partly because his wife, Mary, is experiencing Alzheimer's and needs more care. They're together, just as they've been for sixty-four years. They're the parents of four

children. Look at them and they, too, have that remarkable bright-
ness in their gaze, a look that exudes cheerfulness. If you have those
eyes, you're comfortable in your own skin and others can see it.

But somewhere in his heart, Vining is still piloting the B-26 that
was shot down by a Messerschmitt Me 262.

February 21, 1945

Robert Des Lauriers, copilot of a B-17G Flying Fortress four-engine
heavy bomber coming away from a bomb run on Nurnburg, saw an
Me 262 approaching his formation. Des Lauriers, a first lieutenant,
saw "a khaki gray blur with some kind of symbol on it," he recalled,
coming toward him in front of his right wing. "He was moving very
fast and he kept going right past us and hit the group behind us,
which was the 100th Bomb Group," he said. Des Lauriers's own 34th
group was unscathed but shook up: "We had heard about jets, but we
had not seen any before."

The Me 262 came up on the tail of a B-17 at such high speed that a
collision looked certain. The planes didn't collide, but the cannons in
the nose of the German jet opened up. The muzzle flashes were visible from the distance. Pieces of the number three engine on the B-17
began flying loose. Crewmembers began tumbling out. Parachutes
snapped open and drifted with the wind.

At this late juncture in the war, fully operational German jets
were claiming aerial victories over U.S. bombers almost every day.
On one day, there were half a dozen kills.

Moments later Des Lauriers saw an Me 262 climbing straight up
with a P-51 Mustang behind it. He has always wondered whether
the P-51 pilot was successful. No official credit for an aerial victory
corresponds to this event, so it's likely the Mustang pilot did not get
a kill. The jets, however, claimed several bombers. That day, 1st Lts.
Harold E. Whitmore and Russell N. Webb of the 361st Fighter
Squadron, 365th Fighter Group, tangled with an Me 262 pilot who
apparently was Oberfeldwebel (First Sgt.) Gerhard Ronde. After
Ronde apparently shot down an F-5 Lightning reconnaissance

aircraft, Whitmore closed in on the Me 262 with Webb close behind. Whitmore fired a long burst from four hundred yards that set the jet afire. The two American pilots watched it disintegrate and Whitmore was credited with the kill.

Jerry Wolf, a top turret gunner on a B-17 who was visiting Berlin for the *fourth time* on February 21, 1945, looked out and saw a Messerschmitt Me 262 coming up behind him. "That thing was so fast, we needed two guys to describe it—one to say, 'Here it comes!' and one to say, 'There it goes.' " I had never seen one before and I reacted quickly—too quickly. My brain and my head were turning to follow the jet, but my gun mount was stuck in the forward-firing position. I saw this jet get hits on a B-17 and then it was gone. I didn't see the B-17 or the Me 262 again."

Des Lauriers, Wolf, and the tens of thousands of airmen who fought in the freezing air high above the Reich were well aware by early 1945 that the B-17 Flying Fortress was no match for an Me 262. They knew that a quick burst from the jet's four 30mm cannons could inflict so much damage to a B-17 or B-24 Liberator that the bomber crew would have little chance of making it safely home.

Des Lauriers, Wolf, and other B-17 crewmembers also witnessed the fast, blurry flying disks of indeterminate size that after the war would be known as unidentified flying objects, or UFOs. During the war, they were called foo fighters. American airmen wondered if they were some new and mysterious German weapon. They had no idea that German pilots looked at these objects and wondered if they were some new and mysterious American weapon.

The foo fighters were luminous flying objects witnessed by both Axis and Allied airmen in the skies over Europe. According to one description, they were balls of light that followed and hovered around aircraft in flight, day and night. Some of these sightings undoubtedly were misperceptions by men caught up in combat, but perhaps not all.

A radar operator in the 415th Night Fighter Squadron, Donald J. Meiers, gave the objects their name—from the cartoon-character firefighter Smokey Stover, drawn by Bill Holman, who declared, "Where there's foo, there's fire." The word *foo* itself was a nonsense term widely used in the 1930s and 1940s. In at least some cases, Allied intelligence reported that foo fighters reported in the European theater represented advanced German aircraft or weapons.

In a debriefing following a November 27, 1944, night mission, Capt. Fritz Ringwald, the 415th squadron's intelligence officer, stated that Don Meiers and Ed Schleuter had sighted a red ball of fire that appeared to chase their Bristol Beaufighter through a variety of high-speed maneuvers.

In *Black Thursday*, his account of a fateful B-17 bombing mission, Martin Caidin wrote of members of the 384th Bombardment Group seeing clusters of disks that were silver-colored, an inch thick and three inches in diameter:

> And then the 'impossible' happened. B-17 Number 026 closed rapidly with a number of discs; the pilot attempted to evade an imminent collision with the objects, but was unsuccessful in his maneuver. He reported at the intelligence debriefing that his right wing 'went directly through a cluster with absolutely no effect on engines or plane surface.'
>
> The intelligence officers pressed their questioning, and the pilot stated further that one of the discs was heard to strike the tail assembly of his B-17, but that neither he nor any member of the crew heard or witnessed an explosion.

Critics question Caidin's report that foo fighters made an appearance over Schweinfurt. No one disputes that sightings were reported during other missions in Europe, though.

February 25, 1945

In numbers the Americans hadn't seen before, the German jets swarmed into the air in 1945. Supporting the front-line 104th Infantry Division near Duren, Germany, was the 386th Fighter Squadron of the 365th Fighter Group, "Hell Hawks," with P-47D Thunderbolts. First Lieutenant John H. Rogers, leading eight of the Thunderbolts, was pulling off of one ground target and headed for another when ground control, call sign Sweepstakes, informed him that Me 262s were operating near Duren.

Rogers had been briefed on the capabilities of the Me 262— American airmen in some combat groups were, airmen in others weren't, for no apparent reason—and believed he could engage a jet fighter. Rogers and his fellow Thunderbolt pilots had seen a British report, based on captured wreckage of an Me 262, that told them what to expect. In part, it read:

The outstanding advantages of the Me 262 are its high level speeds, very high diving speeds and probably high ceiling. [These] give it a good performance at 35,000 feet. Its disadvantages are due chiefly to its high wing loading—namely a high takeoff speed requiring a long takeoff run, a high stalling speed and poor maneuvering qualities. It will also tend to overshoot its target at high speed like any jet-propelled fighter.

The Me 262 will have the usual poor performance of a jet fighter at low speed. Thus, it can be attacked most easily by fighters now in service when it is cruising or climbing. In maneuvers, the Me 262 should be forced into tight turns or into a zoom, unless the altitude at which it is encountered is near the ceiling of the attacking aircraft.

When conventionally engined aircraft are avoiding the Me 262, they should not dive since the Me 262's acceleration in a dive will be larger than that of a conventional fighter, enabling it to escape the attack, or to press home an attack on its opponent. If jet-propelled aircraft are used against the Me 262 [something that never happened], diving tactics may of course be employed. In fact, both aircraft can carry out the same maneuvers. British jet-propelled fighters now in service [Gloster Meteors] have a lower wing loading than the Me 262, and thus

better turning qualities. They should be able to out-maneuver the
Me 262.

Rogers and his P-47 flight made visual contact with no fewer than
fifteen Me 262s. First Lieutenant James L. "Mac" McWhorter led
some of the Thunderbolts in a climb hoping to reach the jets' altitude. Just when an eyeball-to-eyeball encounter seemed imminent,
McWhorter's wingman, 1st Lt. Albert Longo, encountered engine
trouble and had to turn for home. As he crossed the Roer River,
Longo looked back to his right and saw an Me 262 firing at him.

Longo made an abrupt turn to the left. The Me 262 overshot him.
The Me 262 pilot veered to the left as well, enabling Longo to latch
onto his six o'clock position and line him up in the Thunderbolt's
gunsight. Too focused on the foe and not enough on his own instruments, Longo was firing a prolonged burst from his eight .50-caliber
guns when his aircraft lurched into a stall.

He'd hit his mark. Longo saw debris fly loose from the Me 262.
The German pilot went into an abrupt climb, apparently seeking to
hide in a blanket of stratus above them. If a jet couldn't outmaneuver
a Jug, its pilot was going to outrace the heavily armed Thunderbolt.
The jet fighter plunged into the white cloud and vanished. Longo
turned for home but remained alert, wondering if the German would
come back. Longo didn't know what happened to the jet, didn't claim
a kill, and wasn't credited with one.

McWhorter was at four thousand feet in his Hell Hawks P-47
when he spotted two Me 262s diving at him from behind, perfectly positioned to lock in on his vulnerable six o'clock position.
McWhorter racked his Thunderbolt around in a violent turn with
the wings vertical to the ground. He turned into the pair of German
jets. "I never felt so intent," he said.

"I turned into them. We were in a head-to-head pass. Those two
Me 262 pilots were a pair of brave men, I'll tell you. They were fully
prepared to play a game of chicken with me. They came straight at
me. I shot at them, but most of my attention was devoted to avoiding

a collision," he said. "Just try to imagine a Jug and an Me 262 coming together at a combined closing speed of almost a thousand miles per hour."

McWhorter was certain his guns were scoring hits on both of the onrushing jets. His glimpse of this used up a split-second. And then, the moment was gone: McWhorter's P-47 and the pair of Me 262s whipped past each other with very little space to spare. He estimated that they were twenty feet apart. McWhorter cranked his robust Thunderbolt around into another tight turn intent on pursuing the two jets, but they were speeding away. He knew a tail-end chase would never succeed.

McWhorter added throttle and climbed over Duren. At twelve thousand feet, he observed another Me 262 making a firing pass on a brace of Thunderbolts. He pulled up and fired a ninety-degree deflection shot from two thousand yards. He continued to pull lead, closing to one thousand yards and observing many strikes on the Me 262. The German jet wobbled and emitted spurts of black smoke. The German pilot banked to the left and settled on a heading that would take him north of Cologne. With his maneuvers, McWhorter had now slowed the speed of his Thunderbolt and had no realistic possibility of chasing after the faster jet. He abandoned the chase and returned to his Hell Hawks Thunderbolt formation.

As the P-47 group reassembled in the sky high near the front lines, the American pilots saw an Me 262 that appeared to be strafing ground troops. Flight leader Rogers was contemplating a fast dive to try to catch the Me 262, but it flew away before anyone could act. No more enemy aircraft appeared to be nearby and fuel was low, so the P-47s returned to their airfield on the continent.

The Hell Hawks were in the air again later in the day, with flight leader 1st Lt. Lowell Freeman Jr. up front. The members of the 365th group's 386th Fighter Squadron received orders from a ground controller and were preparing to dive-bomb a ground target when a radio call announced that more Me 262s had been spotted.

Too distant to engage, the Americans watched two Me 262s fly over Duren, arrive at the front, and make a strafing run on friendly ground troops. The Hell Hawks were unable to pursue.

February 25, 1945 (continued)

This busy day was not, however, over for the fighter pilots of the Eighth Air Force, including those of the 55th Fighter Group. Captain Donald E. Penn covered the fray in an after-action report:

> I noticed two Me 262s airborne and two more taking off from Giebelstadt airdrome. We were flying at 13,000 feet and I ordered the squadron to drop tanks and engage the enemy aircraft, dived on one jet, using fifty inches of mercury and 3,000 RPM.
>
> He was making a slight turn to port at 1,000 feet, heading back toward the drome, so I leveled off 3,000 yards behind him and went to full power. My indicated air speed was about 500 miles per hour and I expected him to use full-power, as well, to attempt to pull away from me. However, I closed rapidly from 1,000 yards.
>
> At 500 yards, I observed the 262 had his wheels down. I cut down on my power and at 300 yards started striking the aircraft in the power unit. Closing to 50 yards, I broke sharply over the top of the jet, watching him as he rolled over, went straight in, and exploded.

Other P-51 Mustang pilots who had success fighting Hitler's jets included Capt. Donald M. Cummings, who bagged two Me 262s, and 2nd Lt. John F. O'Neil, who was credited with one. First Lieutenant Milliard O. Anderson, 2nd Lt. Donald T. Menegray, and 1st Lt. Billy Clemmons were other 55th group pilots who shot down Me 262s. A member of Donald Blakeslee's 4th Fighter Group, 1st Lt. Carl G. Payne, also knocked down an Me 262 that day.

April 10, 1945

On April 10, 1945, no fewer than 1,300 bombers of the Eighth Air Force set out to destroy the last of the Luftwaffe's jet force. However, unknown to the bomber crews and their fighter escort, the enemy jets were already airborne and waiting to spring their deadly trap. As the war in mainland Europe entered its final, bloody phase, the German armies defending Berlin fought on with a savage determination, slowly disintegrating before the mighty weapon of war unleashed against them. What remained of the Luftwaffe was mercilessly pounded from the air, their airfields hammered relentlessly. Aircraft, fuel, spare parts, ammunition, and pilots all were in short supply, but still they fought on, with deadly effect. At the forefront of the German offensive, and pivotal during the defense of the Reich, were the highly advanced jet fighters of the Luftwaffe, and in particular the Me 262.

"They must have thought it was a fearsome weapon," said medium bomber pilot Jim Vining. Considering what was about to happen to him, he should have been more impressed. But Vining had a lot of faith in his own airplane.

"The B-26 was our best twin-engined bomber," said Vining. "It was almost as maneuverable as a fighter." At low level, where much of the war on the European continent was fought, the B-26 Marauder was a hot, metal-smelling, cramped, sweaty airplane with six men busily occupied keeping it aloft and defending it with guns. At high altitude, it was cold. In the war in Europe, it was always cold.

"It was a cold, wet day, like so many of them, but above the weather it wasn't a bad day for flying," Vining said.

He was referring to the fact it was Hitler's fifty-sixth birthday.

WONDER WEAPON
April 20, 1945

The Messerschmitt Me 262 *Schwalbe*, or Swallow, looked like a shark. In dense green camouflage sullied by rain from low-hanging clouds, Hitler's *Wunderwaffe* was almost the color of the ocean predator it resembled. The twin-engine jet fighter looked grimly functional and weather worn.

Me 262 pilot Adolf Galland, until recently wearing the title General of the Fighter Force, or General der Jagdflieger, was considerably higher rank than Unteroffzier (Corporal) Eduard Schallmoser, and Galland's dark features and moustache gave him a grimly serious look in contrast to Schallmoser's boyish smile. The two were brothers in a way that transcended military rank. They were among the couple of dozen who had been at the controls of a jet fighter in combat—and they would be again today. Their outfit was Jagdverband 44 (JV 44), also known as "Der Galland-Zirkus" (The Galland Circus), and was stationed at Munich-Riem. It was the place to which Reichsmarshall (Marshal of the Realm) Hermann Göring dispatched the inconvenient Galland in the fond hope Galland would be killed in action. Another of their brotherhood was Unteroffzier (Cpl.) Johan "Jonny" Müller, who would later believe himself, incorrectly, to be responsible for shooting down Jim Vining's B-26. Another still: the 1,100-sortie, 196-kill air ace Hauptmann (Capt.) Walter Krupinski.

Gifted with a better sense of humor than Galland, even on this brooding day, Schallmoser couldn't resist a complaint about the unreliable Jumo turbojet engines that were the main flaw of the Me 262. "I may have to ram an American plane," Schallmoser said, "if I want to get a new plane of my own with engines that work." It wouldn't be the first time. Two weeks earlier on April 4, Schallmoser racked up the first aerial victory for his flying unit by colliding with the prominent twin tail of a P-38 Lightning in an ear-grating collision that sent the P-38 tumbling wing-over-wing toward the ground. The P-38 pilot bailed out. Schallmoser saw his parachute, a gray-white blemish, drifting across farmland. Schallmoser limped partway home and bailed out too—but in massive battles with P-51 Mustangs, the Me 262 force lost eight aircraft in a single day. Now, Schallmoser was getting into the air again.

On April 20, 1945, Vining and his crew tromped through a damp drizzle to sit down for a briefing at Valenciennes-Denain airfield, also called A-83, in France. They were members of the 454th Bombardment Squadron, part of the 323rd Bombardment Wing, which came ashore just after D-Day and had been caught up in heavy fighting, including the Battle of the Bulge, while the men struggled with the discomforts of living with crude accommodations on the continent. Vining was twenty years old and was about to command his crew of six while flying his fortieth combat mission. As predicted, the weather began to clear when the men walked to the revetment where their B-26 awaited.

"It shouldn't have been a bad day for me," Vining said. "Sure, there might be flak over our target, the railroad marshaling yards at Memmingen in southwestern Germany, but we had flown through flak before. Sure, we had been briefed that the Germans had a new jet fighter, the Messerschmitt Me 262—we had seen one in the distance, two weeks earlier—but we felt we could handle ourselves."

To everyone except perhaps those in Hitler's bunker in the German capital, it was apparent that the war was near its end. For a month, the Red Army had been hammering at the outskirts of Berlin. On this date, April 20, 1945, Soviet artillery reached inside the German capital for the first time, beginning the Battle of Berlin, which would last for a dozen days. Hitler and his minions, ensconced in the Führerbunker, were shielded from the shelling, unlike almost everyone else in the capital. And on this date, a weathered-looking Führer made what most historians agree was his final, above ground appearance to award Iron Crosses to boy soldiers of the Hitler Youth. A handful of conspiracy theorists suggest that Hitler was making an escape and that the faux Führer who made this final public appearance was a double.

Either way, Vining and other American airmen went into action aware of a situation that Vining called a mixed blessing—the Allies absolutely dominated the skies, yet the jet fighters flying in the defense of the Reich were taking a heavy toll of friendly aircraft. The Eighth Air Force, which began with a handful of airmen back in the early days, could now put a thousand bombers over a target anywhere within what remained of the Reich. The Ninth Air Force, to which Jim Vining and his fellow Marauder Men belonged, was on the ground, on the continent, blasting away at withering resistance on the Western Front. At least a few German pilots were deserting or defecting, but the Luftwaffe remained formidable and was still able to put its sharklike Me 262s aloft to challenge the conquerors.

"My regularly assigned bomber wasn't available, so I was piloting a borrowed aircraft," Vining said. "Usually, when you had to borrow a plane, they gave you a hangar queen. They gave me a plane with the name *The Ugly Duckling* painted on the side. It just didn't have the smooth, easy performance of the Marauder I was accustomed to."

In the front right seat next to Vining was copilot 1st Lt. James R. Mulvihill. Looking ahead from behind the Plexiglas nose cone of the Marauder was the togglier, an enlisted version of a bombardier, Staff Sgt. J. D. Wells, who was geriatric at age thirty-three and had never been inside an airplane before joining the army. Unlike the others aboard the B-26, neither Mulvihill nor Wells trained with Vining stateside, but this crew had been together in the combat zone for some time now. Vining was aware of small tensions among the men, but for the most part the crew performed well.

Filling out the six-man Marauder crew were three who had been with Vining in the United States—engineer/gunner Cpl. Henry C. Yates, radioman/gunner Cpl. Newton C. Armstrong, and gunner Sgt. William "Bill" Winger.

Vining said the Marauder was far from comfortable. On combat missions, crews flew without heat because the heaters were built around the exhaust stacks, "and if those got hit you'd have carbon monoxide inside the plane," he said. The Marauder was not pressurized.

"Starting engines: We have a guy on the ground with a fire extinguisher, staying on alert in case of fire. He signals the pilot to start the prop. You start with the left engine, the number one engine. We begin each combat mission knowing when we're expected to taxi out; you have to be in the right place at the right time because we take off in twenty-second intervals," he said. "You get up and get into a formation and headed out."

But before all that, the crew just had to get into the B-26.

"How do you get into a Marauder?" Vining said reflecting on his time in the B-26. "We climb up through the nose wheel well. The guys in back climb into waist windows. You have to be acrobatic: they don't have ladders for the waist openings.

"You can move back and forth between the front and back of the fuselage by going through the bomb bay. The crew consists of six men: pilot, copilot, bombardier (or toggler), and three gunners, one each with additional duty as a radioman, an engineer, and an armorer."

Forty-eight B-26s were part of a larger strike force hitting hard from the air. In a memoir, Louis S. Rehr, who was commander of a Marauder squadron, wrote, "Our initial point was a town called Kempten, south of Memmingen. Here we tightened up our individual groups of six for a four-minute bomb run. We opened the bomb bays and held steady. Arcs of light flak, probably from positions in the higher terrain, crossed our path. Fifteen more seconds until the drop."

"Suddenly, an aircraft ripped the skies directly overhead. Instantly, all hell broke loose. Within seconds, flames billowed from the left engine of a Marauder flying directly behind box leader Smith," he added. Rehr was referring to Me 262 ace Krupinski's 197th and last aerial victory of the war, a Marauder that careened to earth on fire, taking its crew with it.

In a history, Robert Forsyth wrote that when Schallmoser, flying a jet marked as *White 11*, attacked one of Jim Vining's fellow B-26 pilots, his MK 108 cannon jammed. "Schallmoser quickly looked down at his gun firing button, and, as he did so, the Me 262 took him dangerously close to the bomber formation. When Schallmoser looked up, it was too late.

"Attracting fire from the Marauder gunners, *White 11* scraped into the starboard engine propeller of the B-26 piloted by Lt. James H. Hansen. On impact, the jet rolled over and nosed down through the enemy formation streaming black smoke, with pieces of its own debris falling behind it. One American gunner reported seeing 'parts of the right wing break away.' "

Hansen struggled mightily and succeeded not only in keeping his bomber aloft but in keeping the right engine turning over, even though the propeller was badly smashed. This was a very bad day for Marauder Men, but not for Hansen and his crew, who made it safely back to their base.

Vining peered through his windshield and saw an Me 262 spitting 30mm cannon shells at him and his crew. He decided to fight back.

"You were supposed to turn and run. I wasn't going to do that," Vining said.

Vining slid his B-26 out of formation. This gave him a good aim at the Me 262 in front of him and he squeezed off a burst from his bomber's four fixed .50-caliber machine guns.

Cannon fire from a second Me 262 caught Vining's B-26. The crack of an explosion in the cockpit stunned him. Hit, but feeling no pain, he realized the B-26 was falling now, its right propeller windmilling. Vining turned control over to copilot Mulvihill, jettisoned his bombs, feathered the right propeller, and trimmed his rudder to counteract the yaw.

Vining looked down at his right foot. It was dangling from his leg by remnants of flesh. The cockpit floor was slick with his blood. "An artery was pumping out more like a fire hose," he said.

Vining used both hands to squeeze his lower thigh "tight enough to get it down to a trickle." His radioman Armstrong came forward and improvised a tourniquet from a headset cord.

Another flight of Me 262s stalked the Vining's now-crippled bomber. While Vining gave his inexperienced copilot a rapid tutorial on landing a B-26 on one engine, his crew called in warnings of fresh jet attacks. Vining used the interphone to coordinate the bomber's defensive gunfire and evasive maneuvers.

Like the cavalry coming to the rescue, a pair of American P-51 Mustang fighters arrived. In a series of rapid, high-speed maneuvers, the P-51 pilots shot down one of the German jets and chased away the rest.

Vining and Mulvihill headed for the big, U.S.-held airfield at Trier, Germany, but "we were down to 3,000, and the mountains between us and Trier were 3,500 feet high," Vining said. Feeling the effects of blood loss and shock, Vining took the controls again so the crew could prepare for a forced landing.

But Vining was too weak from loss of blood to stay on the controls. Lined up on a seemingly flat stretch of farmland near Uberherrn, Germany, Mulvihill was about to belly in when the crew saw a deep antitank ditch in its path. It was too late, though. The Marauder slammed into the ground with tremendous force. "We pancaked into that ditch and the ship broke into three pieces," Vining said. The impact killed top gunner Staff Sgt. William Winger.

Vining's battered crew pulled their critically wounded aircraft commander from the wreckage. By sheer luck, army medics were nearby. They gave first aid and sent Vining on a three-hour Jeep journey to a hospital in Metz, France. "When I got there, I had no vital signs," said Vining. A doctor told him, "It would have been easier to pronounce you dead." Surgeons removed his right leg below the knee, but Vining recovered to walk—and fly—again. Having earned the Silver Star, the nation's third highest award for valor, he retired in 1946 as a captain.

In 1981, Jim Vining retired from a thirty-year career with the Central Intelligence Agency. He doesn't talk about the CIA, but he will say working there wasn't as interesting as fighting Hitler's jets.

FIFTEEN

DOGFIGHTS

Although he spent little time in Berlin throughout the war, Adolf Hitler took up residence beneath the city's surface on January 16, 1945. Weeks later, on the day before jet fighters rose to defend his capital against one of the Allies' largest bombing efforts, Hitler met in his apartment in the Führerbunker, the air-raid shelter twenty-eight feet below the garden of the old Reich Chancellery building, with a dozen mostly military men, some of them quite junior. It was March 23, 1945.

Surrounded by high-quality furnishings and with a portrait nearby of his hero Frederick the Great, the Führer talked with the military men as if his "wonder weapons" and his Luftwaffe would still be able to save the day. In a reference to fighting along the Rhine River, Hitler asked, "Is the entire Luftwaffe here to eliminate this at least?" The word "here" referred to his pointing at a map.

The portrait of Frederick II was always present. The Führer was intrigued with this historical figure and with likenesses of him. When Hitler traveled in his railway car, the Anton Graff painting of Frederick the Great traveled with him. When Hitler flew aboard his Junkers Ju 52, the portrait flew, too, to the dismay of personal pilot

Hans Baur, who complained that the picture was usually packed in a bulky crate that scratched the plane's leather seating. Hitler was, of course, a connoisseur of art who collected priceless paintings and whose soldiers pillaged every private collection and museum gallery in occupied Europe.

Colonel Nicolaus von Below, the air adjutant, who felt comfortable speaking truth to the Führer—he may have been the only officer ever to overcome Hitler's dislike of men with an aristocratic background—probably wished he were anyone else at that moment.

"My Führer," Below said, "today Me 262s and Arado 234s were sent out as well as Otto fighters." Otto was Below's personal term for a plane with a propeller. "The fighters barely got through, though, because they became involved in aerial combat . . ."

German jet pilots were fighting at the river crossing. Messerschmitt Me 262 pilot Hans Busch, who was still in training, watched other 262 pilots scramble into their cockpits and go aloft. "They were going to unleash those powerful 30mm cannons on American GIs crossing the river," Busch said. Instead, the Me 262s ran into P-51 Mustangs. They tangled and fought, but not on a scale of the battles to come the following day.

In his bunker meeting with the military, Hitler said he wanted more focus on where the air effort should be. Hitler, who knew military terminology well, wanted air action focused on Patton's forces at the Oppenheim bridgehead. Hitler was frustrated at heavy air losses that were not being properly accounted for.

To von Below, the Führer said, "What shocks me with the Luftwaffe are the so-called numbers of aircraft missing where it just says, 'Missing'—over German Reich territory! One can't imagine them to be completely blown up so that nothing can be found." He added concern that "they don't report on these things any more; they maintain complete silence." Hitler was expressing his fear that some German aircraft were defecting to the Allied side, a fear that was totally unfounded.

As for von Below, he had plenty to feel not so good about. With the seizure (back on March 7) of the Ludendorff Bridge at Remagen—

undeterred by Arado Ar 234 jets overhead—the Allies already had a foothold on the east side of the river. Now they were coming on strong: the previous night, von Below knew, Gen. George S. Patton's U.S. 5th Division had crossed the Rhine and established a six-mile deep bridgehead across from Oppenheim, near Darmstadt, and had grabbed up nineteen thousand demoralized German prisoners. Field Marshal Gerd von Rundstedt's defending armies, prohibited in an order from Hitler from improving their situation via a tactical withdrawal, were now being pounded hard.

To make matters worse, a new report had crossed von Below's desk about something German leaders didn't want their own citizens to know: some of the American fighter pilots causing so much trouble for the Luftwaffe were . . . black.

This wasn't news to von Below, who for months had overseen efforts to prevent black prisoners of war from being placed in locations where people could see their skin color. The Germans were in fact very well informed about the African American pilots. When they captured 1st Lt. Harold Brown, an interrogator rattled off personal details about several of his fellow pilots. And added: "Tell me, Brown, why are you fellows so willing to fight for the United States? I know how colored people are treated in the United States and especially in the South. We are considered enemies . . . yet our boys receive better treatment in the United States than you. I can't understand you fellows!"

Yes, von Below knew about these men, but he hated being reminded that this was a difficult day to be a defender of the master race.

March 2, 1945

With KG 51 at Neuburg, Oberfaehnrich (Senior Officer Candidate) Hans Busch was beginning to believe that in spite of his many combat sorties in various kinds of warplanes (culminating with the Messerschmitt Me 262 jet fighter), he would never have an opportunity to shoot down an Allied aircraft. He was right in that respect. The overwhelming majority of fighter pilots in air combat never score an aerial victory, although Busch had more flying experience in more aircraft types than most who end up with a tally of zero.

Busch was not immune to the difficult and painful things that can happen to a fighter pilot, however.

With his best friend Oberfaehnrich (Senior Officer Candidate) Horst Netzeband, Busch was "bonded like a brother," he said later. The two young men shared a room and a wall locker. They spent their spare time together. Each wrote to his parents about the other. When Netzeband suffered a minor injury while flying—a canopy blew off in mid-air and a guide wire cut his throat—Busch helped him in bandaging his face and encouraged him to recuperate. Both were now gradually piling up hours in the Me 262 cockpit. They were no longer the newest or the youngest flying Hitler's jets. As Netzeband's blown-canopy mishap demonstrated, they were doing the difficult things that produced the seasoning in a mature fighter pilot.

On March 2, 1945, Netzeband was scheduled for an early-morning patrol at twelve thousand feet, where an oxygen mask was required. At the life support section for their Gruppe in KG 51 at Neuburg, Netzeband sought to check out an oxygen mask but could not find the sergeant in charge. This meant Netzeband had to fly at a lower altitude, which meant a greater fuel burn and thus a lower air speed. He must have been seething with frustration knowing that this was exactly the circumstance under which the Me 262 was vulnerable to the marauding Americans.

Once starting his mission, the original P-51 Mustang outfit, the 354th Fighter Group, was coming straight at him in no time. Captain James P. Keane was in the lead of four Mustangs. First Lieutenant Theodore W. Sedvert was one of the other P-51 pilots. Sedvert, a Marylander just shy of his twenty-fourth birthday, was strafing a locomotive when he pulled up to see Netzeband's Me 262 sitting large and slow and steady in front of him.

In his memoir, Busch wrote that four Mustangs shot Netzeband down (in fact, Sedvert did), and "apparently he attempted to bail out

[and] unbuckled his seat belts but because of a bullet that had pierced his hip he was unable to lift himself up and out of the cockpit. At 9:35 a.m., near the small town of Dillingen the aircraft hit the ground and Horst was catapulted out of the aircraft and his body was found several hundred feet from the crash site." Busch and one other pilot were the only people at Netzeband's funeral.

March 24, 1945

On March 24, 1945, a formation of P-51s led by Col. Benjamin O. Davis, took off from Ramitelli Airfield on Italy's Adriatic coast on the longest escort mission their crews would fly during World War II. Davis was commander of the 332nd Fighter Group. His men were the Tuskegee Airmen, called Negroes in the polite language. They were American fighter pilots here in the war zone after training in an America that would still be segregated by race on the day the war ended. They were formidable opponents for Hitler, Göring, Galland, von Below, and proponents of Aryan superiority.

To confront the Allies, Jagdgeschwader 7 (Fighter Group 7), "Nowotny," launched about thirty Messerschmitt Me 262s from Brandenburg Briest near Berlin. This jet unit was nicknamed Windhund (Wind Hound), the German name for Greyhound, which was the mascot, and Windhund Nowotny in honor of its first leader. The jet pilots had been very busy. They were becoming an all-too-familiar sight among American bomber formations.

The forty-three Mustangs, together with Mustangs from other units, were in the air to help B-17 Flying Fortress heavy bombers run a gauntlet of more than 1,600 miles into the heart of Hitler's Germany and back. The bombers' target, a massive Daimler-Benz tank factory in Berlin, was heavily defended. Some twenty-five aircraft defended the plant, including battle-tested Focke-Wulf Fw 190 radial propeller fighters, the Messerschmitt Me 163 *Komet* rocket plane, and the Me 262 jet. On this particular day, the *only* German aircraft to get into the air were Me 262 jets. The massive bombing strike by the Americans in daylight, to be followed by another by the British that night, was intended to distract the Germans from the crossing of the Rhine some three hundred miles to the west.

Although the Reich never had more than 82 of its 1,294 Me 262s ready to fight (although von Below gave the figure 187 in a meeting with the Führer), it seemed to the Americans that there were far more and that all of them were defending Berlin on this day. Davis repeatedly told his men that the German pilots were good and would do everything in their power to take advantage of their speed and heavy guns.

When another fighter group missed a rendezvous (as noted later in this text), Davis instructed his pilots to continue toward the German capital. Before reaching Berlin, though, Davis reported engine trouble and was forced to turn back toward Italy. Captain Armour G. McDaniel Sr. took command of the escort-fighter formation. First Lieutenant Roscoe Brown (no relation to prisoner of war Harold Brown) commanded the portion of the formation that came from the group's 100th Fighter Squadron. Among pilots in the air with McDaniel and Brown were 2nd Lt. Charles V. Brantley and 1st Lt. Earl R. Lane.

The 332nd's pilots grew up in a world that treated them as second-class citizens. Still, those who had completed the arduous passage into fighter cockpits considered themselves elite. It would be misleading to think of them as typical of African-Americans of their era. Unlike many white fighter pilots, all of the blacks had been required to have a college degree merely to gain entry to pilot training. Their Tuskegee, Alabama, training center achieved remarkable efficiency as the only base that combined all three flight-training functions, primary, basic, and advanced, at one location. The Tuskegee alumni were some of the best pilots in the U.S. Army due to a combination of prewar experience and the personal drive of those who overcame hurdles to be accepted for training. Nothing about them was ordinary.

And they knew their German aircraft.

They knew the Me 163 and Me 262 were faster than their P-51s, but they also knew they had greater maneuverability. They knew the "wonder weapon" fighters tended to run out of fuel more quickly than their Mustangs.

Since eight Me 262s fell in that battle (out of sixteen claimed by fighter pilots and bomber gunners), some have alleged that this was more a "turkey shoot" than a fair fight. The supposition that this was the second team in the German fighter force was, however, incorrect; of the dozen Me 262 pilots in the air that day, about half were aces. Far from being an easy day, the battle over Berlin became a triumph of Americans seizing advantage of what they knew to be the vulnerabilities of Hitler's super weapon.

It appears the first pilot to encounter a jet was Flight Officer Thurston L. Gaines Jr. of the 332nd group's 99th Fighter Squadron. Gaines's after-action report read:

I was flying number four position in Yellow Flight furnishing penetration cover for B-17s. At approximately 1210 hours, we were escorting B-17s at an altitude of 27,000 feet about 30 miles southwest of the target when three Me 262s were seen diving on the bomber formation from about 30,000 feet. The Me 262s were in string and made their attack from five o'clock high at the rear section of the bombers. The first jet missed his bomber apparently and continued his flight under the bomber formation without altering his course. The second jet made his attack in a glide and after firing a burst from his guns applied power to his engine. This was evidenced by the fact that a puff of dark smoke emitted from the jet nacelles. This jet continued his attack under the bomber formation and started a turn to the right. Immediately after observing the puff of smoke from the jets, a B-17 was seen to do an abrupt high wingover to the right and started to spin in the same direction. The second Me 262 to make a pass at the bomber fired from approximately 1,500 feet. By the time I released my wing tanks, the jet aircraft had made his pass and I gave pursuit.

Gaines wasn't going to catch an Me 262 by following it from straight behind. His report continued:

> I soon discovered that his rate of speed was too fast for me to close in on him. Consequently, I started a climbing turn to the right at approximately 20,000 feet when I observed another Me 262 in a steep right turn at about one o'clock, slightly high. I pulled the nose of my aircraft up and started firing from about 2,000 feet with thirty-five degree deflection. No strikes were observed, nor did the enemy aircraft attempt evasive action. It appeared that the jet pilot did not see me because he made no attempt to bear his guns on my aircraft but instead continued in his steep right turn. The rate of closure was not exceptionally fast for an almost head-on approach and I would estimate that I fired a good three-second burst in my climbing deflection shot.
>
> All of the Me 262s that I observed in the area appeared to be black with blue-gray under surfaces. No markings, belly tanks or rockets were observed and I did not observe contrails during the encounters.

Maybe it was the greatest frustration imaginable for a fighter pilot: Gaines had fired and missed. Wrote Brown in an official report:

> We were leading a formation of B-17s. The 52nd Fighter Group [which had been scheduled to replace the 332nd on the final leg of the trip to Berlin] had arrived at the rendezvous point too late. Then Ben Davis had engine trouble and the next thing I know I'm leading the 100th Fighter Squadron.
>
> All of a sudden at nine o'clock I saw these streaks. I ordered, 'Drop your tanks and follow me.' " There had been a scandalous shortage of 110-gallon auxiliary fuel tanks at Ramitelli, which resourceful maintainers had resolved by both hook and crook and now those fuel tanks, each worth the price of a new Chevrolet sedan, went tumbling into the void.

Ten-kill air ace Oberleutnant (Lt. Col.) Franz Kulp, who was about to enter the crosshairs of Brown's gunsight, could not know that the Tuskegee pilots had been thinking ahead. After being briefed on the Me 262 by intelligence officers, Brown and his flying mates had devised a maneuver, as Brown put it, "where when the jets were coming up, instead of going right after the jets so they could get away from us, cause they were faster, we would go down under the bombers away from the jets, make a hard turn, and put the jet into our gunsight—and boom! It was a good maneuver because the jets were faster than we were, but we were more maneuverable."

Brown's after-action combat report, written two days later, differs in some detail from accounts he gave later, including his interview with the author of this book. Brown wrote:

I was on the west side of the third and fourth sections of B-17s of the 5th Bomb Wing at about 27,000 feet when at 2125 hours we noticed three Me 262s coming in at the bombers at eleven o'clock, breaking to one o'clock. The attack was below the bombers. The jets were attacking individually rather than in formation. I called the flight to drop tanks and peeled right on the three Me 262s. I fired at one from 2,400 feet, having him in the extreme range of my K-14 gunsight. He went into a dive and I went with him down to 22,000 feet where I broke off pursuit because of the exceptional diving speed of the jet. I climbed back to 27,000 feet. It was then that I sighted a formation of four Me 262s under the bombers at about 24,000 feet. They were below us going north. I was going south. I peeled down on them toward their rear but almost immediately I saw a lone Me 262 at 24,000 feet, climbing at ninety degrees to me and 2,500 feet from me. I pulled up at him in a fifteen degree climb and fired three long bursts at him from 2,000 feet at eight o'clock to him. Almost immediately, the pilot bailed out from about 24,500 feet. I saw flames burst from the jet orifices of the enemy aircraft.

The attack on the bombers was ineffective because of the prompt action of my flight in breaking up the attack. The jets appeared unaggressive to [my fellow pilots and me] and used diving speed as evasive action. They seem to employ the tactic of attacking bombers from below where they are not easily visible to our fighters.

In a different account, Brown said, "I did a split-S, went under the bombers, did a hard right, pulled up, shot the jet, blew him up, and that was the first jet victory for the Fifteenth Air Force."

The Tuskegee Airmen fought brilliantly but would later add gloss to their outstanding record by making claims that were exaggerated. This was one. Brown in reality scored the fourth jet victory for the Italy-based Fifteenth. First Lieutenant Eugene P. McGauflin and 2nd Lt. Roy Scales of 31st Fighter Group (on December 22, 1944) and Capt. William J. Dillard, also of the 31st group, two days earlier (on March 22, 1945) were all credited with shooting down Me 262s. In later years, Tuskegee Airmen Inc., a foundation dedicated to preserving the history of America's first black military airmen, would claim never to have lost a bomber the airmen were escorting. And they would claim not merely to have gotten the first Me 262 for the Fifteenth, but the first Me 262 by an American. Brown made the latter claim in an interview with the author of this book.

Brown's victim in that air duel, Kulp, wriggled out of the Me 262 and descended to earth beneath a parachute canopy, while grappling with severe wounds that kept him out of the rest of the war.

The Tuskegee pilots' achievements needed no amplification. As the battle high over Berlin unfolded, 1st Lt. Robert W. Williams and 1st Lt. Samuel W. Watts Jr. tangled with an Me 262 they said was flying at 450 miles per hour. They fired, broke, fired again, and like Gaines were unsuccessful in bringing down the foe. Making the most of their limited advantages, 332nd pilots Brantley and Lane joined Brown in tallying up victory claims against the vaunted Me 262 jet.

Brantley was from St. Louis, Missouri. He was luckier than Gaines and had to work harder than Brown. He wrote: "Between 1200 and

1220 hours . . . my element leader and I encountered an Me 262. We were at an altitude of 25,000 feet flying practically abreast when two Me 262s came in from behind and slightly below us. Both aircraft appeared to be coasting as I saw no indication of power. One jet was between us and the other was to my flight leader's right. I dropped my nose, being well within range, and made several bursts on the ship that was in front of me from dead astern."

Brantley was really working at this. He added:

> The jets broke in a slow turn in opposite directions, pulling us apart. I followed my target in a dive for a short while observing hits on the fuselage. I then broke off to join my flight leader. The dive was very shallow and at no time did I go below 20,000 feet. As I broke away, the Me 262 steepened its rate of turn and dive. It was seen by my flight leader and other pilots to go down in flames. I encountered another Me 262 while joining my flight leader. This Me 262 passed me at approximately ninety degrees. I fired but no hits were observed. I was unable to pick up the correct lead and could not turn fast enough because of one wing tank, which was stuck. The jets were able to pull away from us without using power. Altitude is essential in combating the fast jet aircraft.

Brantley's six .50-caliber machine guns chewed up his Me 262 and killed an accomplished German ace, Oberleutnant (Lt. Col.) Ernst Wörner.

Lane had great eyesight and scored his victory from an extraordinary two thousand–yard distance in a deflection shot while in a tight, left-hand turn, leading far ahead of the jet. His adversary was seven-kill ace Leutnant (2nd Lt.) Alfred Ambs.

Lane, who entered the battle in the number three position in a flight of four P-51s, wrote:

> At 29,000 feet at about 1210 hours I noticed four aircraft, apparently enemy, in string passing from three o'clock to nine o'clock

under the bombers. They were completely out of range. I did not notice any damage to the bombers.

After seeing these aircraft I began looking around. We "S'ed" across the bombers and made a turn back to right when I saw an Me 262. The Me 262 was in a thirty degree drive, coming across the bomber formation. He appeared as if he was peeling for an attack on the bombers. I came in for a thirty-degree deflection shot from 2,000 feet.

He did not quite fill my gunsight. I fired three short bursts and saw the plane emitting smoke. A piece of the plane, either the canopy or one of the jet orifices, flew off. I then pulled up and circled over the spot where he went down. I saw a crash and a puff of black smoke. Two seconds later, I saw another piece hit close to the first piece. I was at 17,000 feet when I broke off the encounter. The jet was a steel blue-gray camouflage.

After this encounter I teamed up with another friendly aircraft and headed for home. Before leaving the area, a black P-51 with German markings approached us at 22,000 feet at five o'clock. The friendly pilot I was with yelled, 'Break right!' I did so and the enemy [P-51] broke off and flew north.

Lane must have seen a dark green (not black) P-51 operated by the Wanderzirkus Rosarius (Rosarius's traveling circus). Hauptman (Capt.) "Ted" Rosarius operated a unit of captured aircraft. Their primary purpose was to familiarize Luftwaffe pilots with Allied equipment—the "circus" had at least two P-51B/C and four P-51D fighters—but they were also used to spy on bomber formations. Kampfgeschwader 200 (KG 200, or Battle Wing 200) operated other captured aircraft.

As for the Me 262 pilot who fell in front of Lane's guns, Ambs bailed out at seventeen thousand feet and came to rest entangled in the branches of a tree. Reported by some sources to have lost his life that day, Ambs actually walked away from the experience and lived a long life (he would live to see history buffs build and fly an Me 262 replica in flight in a new century), but he never fought again.

In an interview with Colin Heaton, group commander Davis later said, "Not only had we destroyed the myths that blacks could not fly or compete in a white military world, we proved we could even exceed those expectations and rise above our white peers." Here, again, was the Tuskegee tendency to exaggerate. "The March 24, 1945, mission was also the longest fighter escort mission of the war"—another exaggeration— "with a round trip of something like almost two thousand miles . . . it was also one of the best missions ever, because our group of fighters kept the German fighters away and we did not lose a single bomber or fighter on that mission. Any time you took off and came back with no losses was outstanding," Davis added. In fact, two bombers and five fighters were lost that busy day.

One of the jets scored hits on a P-51. McDaniel parachuted from his burning aircraft. McDaniel became a prisoner of war and later pursued a successful career in the air force.

The Tuskegee Airmen belonged to just one of the 280 combat groups fielded by the Army Air Forces during the war. They would have to wait until 1948 to see the U.S. armed forces desegregated, and even then the process would be slow and painful. Although he never found himself fighting Hitler's jets, the high-scoring fighter pilot among the Tuskegee pilots was Capt. Lee Archer, with four aerial victories. Archer came home after his combat tour and traveled with his wife by train from Atlanta to his next duty assignment in Washington—only to be refused service in a railway dining car because of the color of his skin. Arriving near Washington, Archer and his wife found a Virginia restaurant with a sign on its front door: "Due to our facilities, we are unable to service colored patrons." It was a sign of progress. "A few years earlier they'd have conveyed the same message with two words," said Archer.

Five Americans with the 31st Fighter Group also shot down Me 262s on the same day as the Tuskegee fliers—Col. William A. Daniel, 1st Lt. Forrest M. Keene, 1st Lt. Raymond D. Leonard, Capt. Kenneth T. Smith, and 2nd Lt. William M. Wilder.

April 1945

April 1945—the final, full month of the war—was something of a turkey shoot for American fighter pilots who by now had clearly defeated the German fighter forces participating in the Defense of the Reich. In the first eight days of April, American fighter pilots were credited with shooting down thirteen Me 262s.

The B-26 Marauder medium bomber was always a tempting target for Me 262 pilots. On April 9, 1945, they shot one up and shot one down.

Also on April 9, 1945, Edward Giller, having long ago transitioned from the P-38 Lightning to the P-51, and still a member of the 55th Fighter Group, was in the air near Munich when he saw two Mustangs chasing an Me 262 down below.

"Usually, the only way we could get those guys was to sneak up on them," said Giller. "The other way was to get them when they were trying to land.

"I'm at twelve thousand feet and see this jet way off and down below me. I observe other Mustangs chasing this guy, but my flight has the advantage of altitude and speed. I opened the throttle wide open and down I went. It took about five minutes for me work my way down to where I was at about five thousand feet and the Me262 was at one thousand. I ended up ahead of the pack just when he put his gear and flaps down." The Me 262 pilot, unaware that he was being stalked, was on final approach for Munich-Riem airfield.

Giller pressed the trigger when the Me 262 was over the airfield perimeter at less than fifty feet of altitude. "I got my shots in at him. He crashed on the runway. I kept going at ten feet of altitude and 450 miles per hour and got the hell out of there," he said. The Me 262 pilot is not identified in available literature, but after the war Giller was told the pilot climbed out of his aircraft, left the wreck, left the airfield, and went away and was never seen again. That was happening increasingly in the German armed forces. An Me 262 pilot probably would not have known, but some in the Reich military were surely aware that Hitler aide Martin Bormann was exploring ways the Führer and a few other top leaders would be able to escape when the end came.

April 14, 1945

Clayton Kelly Gross was on his second combat tour in Europe, an ace, having flown both Mustangs and Thunderbolts in combat by April 14, 1945, when he led eight P-51s on a fighter sweep in the Hersfeld, Mulhausen, Weimar area of Germany. A captain filling the responsibilities of a major or a lieutenant colonel, Gross was flying, scanning, and deliberately hunting for the Luftwaffe. He dispatched a flight of four Mustangs to patrol southward and led the other quartet to the north. He was flying from the airfield known as A-66 at Gael, France—"a dirt field with wire mat superimposed," he recalled—and journeying into German airspace with 1st Lt. Russell Kline, 1st Lt. George N. Kinmon Jr., and 2nd Lt. Berne A. "Danny" Glover at twelve thousand feet in an unusually clear sky. Gross recalled piloting his assigned Mustang, named *Live Bait*, but records appear to show him at the controls of a different 354th Fighter Group aircraft.

Gross's fighter group achieved a number of distinctions. According to the book *Air Force Combat Units of World War II*, the 354th "was instrumental in the development and execution of long-range missions to escort heavy bombers . . . deep into enemy territory." After moving to the Continent, the 354th group, the book notes, "assisted the Allied drive across France by flying fighter sweep, dive-bombing, strafing, and escort missions." The unit supported Allied ground troops during the Battle of the Bulge, by conducting armed reconnaissance operations to destroy enemy troops, tanks, and rail lines. Now, the largest land battle ever fought by Americans was two months behind and Germany was below.

Looking over his nose at the Elbe River, Gross lowered his gaze and spotted what appeared to be an airfield, one that hadn't been covered in any briefing. Something was in motion down there, moving across the patchwork of farm and forest south of the river. Gross did a double take, checked his mental register, and realized that he was looking down at a Messerschmitt Me 262. Gross had an advantage of about ten thousand feet of altitude over the jet, which was cruising at two thousand feet, its pilot apparently unaware.

Gross called out the sighting. Thanks to better intelligence and experience, he was thoroughly briefed, now, on the capabilities of the Me 262. He rolled, pulled the stick back to start straight down, and left his throttle open. He remembers his air speed indictor touching 450 miles per hour. Gross doesn't remember the words he spoke over the radio, or whether he was thinking of his wife, Gwen, or of the movie *I Wanted Wings*, but he was pointedly conscious that something very important was happening, that he was on top of it, and that he was in charge.

It had not been easy, getting this far. Gross had shot down five Messerschmitt Bf 109 propeller-driven fighters, two on May 11, 1944, and one each on May 28, June 14, and October 29, 1944. "Our group lost 187 men who were shot down and killed or captured," Gross said. "That's about twice as many as we started the war with."

He was confident now—having been in the war longer than most other fighter pilots, there was no other way—but Gross also was in a state of compressibility.

That was the term for the condition of air resistance up close to the sound barrier that would become so familiar to Chuck Yeager, Hans Guido Mutke, and others. The disruption to normal airflow over the leading edge of his Mustang's thirty-seven-foot, laminar flow wing meant that, for a temporary time at least, Gross's stick and rudder pedals were useless. He tried various control movements and nothing happened. He felt his Mustang was diving up against some invisible force that would break it into pieces. Gross still had one tiny little notch left on the throttle and now he rammed it all the way forward.

Abruptly, he began to feel forces working on the stick. He was coming out of it. And he was still boring down on an unsuspecting Me 262 jet, piloted by Kurt Lobgesong.

"This Me 262 had a big red number one painted on it," Gross recalled in an interview. "The Germans identified their planes by ranking number. The *staffel* [staff] commander's aircraft was number one. His second in command was two, and so on. The bigger the number was, the lower in rank the pilot was.

"I did a little praying. At lower altitude, I finally regained control and, lo and behold, the 262 was right in front of me. I shot at very close range. I opened fire from very close range and saw strikes on his left side. A fairly large piece of his left wingtip came off and the left jet engine began burning. I had to pull off right to avoid collision, and when I rolled back, I found him climbing straight up.

"I hit him again. He burst into flames. Then, I shot again, and he burned some more. I had sight of him in his cockpit. He climbed another thousand feet or so and, then, seemed to stop in mid-air. The canopy came off. The pilot ejected. I was thrilled as hell. His aircraft fell apart and he went down in flames and smoke.

"I tried to make a pass around the parachute, but we were over a German airfield by this time and the antiaircraft was opening up at me. I thought the guy lived. I was told after the war that he was been killed that day. Years later, I was at a reunion of German fighter pilots. I met the pilot I'd shot down. Kurt Lobgesong. The big red one on the nose of the jet belonged to him, a German commander. He thanked me for saving his life. He had been wounded in the left side and didn't have to fly any more, which meant he lived through the war—something a lot of his mates did not do." When he was shot down, Lobgesong was all of nineteen years old and a member of JG 7.

April 25, 1945

A standout among a flurry of last-minute air-to-air engagements before war's end was the fight in which 1st Lt. William B. "Brad" Hoelscher found himself, after 8:00 a.m. on April 25, 1945. Just a few days earlier, Hans Busch's outfit, KG 51, had moved a few Me 262s to the main airport near Prague, Czechoslovakia. The jet-propelled Me 262 was now a dark threat to Eighth and Fifteenth Air Force airmen attacking targets in the region around the Czech capital.

That morning, a mere five Me 262 pilots were credited with aerial victories over six B-17 Flying Fortresses. This mismatch was evidence of how much harm the jets could inflict, and of how much more impact they might have had, had they been introduced earlier.

Hoelscher was part of Cobweb Flight of the 334th Fighter Squadron, part of Col. Don Blakeslee's fabled 4th Fighter Group. As "Cobweb Blue Three," he was an element leader in his P-51D Mustang. He and his fellow Mustang men were near Prague when black puffs of antiaircraft fire—flak—began to swirl around them.

Hoelscher later wrote: "I broke to get out of a flak barrage, and saw an Me 262 that apparently had just taken off from an aerodrome. I broke onto his tail, missed with my first burst, and then started getting hits all over him. I kept firing three-second bursts at a range of about 500 yards, getting hits. I chased him all around the aerodrome. My indicated air speed was 375 miles per hour and altitude around 1,000 feet."

While Hoelscher was pursuing the Me 262, shrapnel from flak bursts damaged his wing root and tore part of his tail away. Fully aware that he was seriously damaged and in jeopardy, he kept after the Me 262 and continued firing short bursts. He saw the Me 262 go out of control and begin to burn and smoke. The jet rolled over on its back.

Second Lieutenant Gordon A. Denson, who was behind Hoelscher in a P-51 named *Priscilla*, wrote: "I saw a large explosion near the edge of the aerodrome under us, where the Me 262 went down out of control on his back."

According to an account that would later be published in today's Czech Republic, another pilot saw the Me 262 strike the ground at 8:50 a.m. Hoelscher is not officially credited with an Me 262 kill that day, but he would believe all his life—he flew F-86 Sabres in the Korean War and A-1E Skyraiders in Vietnam—that he had scored an aerial victory near Prague that morning. German records reflect the loss of an Me 262 and its pilot, Leutnant (2nd Lt.) Sepp Huber.

According to a Czech publication (not available in English), Oberleutnant (1st Lt.) Stürm set forth from KG 51's deployed location at Prague airfield in a motorcycle to attempt to rescue the pilot of Me 262. The jet fighter exploded. The blast badly wounded Stürm and killed Huber.

Hoelscher fought to save his Mustang, couldn't, and bailed out. He may not have known it, but he had plenty to worry about. The situation for captured U.S. flyers in the Sudetenland was not good. One week earlier, (on April 17, 1945), fellow U.S. fighter pilot 2nd Lt. John H. Banks III was shot down near Prague, taken prisoner, and executed. One source reports that local police tied Banks to a tree and refused to allow the local citizens to bring him food or water. Banks died of exposure days later. He had been on his first mission.

In Hoelscher's case, local citizens helped him evade capture. Missing in action for almost two weeks, he reported to the 14th Armored Division in Pilsen on May 7, 1945.

SIXTEEN

SUPERSONIC SPEED AND SUPER SCIENCE

April 9, 1945

German jet pilot Hans Guido Mutke flew faster than sound long before any American achieved that claim—or so he claimed.

So who really was first to achieve this feat?

It's almost certain that Lothar Sieber exceeded the speed of sound (763 miles per hour at sea level) in the Ba 349 *Natter* (on March 1, 1945), but Sieber was already dead so the achievement doesn't count, so to speak.

But did Hans Guido Mütke fly at supersonic speed?

Mütke loomed larger than life to those who knew him. A very experienced but very junior German military pilot, Mütke flew the Messerschmitt Me 262 jet fighter near the end the war. Afterward, "with tremendous charm and enthusiasm," according to author and analyst G. G. Sweeting, Mütke was taken seriously—by some—when he claimed to have become the first person to fly faster than sound. In other conversations, Mütke claimed not to have been first, but to have been only one of a number of German pilots who accomplished the feat.

On April 9, 1945, Fähnrich (Officer Candidate) Mütke was climbing through a bright, cloudless expanse over the Third Reich at the
controls of an Me 262—enjoying very rare clear weather at the controls of his twin-engine jet and reflecting, as many did, how well it
flew when the engines were functioning properly.

A large man who felt a little cramped in the Me 262 cockpit,
Mütke was enjoying the clear sky and the smooth feel of his fighter
in "clean" condition with wheels up and no ordnance or fuel tanks
beneath his wings. In his earphones was the voice of one of the
Reich's top fighter aces, commander of Ergänzungs-Jagdgeschwader
2 or EJG (Training Wing 2), none other than Obersleutnant (Lt. Col.)
Heinrich Bär. A veteran of more than a thousand combat sorties, Bär
had a way of conveying authority while seemingly remaining mild-
mannered. Now, Bär got Mütke's full attention.

"He's under attack, right now . . ."

This was supposed to be a high-altitude training mission, but Bär
was saying that an American P-51 Mustang fighter was firing on one
of their fellow Me 262 pilots in a sector of the sky nearby. Mütke had
been instructed to climb to thirty-six thousand feet after takeoff. He
was near the Me 262's service ceiling, listed on the books as thirty-
eight thousand feet, when he received the call and decided to rush to
the aid of the German pilot who was under attack.

With visibility more than one hundred kilometers (sixty miles),
Mütke easily spotted the P-51. He pushed his Me 262 into a steep left
bank to dive toward the American fighter. Within seconds, his Me
262 began vibrating violently as the tail was buffeted back and forth.
His airspeed indicator was designed for a maximum reading of 1,100
kilometers per hour (684 miles per hour) and now the needle was
jammed up against that maximum number.

The nose pitched down sharply. The plane was no longer controllable.

Mütke told author Walter J. Boyne: "I moved the stick wildly
around the cockpit. For a brief moment, the airplane responded
to controls again momentarily, then went back out of control. The
plane still did not respond to pressure on the stick so I changed the

incidence of the tailplane. The speed dropped, the aircraft stopped shaking, and I regained control." This is a reference to changing the angle of attack of the horizontal stabilizer, a technique that was later associated with other supersonic aircraft.

Tests at the Messerschmitt plant in Augsberg had indicated that the Me 262 had a structural limit of Mach 0.86. At eighty-six one hundredths of the speed of sound, the Me 262 would become uncontrollable. If the pilot continued to accelerate, the aircraft would break up and come flying apart in a thousand pieces. But if the pilot could slow down, he could regain control. The Me 262 wing had a sweep of just 18.5 degrees for trim reasons and probably would have suffered structural failure due to divergence at high transonic speeds.

Later in life, Mütke said he overcame his high-speed dive by adjusting the Me 262's whole tailplane incidence while the aircraft was still at high speed. This, plus Mütke's recollection that he briefly regained control while still accelerating, matches up with later accounts of recorded flights at supersonic speed. Most experts are skeptical that Mütke went supersonic and do not believe any pilot achieved the feat before Yeager.

Mütke insisted. Described as the consummate gentleman, he was nevertheless passionate in his beliefs. Mütke began medical school before the war, completed advanced studies later after a stint as a civilian transport pilot in South America, and became a gynecologist, aviation doctor, and authority on space medicine. In an interview for this book, Boyne remembered Mütke as "brilliant . . . cordial and friendly," but said he "had a way of dominating conversations." Mütke remained a *Fähnrich* throughout the war because he would not become a Nazi, but his experience belied his junior rank.

Before becoming a jet pilot, Mütke flew hundreds of sorties in twin-engine propeller aircraft. He flew the Messerschmitt Bf 110 into British bomber streams to report on their altitude, speed, and flight path. He flew combat missions over Great Britain. He bailed out of a Bf 110 near Paris in a snowstorm. In October 1942, he was at the controls of a Dornier Do 217 he said was sent to shoot down a British aircraft believed to be carrying Winston Churchill. He never reached the British plane and it does not appear Churchill was in the air that day.

Mütke's assertion that he flew faster than sound was not his only claim to fame. On April 25, 1945, after attempting to engage a formation of B-26 Marauder medium bombers, Mütke flew his Me 262 to neutral Switzerland. When fighting in Europe ended two weeks later, Mütke took the position that because the Third Reich no longer existed, he was the rightful owner of the sleek jet fighter.

The Swiss authorities never attempted to test fly the Me 262. They returned it to Germany in 1957, and it's now on display at the Deutsches Museum in Munich. Over the years, Mütke filed several lawsuits asserting his personal ownership of the Me 262—to no avail. During the time he made his mark in the medical profession, Mütke continued flying as a civilian pilot. He hoped to fly one of the Me 262 replicas that began to appear in the United States in 2002. He never got the chance.

Because Mütke was interviewed repeatedly, numerous accounts of his experience have survived. Each is different. None reveals what happened to the fellow German pilot who was under attack by a P-51 on the day of Mütke's most fateful flight.

April 26, 1945

The last Americans to engage and shoot down Me 262s were piloting the same plane that Val Beaudrault liked so much, the portly P-47 Thunderbolt. The last encounter took place on April 26, 1945, just a fortnight before the end of hostilities. It happened minutes after 1st Lt. James J. Finnegan of the 50th Fighter Group pumped hundreds of rounds into an Me 262 piloted by none other than . . . Adolf Galland.

Galland needed all of his virtuoso cockpit skills to bring his jet down to a dead-stick and belly land at Munich-Riem. He clambered out of his wrecked jet and was rescued by a mechanic who came after him with an armored tractor. Finnegan unquestionably defeated Galland in what had to be the final combat for both, and yet

Germany's most famous fighter pilot is not counted as an aerial victory for U.S. forces that day, perhaps because most of the damage to the Me 262 was done on collision with the airfield surface.

Once again—now, for the last time—Me 262s tore into formations of B-26 Marauder medium bombers and wreaked havoc. A fourth Marauder made a crash landing in friendly territory. Three of the medium bombers plummeted from the sky in flames. Captain Robert W. Clark, also of the 50th Fighter Group, engaged a second Me 262 from Galland's outfit, JV 44, maneuvered behind it, and shot it down.

The very last aerial victory over any German aircraft by an American in World War II came a few minutes later. Thunderbolt pilot Capt. Herbert A. Philo pulled away from a strafing pass on a locomotive, spotted an Me 262, and led his wingman in a high-speed chase. Philo fired a burst from too far, drew closer, and fired again.

April 29, 1945

If the Third Reich's first generation of operational jets couldn't turn the tide—although they wreaked havoc on the Allies—a second generation might still save Germany, Adolf Hitler is reported to have said, within a few days of the end of his life.

If salvation was to come, it might have arrived in the form of the Messerschmitt P.1101 single-seat, single-engine advanced jet fighter. Futuristic in its appearance—on drawing board blueprints at least, since the first aircraft was never fully completed—the P.1101 was a product of the Third Reich's emergency fighter program of July 1944 and was scheduled to make its first flight in June 1945. It became a "might have been" when the war in Europe ended.

When American tanks rolled into Oberammergau in Bavaria on April 29, 1945, the war had not yet ended and the American soldiers on the scene were partly distracted by the prospect of more combat to come. The GIs had no idea that they had found a top-secret air test facility that was unknown to Allied intelligence and had never been bombed.

The troops seized a tall figure who called himself Professor Willy Messerschmitt. It was, in fact, the famous plane maker, the man who had passed on an opportunity to tell Hitler that the Me 262 shouldn't become a bomber. The soldiers understood Messerschmitt's importance but paid little attention to the skeletal metal frame of an aircraft that was 80 percent completed but had never taken to the air. Nor had they yet discovered twenty-three miles of tunnels that had been dug, almost certainly by slave labor, and used for jet engine production.

Here, the Americans eventually learned about new German warplanes, some of which they would dismantle and ship home for postwar testing. Here, too, they encountered other well-known figures in the Reich and discovered horrors that went hand in hand with high technology.

Author James Shapiro wrote, "Looking at maps and photos of this installation, located on land that the village had made available to the German military even before the outbreak of war (the majority of village leaders thought it would be good for local business), it's hard to believe that the people of Oberammergau didn't know what was going on. The installation was one of the leading sites for advanced aircraft technology in Germany. It was also the place, Dennis Piszkiewicz has shown, where Wernher von Braun and four hundred other leading rocket scientists were relocated [from Peenemünde] toward the end of the war. They reported to Hans Kammler, the notorious designer and builder of the crematoria at Auschwitz, who had set up headquarters in Oberammergau at the Hotel Alois Lang. The Allied forces' desire to appropriate this scientific booty and know-how may have been one of the reasons that Oberammergau wasn't bombed as the war was winding down. As it turned out, Wernher von Braun and a hundred or so others, most of them Nazis, were subsequently brought to the United States where, two decades later, a number of them . . . helped the Americans win the race to the moon."

Willy Messerschmitt was despondent yet relaxed, depressed yet argumentative, and openly worried about his future. As the

Americans learned when they set forth to exploit his technology, Messerschmitt's reputation as an aircraft designer was somewhat open to question. He was not personally responsible for the engineering work behind the Me 262 jet fighter that bore his name. Messerschmitt's twin-engine Bf 110 was used for long-range escort missions during the Battle of Britain; it suffered heavy losses to RAF fighters then and was all but eliminated from the war later when the P-51 Mustang arrived. According to lore, someone—it is not known who—asked about designing a single-engine fighter like the P-51 with long range and Messerschmitt replied, "What do you want, a fast fighter or a barn door?" Years later, forced to seek shelter together from American Thunderbolts attacking the Augsburg factory, the same person told the self-appointed professor, "Those are your barn doors!"

So the Americans had found the Messerschmitt P.1101, possibly the most advanced piece of German hardware ever to fall into Allied hands. It was an extraordinary airplane that was far more advanced than anything the Allies possessed.

By the time they began hunting documents about the P.1101, French agents had already retrieved huge amounts of microfilm in watertight containers from a nearby cave and had spirited them off to Paris. In the period that followed, French authorities refused to turn the P.1101 microfilm over to American experts.

The P.1101 was a single-seat, swept-wing jet fighter powered by a 1,962-pound thrust Junkers Jumo 004B turbojet engine intended to offer the same endurance and range as Messerschmitt's better-known Me 262. An operational version would have been armed with four Mk-108 30mm cannons. The P.1101 had variable-sweep wings (with a maximum span of 27 feet 0.5 inches), but only technicians on the ground could adjust the angle of sweep. Having the wings swept forward improved performance when taking off or landing; having them swept back increased speed and performance at altitude.

Robert J. Woods, Bell Aircraft Corporation's chief design engineer and a key figure in the exploitation of German technology, became interested in the P.1101's variable-sweep wing and tried to have the prototype completed in Germany under American supervision. With the French withholding documents and pieces of the prototype nabbed by GIs as souvenirs, the idea of flying the P.1101 at Oberammergau failed to materialize.

The P.1101 and a second set of wings were shipped to Wright Field, Ohio. Air force technical experts spent some time studying it, could find no further use for it, and transferred it to Woods's company in Buffalo, New York, which was already making its mark in technology with rocket-powered research aircraft.

After further, fruitless efforts to find a way to fly the original, Bell proposed a new aircraft based on the P.1101 but with the capability for the pilot to adjust wing sweep while in flight. Basking in the success of Capt. Charles E. Yeager's first supersonic flight in the rocket-powered XS-1 on October 14, 1947, and with the company's X-1A and X-2 rocket planes about to make headlines, plane maker Larry Bell and right-hand man Bob Woods believed the P.1101 gave them the makings of the fighter of the future. Had they been right, a Bell version of the P.1101 might have been ready in time to fight the Soviet MiG-15 in Korea.

The F-86 Sabre, which was influenced by the Messerschmitt Me 262, filled that role. The MiG itself was also influenced by the Me 262 and another German design, Kurt Tank's Ta 183.

Air force officials saw promise in a proposed P.1101 derivative but believed it would lack the capacity to carry guns or ordnance. With strong backing from the National Advisory Committee for Aeronautics (NACA), the new Bell aircraft became a research plane, the X-5, powered by a five thousand–pound thrust Allison J35-A-17 turbojet engine. It was planned to replace the J35 with a Westinghouse J40 eventually, but the latter engine became a spectacular failure so the powerplant change was never made.

Bell built two X-5s and flew both at Edwards Air Force Base, California, the first on June 20, 1951, with company test pilot Jean "Skip" Ziegler at the controls. (Ziegler lost his life in the explosion of an X-2 rocket plane while a B-50 Superfortress was carrying it on May 12, 1953.) The wingspan of the X-5 was twenty feet nine inches at maximum sweep (fifty-five degrees), thirty-three feet six inches when nearly unswept (at thirty degrees). A "glove" designed by Woods moved fore and aft along the fuselage on rails with changes in wing angle in order to assure stability.

The X-5 proved difficult to fly, even at the hands of test virtuosos such as Ziegler, Yeager, Albert Boyd, Scott Crossfield, and Neil Armstrong. It was unstable under certain conditions and had bad stall characteristics. On October 14, 1953, a spin recovery problem led to the loss of the second X-5 and caused the death of Maj. Raymond Popson. The first ship continued research flying with NACA, but an attempt to revive a fighter version went nowhere.

In Sweden, the SAAB design team under Lars Brising acquired P.1101 data and used it to explore the swept-wing configuration with an experimental version of the SAAB 91 *Safir*. This led to development of the SAAB 29 *Tunnan* (Barrel), designated J29 by the Royal Swedish Air Force and first flown on September 1, 1948, with British test pilot Robert A. Moore doing the honors. While it had roots in the P.1101, it did not employ variable-sweep technology. SAAB built 661 *Tunnans* between 1950 and 1956, and despite its portly appearance, the *Tunnan* was very comparable to the F-86 and MiG-15.

Many other jet warplanes from the 1950s onward mirrored the size and shape of the P.1101. The Messerschmitt airplane's most significant feature, the swing wing, found its way to many subsequent aircraft, including the MiG-23 Flogger, F-111 Aardvark, F-14 Tomcat, and B-1B Lancer.

May 8, 1945

Two weeks after American troops liberated Oberammergau, the most famous of American aviators, Charles Lindbergh, began a journey through Western Europe with a U.S. naval technical delegation. At Oberammergau, Lindbergh met a haggard and depressed Willy E. Messerschmitt. The plane maker, who had seemed businesslike and attentive when Lindbergh visited the Augsburg aircraft factory in 1939, was now, six years later, a worn-down and despondent version of his former self.

He was a broken man.

Lindbergh, as A. Scott Berg wrote, "learned the once-revered designer's country home had been 'liberated' by American troops; and he found him living with his sister's family in a village farther into the country, reduced to sleeping on a pallet in a barn." Added Berg: "A visibly broken man, he told Lindbergh that he had been concerned about defeat as early as 1941, when he saw America's estimates for its own aircraft production. Lindbergh further learned that Messerschmitt had only recently returned from England, where he had been a prisoner of war. Both the British and the French had asked him to serve as a technical advisor." Messerschmitt, as it turned out, remained in Germany during the postwar years and never recovered financially or emotionally from the setback of being on the losing side in the war.

May 8, 1945

Many of the things that never happened filled the pages of magazines such as the *Police Gazette* that Val Beaudrault read after war's end. Did Adolf Hitler escape from Berlin in a Junkers Ju 290 aircraft and make his way to the secret Nazi base in Antarctica, together with German antigravity and time-machine technology, including the mysterious device known as Die Glocke (the Bell)? Did he take refuge at the SECRET NAZI BASE, always spelled with upper-case letters in postwar American pulps? In a different version, Hitler reportedly escaped from Berlin in a Ju 290 and made his way to Madrid, where his old pal Francisco Franco gave him lodging in a secure wing of the dictator's residence.

In yet another story, Hitler, Eva Braun, and a small party flew in a succession of Junkers transports from the bombed-out center of Berlin to Denmark, to Spain, and to the Canary Islands, where they boarded a U-boat that transported them to Argentina. According to this scenario, Hitler was alive in Argentina until 1962, exactly as P-47 Thunderbolt pilot Beaudrault read in the *Police Gazette*. This version of events, with an impressive roster of documentation, is the core of the book *Grey Wolf: The Escape of Adolf Hitler*, by Simon Dunstan and Gerrard Williams.

A September 4, 1944, Federal Bureau of Investigation memorandum sent up through channels to FBI director J. Edgar Hoover noted that, "a large, wealthy colony in Argentina affords tremendous possibilities for the providing of a refuge for Hitler and his henchmen." The memorandum speculated that Argentina could "serve as a terminus for Hitler after a non-stop flight of 7,376 miles from Berlin to Buenos Aires in an especially constructed plane or as a passenger in a long-range submarine."

None of this happened, did it? After all, Hitler's personal pilot Hans Baur survived the war and contributed to a biography of himself, so his movements all seem to be accounted for and he couldn't have flown the Führer to safety. Remember that Hitler often said he would never fly with anyone else. Most historians generally accept the widely published account of Hitler's suicide in his Führerbunker in the German capital on April 30, 1945, when he shot himself in the head with his personal Walther PPK 7.65mm pistol.

The facts are known. Aren't they?

The Ju 290 wasn't a jet and wasn't the highest-technology German weapon, but it does figure prominently in this tale of Hitler's jets, his *Wunderwaffen*, and the plans formulated by some of his subordinates for his escape after the defeat of the Reich.

Hans Baur, who gave personal recollections of the Insterburg event for chapter one of this narrative, was "a nice, gentle family man you'd enjoy having next door," said his biographer G. G. Sweeting, "but he was a member of the Nazi Party from 1926 on and remained steadfastly loyal to Hitler until his dying breath." Baur never participated in the heinous atrocities of the Reich and he despised Himmler, Goebbels, and especially Göring; however, he was far more than just an aerial chauffeur.

Hitler often turned to Baur for advice about air war policy and technical developments. Baur's special squadron (*Die Fliegerstaffel des Führers*) was not part of the Luftwaffe—and on paper, Bauer was a *Standartenführer* (colonel) in the SS, so Baur could offer words of wisdom without Göring being any the wiser. By 1945, Baur was one of a handful of people on earth who were genuinely close to Hitler. Bauer was a *Gruppenführer* (lieutenant general) in the SS but, far more importantly, he was the closest thing to a friend the Führer ever had.

Baur repeatedly devised plans for an escape from beleaguered Berlin for the Führer, only to have Hitler repeatedly rebuff him. Hitler insisted that he would stay until the end.

Or did he?

Baur told Sweeting after the war that he "would gladly have died for Adolf Hitler." He understood that if the Führer were going to secretly escape and take up exile outside Germany, the escape would not remain secret unless the Allies could account for Hitler's pilot. If the world were going to be deceived into believing Hitler was dead while the Führer was actually finding safe haven in another country, Baur would have to be accounted for when the Allies arrived. If Baur were going to whisk the German leader to safety in an aircraft, he—Baur—would have to return to the Führerbunker and become a prisoner when the war ended. Asked whether he would agree to do this even if it meant he would be a prisoner of the Soviets for ten years after the war—which is how it turned out—Baur said yes.

Under Baur's direction, a small aircraft, a two-seat Fieseler Fi 156 *Storch*, was kept on standby, ready to take off from an improvised airstrip in the Tiergarten, near the Brandenburg Gate. The Reich's celebrated and intrepid female aviator, Hanna Reitsch, used the airstrip on April 26, 1945, to bring in Colonel-General Robert Ritter von Greim, who became head of the Luftwaffe after the Führer abruptly sacked Göring. Reitsch transported Greim out of the capital two days later; she, Baur, and others pleaded with the Führer to make his getaway in similar fashion.

Had he gotten away from the immediate pressures in Berlin, Hitler could have been put aboard a much larger aircraft—a plane he'd admired at Insterburg. It was an aircraft that would also be seen at air shows in Ohio after the war, and in both Germany and in the United States, it flew with the swastika painted on its tail.

Hitler was smitten by the four-engine Junkers Ju 290 A-5 he saw at Insterburg along with many other new aircraft and prototypes. He told Göring he wanted a Ju 290 for his personal use. In late 1944, Baur's *Fliegerstaffel des Führers* received a Ju 290 A-7. For Hitler's use, the aircraft was fitted with a special passenger compartment in the front of the aircraft, protected by half-inch armor plate and two-inch bulletproof glass. A special escape hatch was fitted in the floor and a parachute was built into Hitler's seat; in an emergency it was intended that he would put on the parachute, pull a lever to open the hatch, and roll out through the opening. This arrangement was tested using life-size mannequins.

If Hitler was to make a getaway and Baur was to be found by the Allies, how could it be explained that his aircraft was missing? The official version of events is that more than a month before the end, Baur flew the Ju 290A-7 to Munich-Riem airport on March 24, 1945, landing just as an air-raid alert was sounded. Parking the plane in a hangar, he went to his home. Upon returning to the airport, he discovered that U.S. bombs had destroyed both the hangar and the plane.

Only forty-seven Ju 290s were built in transport and maritime patrol/bomber versions. But what if the Third Reich had invested in four-engine heavies on the same vast scale as the British and Americans? If a thousand Ju 290s had been available for the German airlift to Stalingrad—in which 266 smaller and less capable Ju 52 tri-motors were lost in battle—a rash promise made by Hermann Göring of a successful supply effort might have been fulfilled. The outcome of one of history's largest battles might have been different.

The Ju 290 was a tailwheel-equipped aircraft similar in configuration to the U.S. B-17 Flying Fortress or the British Handley-Page

Halifax, but about 20 percent larger than either. Long after 1936, when the Reich abandoned a more ambitious project for a "Ural bomber"—capable of striking Soviet targets to the east beyond the Ural mountain range—the Ju 290 was developed from the Ju 90 airliner and made its first flight on July 16, 1942.

The prototype Ju 290 V1 and the first eight Ju 290 A-1s were unarmed transports and were rushed into service, but only one was available to participate in the Stalingrad airlift. The Ju 290 A-2 was a maritime patrol/bomber warplane with low-band UHF search radar and cannon armament. A Ju 290 A-3 version followed with more guns, giving the Junkers a mantislike appearance with cannons protruding in all directions. A Ju 290 A-4 weapons test ship—the plane that eventually reached the United States—was followed by Ju 290 A-5 and Ju 290 A-7 versions with heavier armament and self-sealing fuel tanks.

The Ju 290 A-5 carried a crew of nine, had a wingspan of 137 feet 9 inches, and was powered by four 1,700-horsepower BMW 801G/H fourteen-cylinder radial engines. It was credited with a maximum speed of 273 miles per hour.

The Ju 290 appears to have been a more than adequate performer, more robust and longer-legged than the Focke-Wulf Fw 200 Kondor. So why were there so few? The limited number of Ju 290s produced—including a pair of six-engine variants, designated Ju 390 that came too late to influence the war—was partly the result of a decree by Albert Speer that was intended to divert all aircraft industry resources to the manufacture of fighters to confront the Allied bombing campaign.

Any date, maybe today

Postwar conspiracy theories—the *Police Gazette*, remember?—apply to fanciful events that could have happened at any point on the calendar after the German surrender.

Or not.

No, the Nazis didn't send vast numbers of scientists and military troops to Antarctica in 1938 to build a "New Berlin" under ice inside a city-sized, warm-water cave. But the Germans did send a ship, the *Schwabenland*, to explore Antarctica's Queen Maud Land. They may have known as much about Antarctica as the Western Allies did. They could have built an ice runway where a Ju 290 could touch down.

The most imaginative of the conspiracy theories applies to Die Glocke (the Bell) and the extraordinary claims made about it. According to researcher Rob Arndt, during tests "various plants and animals . . . decomposed into a blackish goo without normal putrefaction, within a matter of a few minutes or hours after exposure to its field effects."

It's necessary to wallow through a lot of fantasy literature and, only thereafter, to ask whether the same brilliant minds that produced the V-2, Me 262, and the misguided *Natter* might also have produced a secret doomsday weapon. Or is the Bell merely a fantasy concocted by postwar pranksters armed with Photoshop?

To Nick Cook, author of *The Hunt for Zero Point*, Hitler's Nazi Germany developed Die Glocke—named because it was roughly the shape of a bell—as part of a search for antigravity technology. To other researchers, the Bell was just one of dozens of *Wunderwaffen*.

The Bell was a purported top secret experiment with a mysterious purpose carried out by Third Reich scientists working for the SS in a German facility known as Der Riese ("The Giant") near the Wenceslaus mine. The mine is located about thirty miles from Breslau, a little north of the village of Ludwikowice Kłodzkie (formerly known as Ludwigsdorf) close to the Czech border.

Exactly what was the Bell? Maybe it was an antigravity device. Maybe it was a shortcut toward enriching uranium for weapons-making purposes. Maybe it was a time machine. Or, in the view of many, the Bell is a myth created long after the war by writers like Polish historian Igor Witkowski and Cook.

One Nazi scientist said to have worked on the Bell was Kurt Heinrich Debus, described by one writer as "a particularly nasty SS officer and electrical engineer." Debus is better known for his humorless personality, said by critics to be akin to Hitler's, and for his work on the V-2 rocket, developed at the secret northeastern German rocket facility Peenemünde on the Baltic coast. Debus led the Test Stand Group personnel at Peenemünde and was the engineer in charge at Test Stand VII, which would be called a launching pad in today's jargon. Several versions of Debus's life story—widely available because he became a key U.S. scientist after the war—have him remaining at Peenemünde until within weeks of war's end and then making a dramatic escape that put him in the hands of the advancing American 44th Infantry Division near Oberammergau in Bavaria— itself a site of secret weapons projects and a base the Allies didn't know about until they reached it.

So what is the truth? "The Nazi Bell was nothing to do with UFOs, or antigravity except in the imaginations of impressionable people," wrote one researcher who publishes extensively on the Internet but does not provide his real name or whereabouts. "It was, however, the most top secret arm of Nazi nuclear research, and as a result of secrecy or ignorance, many people have filled in the blanks with their imaginations."

This writer also claims, "The Nazi Bell was a spherical Tokamak plasma generator. The Nazis were using it for transmuting Thorium 232 to Uranium 233 (and possibly Uranium 238 to Plutonium 239) using photo fission. Originally the project was under the control of Heereswaffenamt as Projekt Thor, led by Gerlach whose role was procurement of enriched uranium for the German A-bomb. Following the failed assassination attempt against Hitler on July 20, 1944, the SS took control of all nuclear projects on 22 July and at that point the project became Projekt SS/1040 Charite Anlage."

Say what? Could the Bell in some odd way be connected with the futile and failed efforts of Hitler's minions to develop an atomic bomb?

No date, not ever

Never fully understood or fully supported by Hitler, the German attempt to develop the bomb, called the Uranverein (Uranium Club), began shortly after the invasion of Poland. Scientific teams were formed, of which two rival teams stood out as they struggled to make an atomic pile critical—one consisting of theoretical scientists under Werner Heisenberg and the other a more empirical team under the program's administrative director, Kurt Diebner.

Many of the Reich's scientific advances made dramatic progress in spite of Hitler's abrasive and divisive leadership style. The nuclear weapons program did not. Authors Simon Dunstan and Gerrard Williams, who believe Hitler escaped to Argentina after the war, described the challenges facing atomic scientists before the war: "In reality, the Germans lagged far behind largely due to the divisive nature of Nazi governance. Unlike the Manhattan Project, with its strictly centralized control under Gen. Leslie Groves, German researchers reported to several bodies, including the Army Ordnance Office, the National Research Council, and even the Postal Ministry. Furthermore, the scant resources were divided [among] nine competing teams all pursuing different agendas." Dunstan and Williams also wrote that many leading physicists in prewar Germany were Jewish. They either escaped or were killed.

The Heisenberg and Diebner teams wrongly believed that graphite could not be used as a moderator in an atomic pile (now called a nuclear reactor). This left only "heavy water" (deuterium oxide) as the only alternative. The Germans' heavy water plant in Norway, which came under frequent Allied attack, could not produce enough of the substance. Heisenberg's men, nevertheless, began building a rudimentary pile in a cave at Haigerloch in southern Germany. They made little progress.

History captures the imagination precisely because it all could have turned out differently, so that the study of past events is also the study of "what if?" Imagine this: What if the atomic bomb had been developed near the *beginning* of World War II instead of near its *end*? Nothing more needs to be said about that possibility. It speaks for itself.

What if Gen. Henry H. "Hap" Arnold's staff had gotten its way and prevented the P-51 Mustang from arriving in England at the time the Eighth Air Force was reeling from the defeat of its bomber forces in August and October 1943? Imagine that instead of "Big Week," in which bomber formations pounded German aircraft facilities and fuel supplies, the Western Allies had experienced "Bad Week" in February 1944, with formations of German jets decimating the bomber swarms. Used earlier, more smartly, and in greater numbers, jet fighters had the potential to halt the daylight bombing offensive and delay the Allied invasion of occupied Europe.

This in turn might have enabled even more jets to become available for the defense of the Reich.

Or not.

SEVENTEEN

THE AIR SHOW, PART II

November 8, 1950

"**D**amn! I'm going to get him!"

Those six words boomed in the earphones of American pilots high over the Yalu River as an air battle raged.

The speaker was 1st Lt. Russell J. Brown. He was pilot of an F-80 Shooting Star, the plane that had been called the P-80. He was in a screaming vertical dive with five of his six .50-caliber guns jammed. He must have thought it impossible to defeat a more advanced fighter with just a single gun working. But Americans had been up against more advanced fighters before.

In Brown's gunsight was a MiG-15, a silvery, swept-wing jet that had entered the Korean War only in the past few days. A Soviet engineering team had designed the MiG-15 with access to German wartime jet technology. Kelly Johnson's Lockheed team had designed the F-80 without that advantage.

At this juncture, Americans thought the men in the cockpits of Soviet-built MiGs were Korean or Chinese. They were Russians. Brown, of the 51st Fighter Group, was battling the Soviet Union's 151st Guards Fighter Aviation Division.

Brown's single gun emitted its buzz-saw sound. Brown's bullets struck the MiG. Several people in his F-80 flight saw the MiG go down. The air force officially credits Brown with an air-to-air victory.

At the end of World War II, with the Gloster Meteor in Britain, the P-80 in Italy, and the Messerschmitt Me 262 in Germany—all fully operational—no jet fighters on opposite sides ever met in battle. What is not in dispute is that Russell J. Brown fought in history's first jet-versus-jet air battle. But the rest of the story is a tale of history gone awry.

May 7, 1945

A weary frown adorned the face of Generalobertst (Gen.) Alfred Jodl as he signed the instrument of surrender at Reims, France. The war in Europe officially ended the next day, but for practical purposes it was already over. On opposite fronts, American and Soviet troops were overrunning concentration camps, military installations, and aircraft factories. American technicians were already beginning to destroy German equipment, the first step in Operation Eclipse, the disarmament of Nazi Germany. At some installations, men working for Col. Harold E. Watson, commander of the Army Air Forces' Air Technical Intelligence Group, dubbed "Watson's Whizzers," were seizing rather than destroying machines of war, including examples of the Messerschmitt Me 262 jet fighter. Watson and his men were undertaking Operation Lusty—a word derived from "Luftwaffe secret technology"—to capture and exploit Nazi technology.

Jodl had not been a big proponent of the Me 262. He was, after all, an artillery officer and did not yet realize that the artillery of the future would unleash its fury from the sky.

September 30, 1945

The jet fighter pursued its shadow across the apron at Freeman Field, Indiana. It sliced through the air at high speed just two hundred feet above the ground.

The war had ended. Adolf Hitler was dead. The thousand-year Third Reich lay in ruins after just a dozen years. Yet the Messerschmitt Me 262 still had a menacing, predatory look and still flew with deliberate purpose. It was never taken for granted and it never ceased to turn heads.

At the controls was Watson. The Americans had given this particular captured Me 262 a name. They called it *Jabo Bait*. Another Me 262, a two-seater, which the Americans dubbed *Ole Fruit Cake*, was on display on the ground alongside an Arado Ar 234. Captured German equipment was everywhere. Freeman Field was handling the overflow of captured Axis equipment from Wright Field.

In a speech prepared for delivery many years later, Watson wrote, "When I first saw the Me 262 I was spellbound. Just sitting there on the ground it looked as though it was doing Mach 1," the speed of sound.

Watson was a Wright Field test pilot and engineer who had been given the job of exploiting German technology and recovering examples of the Third Reich's advanced aircraft and weapons. He was usually self-effacing and unpretentious. He was just the right man to be in charge of Lusty. And now, buzzing the ground, turning heads, howling across Freeman Field, Watson was celebrating his triumph: He had rounded up dozens of German aircraft, including a remarkable large transport (below), and turned them over to U.S. technicians and scientists. His small band of handpicked "Whizzers" had picked the low-hanging fruit of the defeated Luftwaffe and had quietly and discreetly brought it back to America.

Now the time for secrecy had passed. Now, it was time to celebrate.

Watson's low-level demo flight was made in front of a viewing stand full of political, scientific, and technical leaders, all feasting their eyes on the German jet fighter for the first time. In addition to bigwigs, about three hundred print and radio journalists were on the scene. One later said he was unnerved by the lethal appearance of the Me 262. More than a few noticed that the Me 262 was about as capable as the Lockheed P-80 Shooting Star—the American jet fighter

Gen. Henry H. "Hap" Arnold was attempting to save amid a postwar consensus that it was time to sharply reduce U.S. military spending.

The public apparently was not invited to this Freeman Field event, although subsequent events at the same location showed off Watson's war prizes to all. Among those who *were* invited, though, was German Me 262 test pilot Karl Baur, who in a matter of weeks had become a sort of buddy of Watson's, as well as his tutor on the cockpit and instrument layout of the jet. Bauer is the bookend of this narrative. He was at the air show at Insterburg on November 26, 1943, with the Führer. He was at the air show at Freeman Field on September 30, 1945, with Watson. It appears—although we cannot be certain, even from his own papers—that Baur was at Wright Field two weeks later.

As in the aftermath of all wars, treatment of the defeated foe was uneven and inequitable. The artillery officer Jodl, linked to killings of prisoners, was tried for war crimes at Nuremburg and hanged. He may have been a victim of history gone awry. A German court later exonerated him.

Baur, who was an aviation person rather than a warrior, taught Watson and other "Whizzers" how to fly the Me 262 and socialized with them.

October 13, 1945

The Army Air Forces *did* invite the public to the air force fair at Wright Field, Ohio, on the weekend of October 13 and 14, 1945. The public came in droves. Watson came. Karl Baur came. The Me 262 was there and the P-80 was there. Arnold's staff flew up from Washington in a special plane. The German jet was a bigger attraction for the audience than the American jet. Arnold, who was in poor health, considered giving some kind of speech over the PA system and concluded that it wasn't practical to promote the P-80 at a family fun event.

In this era before metal detectors, before photo ID, before guards at the main gate, thousands of civilians brought their cameras and their lunches. There was music. There was cotton candy. People crowded around among displays—some outdoors, some in tents. They included a Heinkel He 162 *Volksjäger*, a Messerschmitt Me 163 *Komet*, and many other war prizes. The magnificent Junkers Ju 290 dubbed *Alles Kaput* (Everything's Lost) was on display—a plane that would have made a wonderful museum piece but was soon, instead, to be scrapped in a senseless act of needless destruction. Beside this great and magnificent transport plane, not fully removed from its packing crate, was a pristine example of the ill-advised and ill-fated Bachem Ba 349 *Natter*.

The show also included a twin-prop Junkers Ju 388L, a Japanese Mitsubishi A6M Zero, and a Kugisho Ohka, the plane known to the Americans as the *Baka* (Fool) and designed to be dropped from a bomber on a one-way suicide mission with an explosive charge in the nose. "They were letting guys climb in and out of the 'Baka' and allowing them to close the canopy over their heads," said veteran army pilot Robert Bush, home from the war and attending the air show as a tourist. "It was amazing to see the remarkable diversity of the captured weapons on display, but for me the star was the Me 262."

In his head, Bush acted out a dogfight that had never taken place, putting himself in an American P-51 Mustang and imagining his opponent in an Me 262, an aircraft he had not seen during the fighting.

He walked among the aircraft. They did not seem warlike, even with their iron crosses and swastikas restored by American painters. He came upon the He 162, which he had witnessed from a distance during a combat mission. "Up close, it seemed so ordinary," Bush said. "Their other jet was more impressive. That great big transport of theirs was a lot more impressive." Bush never realized that he might have passed a German jet test pilot in the crowd.

The air force fair at Wright Field was—it's worth making this metaphor a second time—an unintentional bookend to the display at Insterburg only twenty-three months ago that had been held for an audience of one, Adolf Hitler. Karl Baur, the Me 262 test pilot who attended both events, came into U.S. hands and became a de facto member of "Watson's Whizzers" when the Allies captured Augsburg, home of the Messerschmitt plant (on April 29, 1945), after Baur decided not to accompany Willy Messerschmitt to Oberammergau.

The Americans required Baur and his crew to repair the Me 262s that had been damaged and to instruct American pilots in their operation. Along with other German experts in the field of aeronautics and rocketry, Baur was sent to the United States in fall of 1945. He arrived at Wright Field on September 24, 1945, reached Freeman Field three days later, and returned to Wright Field. Never involved in any of the heinous wrongdoing by the Nazi regime, Baur was able to return to Germany and reunite with his family in December 1945.

May-September 1945

Watson and his team were in Germany even before VE Day (May 8, 1945), rounding up aircraft to be taken home and evaluated by U.S. intelligence. The crown jewel of their efforts was the Me 262, which had an enormous influence on postwar technology. Other choices by the team seem difficult to understand: the "Whizzers" probably would have learned little from the three Bf 109Gs they rounded up. Along the way, Watson's men grabbed up a Junker Ju 290 transport, which was a wonderful curiosity but perhaps not more or less by accident.

Watson shipped several dozen German aircraft back to the United States by sea. Many contributed knowledge that helped with early U.S. jets. The design team working on the North American XP-86 fighter, which became the F-86 Sabre, had access to the Me 262.

The Arado Ar 234 did not elude Watson's Whizzers and other Allied intelligence collectors. Fully nine Ar 234s were surrendered to British forces at Sola Airfield near Stavanger, Norway. Watson's team collected several of them. One aircraft was flown from Sola to Cherbourg, France, on June 24, 1945, where it joined thirty-four other advanced German aircraft being shipped back to the United States aboard the British aircraft carrier HMS *Reaper*. *Reaper* departed from Cherbourg on July 20, arriving at Newark, New Jersey, eight days later.

Watson's pilots took two Ar 234s from the *Reaper* to Freeman Field, Indiana, for testing and evaluation. The fate of the second Ar 234 flown to Freeman Field is unknown. A third Ar 234 was taken off the *Reaper* and assembled by the U.S. Navy for testing, but was found to be unflyable and was scrapped. The first aircraft to be grabbed up by Watson, the only surviving example in this series, the Ar 234B-2 bomber is today on display at the Steven F. Udvar-Hazy Center of the National Air and Space Museum, Smithsonian Institution, at Dulles, Virginia, replete with rocket-assisted takeoff, or RATO, units.

Neither Watson's Whizzers nor any other Allied intelligence officials ever found any clue to the foo fighters, mysterious disks that bomber crewmembers observed in flight over the Reich. They remain unexplained phenomena in the minds of most and a sign of extraterrestrial intelligence to a few. The Air Force Historical Office at Maxwell Air Force Base, Alabama, has records of claimed foo fighter sightings by P-61 Black Widow night-fighter pilots but no record of the foo fighters reported over Schweinfurt by Martin Caidin.

The Ju 290 was impressive but was hardly a technical treasure. It fell into Watson's hands more or less by accident. On May 8, 1945, a Luftwaffe pilot landed the plane at Munich-Riem Airport, which was in the hands of U.S. troops. The pilot surrendered himself, the plane, and a planeload of women auxiliary members of the German air arm. All had flown to Munich from Czechoslovakia, eager to be captured by the Americans rather than the Soviets.

Watson decided to take the Ju 290 to the United States.

It's not clear why. The Ju 290 was a sturdy, practical machine but hardly the latest technology. At best, it might give U.S. experts a look at how Germany had designed a very large aircraft.

Watson and his men confronted a steep learning curve with a plane designed and built in another country. With help from the German pilot, Watson flew the Ju 290 to an airfield near Nuremberg on May 10, 1945.

Watson and others made several test hops in the big plane. Surprised to find the Ju 290 in relatively good condition, Watson decided that he would fly the Ju 290 back to Wright Field.

July 28, 1945

With Capt. Fred McIntosh as copilot and eight more crewmembers aboard, Watson departed Orly Field, Paris, France, on July 28, 1945, to fly the Ju 290 to the United States. By this time, the Americans had painted the name *Alles Kaput* on the nose and had replaced German insignia with U.S. markings.

At their first stop during the flight, Santa Maria Island in the Azores, Watson and McIntosh had a chance to show the Ju 290 to AAF boss Arnold, who happened to be passing through. The flight continued to Bermuda and proceeded directly to Wright Field.

Repainted in German markings for display purposes, the Ju 290 was tested exhaustively and was displayed at open houses and air shows in 1945 and 1946. By the end of 1946, however, this unusual plane was grounded and was being dismantled for specialized study.

The air force was still a branch of the army at that time, and there was no museum program that would provide a resting place for this unusual example of war booty. *Alles Kaput* was scrapped on December 12, 1946. "It would be of interest to a lot of people today," said David W. Menard, a restorer at the Air Force Museum. "It's a pity that an intriguing aircraft like this couldn't have been preserved."

The Reich's jet designs strongly influenced the B-47 Stratojet and F-86 Sabre, the most important American bomber and fighter of the immediate postwar period—and, indeed, almost everything that U.S. industry produced after VE Day. Watson's Whizzers and other intelligence collectors scooped up vast quantities of material on German jets, especially the Me 262. U.S. industry also received help from German engineers brought to the United States in Operation Paperclip, the Office of Strategic Services program that recruited scientists and technical experts of Nazi Germany for employment in the United States. No fewer than eighty-six aeronautical experts from the Reich were transferred to Wright Field, where they provided background knowledge for Me 262s and other items of hardware. The knowledge base, the men, and the captured equipment were lent out to U.S. plane makers, who were eager to overcome an expected postwar slump in business. They would be recovering from one of the great industrial miracles in history.

In separate rocketry and space programs, the United States made use of Operation Paperclip immigrants such as Wernher von Braun, who thrived and prospered in postwar America while men deemed less valuable were prosecuted for war crimes. Von Braun was never held to account for abiding slave labor.

The Germans came to an America with high standards of education and literacy, and thriving industry. In a single year during the war (1944), America's aircraft manufacturing capacity produced just slightly fewer than one hundred thousand warplanes. The heroic machinery of the American heartland demonstrated how true, how prophetic, was a warning often attributed to Japan's Adm. Isoroku Yamamoto. Rather than winning a victory at Pearl Harbor, Yamamoto supposedly warned his fellow officers the attack had merely "awakened a sleeping giant and filled him with a terrible resolve." It hardly matters that Yamamoto never said those words, which were created by a screenwriter for the movie *Tora Tora Tora* (1970). The quote accurately reflects the views of Japanese leaders during an era—now gone—when the United States led the world in almost every field of endeavor.

At Dearborn, Michigan, the Ford company was turning out a new B-24 Liberator bomber every fifty-one minutes. At Bethpage, New York, Grumman was in the midst of delivering 12,275 F6F Hellcat fighters in just thirty months. In Inglewood, California, North American's plant produced Mitchell bombers and Mustang fighters so rapidly the aircraft sat waiting, row after row, while Army Air Forces worked in a frenzy to get them delivered. American factories, workers, and products set a standard for the world.

While the war was being won, American leadership in science (for the word technology was not yet widely used) brought astounding change. It was rumored that a time machine was being developed at the Philadelphia navy yard. It was true that a new bomb of incredible power was being assembled in a remote village in New Mexico. Radical new warplanes were taking shape with both propeller and jet-engine power.

So dominant was American industry that it could afford a luxury: far more experimental planes were built and tested than were needed to win the war. In the California desert at a bleak, sandy outpost called Muroc, bizarre pursuit ships were flying with strange wing shapes and different engines. The Curtiss XP-55 Ascender was pushed, rather than pulled, through the air (by a propeller) and boasted a swept-back wing. The Bell P-59A Airacomet was trucked to the desert with a fake propeller glued to its nose (to fool watching gophers and rattlesnakes) but flew without one. It was a time of miracles. American know-how dominated the world.

But science advanced elsewhere, too. For all their achievements, American engineers could not match German accomplishments in military aviation. The world's most powerful nation, while still planning to unleash the fury of the atomic bomb, is usually listed third among nations producing jet airplanes. The Soviet Union—a backward nation, in so many other ways—was advancing at about the Americans' pace and was hoarding its own cache of German documents, equipment, and scientists.

At the North American Aviation (NAA) facility in Inglewood, the company's confidential design group, under Edgar Schmued, was pondering radically new versions of the P-51 Mustang, which had established itself as one of the most important fighters of World War II. Some of the impetus for Schmued's design effort came from the U.S. Navy, which test-flew a P-51D Mustang from the carrier USS *Shangri-la* (CV-38) in 1944. Looking for a new carrier-based fighter that would exploit the Mustang's proven qualities, Schmued and his colleagues studied several advanced concepts, including a Mustang with swept-forward wings and both turboprop and turbojet power.

The navy said no. Instead, the sea service pressed NAA for a wholly new but far from radical jet fighter, the XFJ-1, later named the Fury. The navy also went ahead with the Grumman F9F Panther, the last carrier-based fighter built in large numbers that did not benefit from German jet technology: the Panther was straight-winged, slow, and clunky. But it was reliable and performed reasonably well on ships' decks.

To maintain full advantage of its very thin, high-speed wing, the Fury was to have a circular nose engine air intake and straight-through ducting, rather than the side or wing air inlets chosen for the Lockheed P-80 Shooting Star, McDonnell XFD-1 Phantom, and Vought XF6U-1 Pirate. Among American jet designs of the period, only the Republic XP-84 Thunderjet had a circular nose air intake. The Soviets, who were wining and dining their own German engineers, used this feature on their MiG-9 and—very importantly—their MiG-15 fighters.

In 1945, the AAF studied the navy's yet-unbuilt Fury, including its thin, straight wing. The AAF gave its aircraft the designation XP-86. It was later named the Sabre.

On May 18, 1945, just a fortnight after fighting ended in Europe and while the war was continuing in the Pacific, NAA received an AAF contract for three XP-86 prototypes. But designers at Inglewood began to think of making a change when they came into possession of German wind-tunnel data that had been obtained by U. S. technical intelligence experts. Schmued's engineers were already aware of the Me 262 and now they knew more about it.

Larry Green, NAA's head of Design Aerodynamics, began attending night school, sharpening his fluency in the German language so he could pore through the wind-tunnel reports. Green also studied interrogations of captured German scientists and engineers. A little later, Green and others on the Sabre project met with German experts.

Finally, a captured Me 262 became available for rigorous study by Schmued's Inglewood team. A pile of documents, a real Me 262, and Green's fast-improving German proficiency all accelerated the pace of change at North American. Engineers, military officers, and corporate decision makers alike, seemingly all struck by a bolt from above, came to the realization that the lackluster performance of the Sabre could be improved strikingly with a swept wing. They were unaware that in the Soviet Union an identical decision had been reached with respect to the future MiG-15.

A thirty-five-degree sweep 5.0-aspect ratio wing with full span leading slats was quickly built and tested in September 1945 on the XP-86 model in North American's low-speed wind tunnel. It had been expected that the wing would show instability at high lift coefficients, and it did, but engineers determined that satisfactory stalling characteristics could be achieved with the slats.

The proposal to overhaul the XP-86 design and install a swept wing was prepared under the watchful eye of AAF project engineer Capt. Roy Mann. NAA's Raymond H. Rice discussed the concept with Gen. William Craigie, head of research and development at Wright Field. Told that installing a new wing would cause a six-month delay in the first flight of what had seemed, so far, a mediocre performer, Craigie said, "Go ahead." The swept wing was officially approved on November 1, 1945.

Even then, the swept-wing XP-86 was to have straight tail surfaces. Details of the leading-edge slat design were debated intensely. Eventually, again based on German data, vertical and horizontal tail surfaces were also swept.

As of November 1, 1945, when many projects were being cancelled after war's end and the AAF was chopping off on a swept-wing XP-86, no warplane with fully swept wings had yet proven successful. Schmued, Rice, and Green did not know about the Soviet MiG-15, only months behind them.

The XP-86 initially was to be powered by a Chevrolet-built, General Electric–designed J35-C-3 or Allison J35-A-5 axial-flow turbojet engine

with four thousand–pound (1,816 kilograms) thrust (originally designated TG-180). The first three XP-86 aircraft were unarmed.

Test pilot for the new fighter, as on many NAA aircraft of the
period, was George Welch. At Pearl Harbor, "Wheaties" Welch had
gotten aloft in a P-40 Tomahawk and had shot down four of the
Japanese attackers. He'd become an air ace in the Pacific theater, raising his total to sixteen kills, before joining North American in 1944.

On September 18, 1947, the AAF became the U.S. Air Force, an inde-
pendent service branch. That week, NAA trucked the XP-86 prototype
from Inglewood to the air force's remote desert installation at Muroc.

Some of what went on at Muroc was secretive—think Bob Hoover
making the one and only test flight in a captured Heinkel He 162—
but much was not. Used for training and checkout of P-38 Lightning
pilots and initial flying of other hazardous aircraft from 1941 on, the
base was quite primitive. The P-38 transition was accomplished here
so that Los Angeles' congested areas would be spared the frequent
crashes by newly graduated fighter pilots.

Muroc had been a secluded hideaway for secret tests of weird
and mysterious airplanes, among them the previously-mentioned
Curtiss XP-55 Ascender pusher-prop fighter with swept wings developed years before German data on wing sweep was available. Now,
Welch made the first flight of the first XP-86 on October 1, 1947, at
Muroc. Years later, the myth would be perpetrated that Welch flew
faster than sound before Capt. Charles E. "Chuck" Yeager achieved
that feat two weeks later on October 14. Based on dozens of interviews with people who worked on the XP-86 program at the time,
the author of this book is certain Welch did not fly supersonic before
Yeager. But Welch did have in his hands the prototype of what would
be the most successful jet fighter in the West in the 1940s and in the
Korean War, and the Me 262 had a lot to do with it.

June 25, 1950

The North Korean invasion across the 38th Parallel ignited a new war.
The term *recall* became all too painfully familiar to former American

fighter pilots who'd thought *their* war was over, who'd come home, started families, and launched careers.

Robert Bush returned to southeast Washington, D.C., married, and had a daughter. He told friends he would never climb into a cockpit again. Like the German with a similar name, Hans Busch, Robert had become a seasoned fighter pilot in combat during the war but wasn't credited with shooting down any aircraft. He considered himself a citizen-soldier. He was working part-time and doing university study when he received the notice that the United States needed him in uniform again. He was brought back into uniform to fly a new jet fighter, the F-86 Sabre, originally the XP-86. As it turned out, Bush, like many recalled during Korea, didn't actually go to Korea—he spent two years boring holes in the sky in the American Southwest and *then* never climbed into a cockpit again. However, the two German-influenced jet fighters on opposite sides, the F-86 and the MiG-15, did make it to Korea.

November 8, 1950

Russell Brown pulled out of his sharp dive with a MiG-15 falling away. He remained in the air force, retired as a colonel, and almost never appeared in public to discuss his role in history's first jet-versus-jet encounter.

On November 10, 1950, two days after Brown's encounter, Lt. Cdr. William Thomas Amen, pilot of a Navy F9F-2 Panther, was credited with shooting down a MiG-15. Years later, Soviet records confirmed that Amen did, indeed, bag the MiG and that its pilot, Mikhail Grachev, was killed. Although credit for history's first jet-versus-jet kill officially belongs to Brown, the credit to Brown is a mistake. Amen was the first pilot to shoot down another aircraft in jet-versus-jet combat.

December 4, 1950

Another American jet that had been designed before German technology became available—a straight-winged, four-jet North

American RB-45C Tornado reconnaissance aircraft. It became the first plane of any kind ever to be shot down by a MiG-15.

Soviet pilot Aleksandr F. Andrianov received credit for the kill. Copilot Capt. Jules E. Young and navigator 1st Lt. James J. Picucci lost their lives in the shootdown. RB-45C pilot Capt. Charles E. McDonough and a Pentagon intelligence officer, Col. John R. Lovell are thought to have bailed out, landed on the North Korean side of the Yalu River, been interrogated by the Soviets, and were subsequently murdered. Lovell was the highest-ranking intelligence officer to be lost during the Korean War.

December 17, 1950

The F-86 Sabre had arrived in Korea. Lieutenant Colonel Bruce H. Hinton, piloting an F-86, shot down a MiG-15. It was the first battle between aircraft that were both influenced by German design. It was the beginning of a thirty-month aerial campaign in which the F-86 would prevail mostly because of the skill of its pilots, racking up a seven-to-one kill ratio over the MiG.

January 27, 1957

It ends here, in the rain.

Outside the main gate of the Naval Research Laboratory (NRL) along the Anacostia River in Washington, D.C., the author of this volume—age seventeen, a high school senior, and already published—arrives to look at two pieces of junk that were once airplanes. Now, they are skeletons of rust, derelict, moistened by the drizzle that hangs in the air.

There is not yet a "warbird movement." No one is yet restoring surplus military aircraft and flying them in military markings. Nor is there a movement, yet, to build and fly replicas of Germany's most famous jet. That will come in a new century. A real Messerschmitt Me 262 will never again take to the air.

Outside the NRL gate, missing pieces of skin, literally falling apart, wet in the rain, in pitiful, forlorn condition, are a Japanese

Kawanishi N1K1 *Shiden* (Violet Lightning) fighter, called a "George" by the Americans, and a Messerschmitt Me 262A-1a *Schwalbe*. In years to come, the George would be saved, refurbished, restored, and displayed in a museum.

The Me 262 would not.

Other Me 262s, none of them airworthy, made it to museums. This one didn't.

When I climbed over that Me 262, sat in what remained of the cockpit, and walked on what was left of the wing, it never occurred to me that I might be among the last people to see it. When I pulled out my Ricoh 35mm camera, back in that era when such a camera was a rarity, it never struck me that I might be among the last people to take a picture of it. Thanks to spotters who keep track of such things, we know that Watson's Whizzers named this Me 262 *Delovely* and that it was assigned the U.S. Navy bureau number 121444, but we do not know its German werke number. We know that the U.S. Navy received it; held it at Patuxent River, Maryland; and studied it at the Naval Proving Ground in Dahlgren, Virginia—but never flew it. One reference work asserts that it was scrapped at Naval Air Station Anacostia in 1947, a decade before I climbed all over it. Another reports that it was displayed at the naval air station, which is a few miles down the road from the NRL, on the other side of Bolling Air Force Base—but it never was.

We do not know what happened to it.

In my fanciful daydreams, that Me 262 is flying around through a dry, bright, blue sky somewhere, not as a weapon of war but as a miracle of aviation, a beautifully performing aircraft that doesn't deserve to have disappeared without a trace.

not meant to be exhaustive, but to show how Americas adjusted to Jets? That they should not have had a chance but did well? Can't this be generalized to all combat?

ACKNOWLEDGMENTS

These first-person accounts of pilots and crews in combat are the result of many interviews completed in 2011 and 2012. This book would have been impossible without the help of many.

The following combat veterans were interviewed for this book:

Frank E. Birtciel, Warren E. "Buzz" Buhler, Don Bryan, Robert Des Lauriers, Robert K. Filbey, Edward Giller, Clayton Kelly Gross, Robert A. Hadley, Jim Kunkle, Warren Loring, John O. Moench, Robin Olds, Robert "Punchy" Powell, Felix M. Rogers, Harrison B. Tordoff, William R. Wagner, Max Woolley, and Jerry Yellin.

Looks like some new material in here in device

On the German side:

Hans Busch and Willi Kriessman.

Thanks also to family members of veterans and scholars of the war, including:

Timothy Barb, Hollis H. Barnhart, Priscilla Beaudrault, Walter J. Boyne, Jack Cook, Tom Crouch, Bob Esposito, Devin Ezersky, Christopher "Zippo" Fahey, Lloyd Fergus, Mike Fleckenstein, Eleanor Garner, John Gourley, Alan Gropman, Jim Hawkins, Colin Heaton, Edward R. Hindman Jr., David Isby, Corey Jordan, James William Marshall, Craig Meyer, Ted Oliver, Paul Schoemacher, G. G. Sweeting, Barrett Tillman, and Nate Wilburn.

appears to take combat claims a step further. appears to present some new sources

A few paragraphs in this book are adapted from material I wrote for *Warplanes of the Luftwaffe*, edited by David Donald and published in 1994. In quoting from after-action reports and other official documents, I've made minor changes in punctuation and spelling for the ease of the reader.

no original source docs appear to
have been used - combat reports - or
at least cited -
- he does mention "official report said"
but appears to be pulling that from
some other book,

MACR?
combat reports?
monographs?

How about the combat chronology?
is it in the bibliography?

This is built around [illegible] in formations -
purpose is combat accounts, to bring you back
to the time when the jets were a threat.
Bookended with air shows is good device -
Germans are this is what will win, ours was
this is what won and what we beat
or has 1,000's of interviews in his literature - he may have
purposely sacrificed precision for theme - find out
what his [illegible] and play it up

BIBLIOGRAPHY

Baur, Isolde. *A Pilot's Pilot, Karl Baur: Chief Test Pilot for Messerschmitt.* Winnipeg: J. J. Fedorowicz Publishing, 2000.

Beevor, Anthony. *The Second World War.* New York: Little Brown, 2012.

Below, Nicolaus von. *At Hitler's Side: The Memoirs of Hitler's Luftwaffe Adjutant, 1937–1945.* Barnsley, South Yorkshire: Pen & Sword, 2010.

Berg, A. Scott. *Lindbergh.* New York: G. P. Putnam's Sons, 1998.

Boyne, Walter J. "Hans Mutke and Mach 1." *Axis Fighters.* Winter 2013.

Busch, Hans. *The Last of the Few: An Me 262 Pilot Remembers.* London: Shelf Books, 2001.

Caidin, Martin. *Fork-Tailed Devil: The P-38 Lightning.* New York: Bantam, 1990.

———. *Black Thursday.* New York: Bantam, 1960.

Cleaver, Thomas McKelvey. "Donald Blakeslee and the Battle of Germany, 1944." *World War II Ace Stories.* http://www.elknet.pl/acestory/blake/ blake.htm.

Donald, David, ed. *Warplanes of the Luftwaffe*. Westport, CT: AIRTime Publishing, Inc., 1994.

Dube, Ron. *Nashua Area Men and Women in WW II*. Nashua, NH: Xlibris Corp., 2011.

Forsyth, Robert, and Jim Laurier. *Jagdverband 44: Squadron of Experten*. London: Osprey, 2008.

Francis, Charles E., and Adolph Caso. *The Tuskegee Airmen: The Men Who Changed a Nation*. New York: Branden Books, 2008.

Fry, Garry L. *Eagles of Duxford: The 78th Fighter Group in World War II*. St. Paul: Phalanx Publishing, 1991.

Gilbert, Christian. "One Man Air Force." *True*, June 1944.

Gross, Clayton Kelly. *Live Bait*. Portland, OR: Inkwater Press, 2006.

Harvey, James Neal. *Sharks of the Air*. Havertown, PA: Casemate, 2011.

Haynes, Richard F. *The Awesome Power: Harry S. Truman as Commander in Chief*. New Orleans: Louisiana State University Press, 1973.

Heaton, Colin D., and Anne-Marie Louis. *The Me 262 Stormbird*. Minneapolis: Zenith Press, 2012.

Heiber, Helmut, and David W. Glantz, eds. *Hitler and His Generals: Military Conferences, 1942–1945*. New York: Enigma Books, 2003.

Hess, William N. *354th Fighter Group*. London: Osprey, 2002.

———. *German Jets Versus the U.S. Army Air Force*. North Branch, MN: Specialty Press, 1996.

Hess, William N., and Thomas G. Ivie. *Fighter of the Mighty Eighth.* Osceola, WI: Motorbooks International, 1990.

Ilfrey, Jack, with Mark Copeland. *Happy Jack's Go Buggy: A Fighter Pilot's Story.* Atglen, PA: Schiffer Military/Aviation History, 1998.

Irving, David. *The Rise and Fall of the Luftwaffe: The Life of Field Marshal Erhard Milch.* Boston: Little, Brown and Company, 1973.

Malayney, Norman. *The 25th Bomb Group (RCN) in World War II.* Atglen, PA: Schiffer Military/Aviation History, 2011.

Morgan, Hugh. *Me 262: Stormbird Rising.* London: Osprey Publishing, 1994.

Pisanos, Col. Steve N. *The Flying Greek: An Immigrant Fighter Ace's WWII Odyssey with the RAF.* Dulles, VA: Potomac Press, 2008.

Powell, R. R. *Ben Drew: The Katzenjammer Ace.* New York: Writer's Showcase, 2001.

Price, Alfred. *The Last Year of the Luftwaffe: May 1944 to May 1945.* London: Arms and Armour Press, 1991.

Ransom, Stephen, with Hans-Hermann Cammann and Jim Laurier. *Jagdgeschwader 400: Germany's Elite Rocket Fighters.* London: Osprey, 2010.

Samuel, Wolfgang. *American Raiders: The Race to Capture the Luftwaffe's Secrets.* Jackson: University Press of Mississippi, 2004.

Shapiro, James. *Oberammergau: The Troubling Story of the World's Most Famous Passion Play.* New York: Random House, 2000.

Speer, Albert. *Inside the Third Reich.* New York: Orion Books, 1970.

Stapfer, Hans-Heiri. *Me 262 in Action.* Carrollton, TX: Squadron/Signal Publications, 2008.

ENDNOTES

Do not locate the quote!

Scently does not locate to some of the narrates — Just a few. Hansha point

"*With a flock of generals and grim-looking SS guards at his side*": *A Pilot's Pilot*, by Isolde Baur, sister of Messerschmitt chief test pilot Karl Baur.

The Reichsmarschall "*took the printed program out of Milch's hands*": *The Rise and Fall of the Luftwaffe*, by David Irving, p. 259.

"*Every month that passes makes it more and more probable that we will get at least one Gruppe of jet aircraft*": *The Last Year of the Luftwaffe*, by Alfred Price, p. 33.

"*Baur was a decent person in many ways*": Author interview with G. G. Sweeting, June 13, 2012.

"*Hitler was always excited about new things*": *The Me 262 Stormbird*, by Colin D. Heaton and Anne-Marie Lewis.

"*I'm more an artist than a mechanic*": Interviews with G. G. Sweeting and David Isby.

"*An opportunist*": Interview with G. G. Sweeting.

"*Urged Willy to join the party*": *Sharks of the Air*, by James Neal Harvey.

* * * * * * * * * * * * *

"A north woods lumberjack or football lineman": Nashua Men and Women of WW II, by Ron Dube.

* * * * * * * * * * * * *

"We possessed a remote-control flying bomb, a rocket plane that was even faster than the jet plane": Inside the Third Reich, by Albert Speer.

* * * * * * * * * * * * *

"I loved the P-38": Interview with Robin Olds, 1988.

"Too complicated for the 'average pilot' ": Report for VIII Fighter Command written by Col. Harold Rau.

"The quality of multi-engine training": Letter from former 1st Lt. Arthur W. Heiden, sent originally to Carlo Kopp with a copy to the author of this book.

"It looked like a beautiful monster": Happy Jack's Go Buggy, by Jack Ilfrey, with Mark Copeland.

"If you were a boy in America, you wanted to fly it": Author interview with Lt. Gen. Winton "Bones" Marshall.

"On December 13, 1943, the target was Kiel": Author interviews with Rogers and Gabay.

* * * * * * * * * * * * *

"I was doing close to 400 mph in a left breaking dive, a customary maneuver": The 25th Bomb Group (RCN) in World War II by Norman Malayney.

* * * * * * * * * * * * *

"A straitlaced, 'go by the book' kind of guy": Author interview with Clayton Kelly Gross, April 18, 2012.

"We all wore seat belts and shoulder harness": Author interview with P-51 Mustang pilot Jerry Yellin, March 23, 2012.

"Prominently hung on Kepner's office wall": *Doolittle, Aerospace Visionary*, by Dik A. Daso.

"A kind of 'Little Caesar' attitude": Interview with Clayton Kelly Gross, April 18, 2012.

"Most fighter pilots played to the crowd": *Donald Blakeslee and the Battle of Germany, 1944*, by Thomas McKelvey Cleaver.

"First use of external fuel tanks": *Thunderbolt*, by Roger Freeman.

"[T]he oxygen system failed": *Eagles of Duxford*, by Garry L. Fry.

"Secrecy was enforced": *The Last of the Few* by Hans Busch.

* * * * * * * * * * * * * *

"It was a warm, sunny day": *Sharks of the Air*, by James Neal Harvey.

* * * * * * * * * * * * * *

"The P-47s' pursuit paid off": *German Jets Versus the U. S. Army Air Force*, by William N. Hess.

"I . . . attempted to jettison the canopy": *Jagdgeschwader 400: Germany's Elite Rocket Fighters*, by Stephen Ransom, Hans-Hermann Cammann, and Jim Laurier.

"We walked up to this mysterious aircraft": *The Last of the Few*, by Hans Busch.

* * * * * * * * * * * * *

"And then the 'impossible' happened": *Black Thursday*, by Martin Caidin.

* * * * * * * * * * * * *

"'Tell me, Brown . . .": *The Tuskegee Airmen: The Men Who Changed a Nation*, by Charles E. Francis and Adolph Caso.

"Usually, the only way we could get those guys": Interview with Edward Giller, March 9, 2013.

"Apparently he attempted to bail out": *The Last of the Few*, by Hans Busch.

* * * * * * * * * * * * *

"Schallmoser quickly looked down at his gun firing button": *Jagdverband 44: Squadron of Experten*, by Robert Forsyth.

* * * * * * * * * * * * *

"Looking at maps and photos of this installation": *Oberammergau: The Troubling Story of the World's Most Famous Passion Play*, by James Shapiro.

"The once-revered designer's country home had been 'liberated' ": *Lindbergh*, by A. Scott Berg.

"I moved the stick wildly around the cockpit": *Hans Mutke and Mach 1*, by Walter J. Boyne.

"In reality, the Germans lagged far behind": *Grey Wolf*, by Simon Dunstan and Gerrard Williams.

APPENDIX A

AIRCRAFT

Messerschmitt Me 262A-1a *Schwalbe*

Type: single-seat air superiority fighter

Powerplant: two Junkers Jumo 004B-1/2/3 axial-flow turbojet engines each providing 2,000-pound (907 kg) static thrust

Performance: maximum speed 521 miles per hour (838 km/h) at sea level; 530 miles per hour (852 km/h) at 9,845 feet (3,000 m); 532 miles per hour (856 km/h) at 26,246 feet (8,000 m); initial rate of climb 3,937 feet (1,200 m) per minute; service ceiling 38,000 feet (11,582 m); range 652 miles (1,050 km)

Weights: empty 8,500 pounds (3,855 kg); maximum takeoff weight 9,742 pounds (4,413 kg); gross weight 14,080 pounds (6,387 kg)

Dimensions: span 40 feet 11 1/2 inches (12.50 m); length 34 feet 9 1/2 inches (10.57 m); height 12 feet 7 inches (3.83 m); wing area 234 square feet (21.73 sq m)

Armament: four 30mm Rheinmetall-Borsig Mk 108A-3 cannons with 100 rounds per gun for the upper pair and 80 rounds per gun for the lower pair; ordnance station for 12 R4M air-to-air rocket projectiles

First flight: April 18, 1941 (Me 262V1); October 17, 1943 (Me 262V6); 1944 (Me 262A-1a)

Messerschmitt Me 163 *Komet*

Type: Single-seat, single-engine rocket-powered fighter

Powerplant: One 3,800-pound thrust (17 kN) Walter HWK 109-509A-2 liquid-fuel rocket engine

Performance: maximum speed 596 miles per hour (1,060 km/h); Rate of climb 31,500 feet per minute; service ceiling 39,700 feet (12,100 m); range 25 miles (40 km)

Weights: empty 4,200 pounds (1,905 kg); maximum takeoff weight 9,500 pounds (4,310 kg)

Dimensions: wingspan 30 feet 7 inches (9.33 m); length 19 feet 7 inches (5.98 m); height 9 feet (2.75 m); wing area 200 square feet (18.50 sq m)

Armament: two 20mm MG 151/20 cannons (Me 163B-0); two 30mm (1.18-inch) Rheinmetall Borsig MK 108 cannons with 60 rounds per gun (Me 163B-1)

First flight: (powered) August 1941

Bell P-39M Airacobra

Type: single-seat fighter

Powerplant: one 1,200-horsepower (895-kW) Allison V-1710 in-line engine driving a 10-foot 4-inch (3.14-m) Curtiss Electric propeller

Performance: maximum speed 386 miles per hour (621 km/h); cruising speed 378 miles per hour (608 km/h); climb to 16,400 feet (5,000 m) in 6.5 minutes; ceiling 36,000 feet (1,0970 m); range 650 miles (1,046 km)

Weights: 5,610 pounds (2,545 kg); normal gross weight 8,400 pounds (3,810 kg); maximum takeoff weight 10,500 lb (4,763 kg)

Armament: one American Armament Corporation T-9 37mm cannon in the propeller hub, plus four .30-calilber (7.62mm) machine guns.

Dimensions: included span 34 feet (10.36 m); length 30 feet 2 inches (9.19 m); height 11 feet 10 inches (3.61 m)

First flight: April 6, 1939 (XP-39); November 25, 1939 (XP-39B); September 13, 1940 (YP-39)

Bachem Ba 349 *Natter* (Adder)
Type: single-seat interceptor

Powerplant: one 4,400-pound thrust (30.15 kN) Walter 109-509 (A-2/C-1) liquid-fuel rocket motor and four 1,200 pounds thrust Schmidding 109-533 solid-fuel jettisonable rocket boosters

Performance: maximum speed 497 miles per hour (800 km/h) at sea level; initial rate of climb 36,415 feet per minute (11,100 m/m); service ceiling 45,920 feet (14,000 m); radius of action 25 miles (40 km)

Weight: maximum takeoff 4,850 pounds (2,200 kg)

Dimensions: wingspan 11 feet 9 1/2 in (3.60 m); length 20 feet (6.10 m); wing area 29.60 square feet (2.75 sq m)

Armament: 24 Henschel Hs 297 Föhn 73mm spin stabilized rockets or 33 R4M 55mm spin stabilized rockets, or (proposed) two MK 108 30mm cannon with 60 rounds total

Blohm und Voss P.170
Type: two- or three-seat bomber or fighter-bomber

Powerplant: three 1,600-horsepower (1176 kW) BMW 801D radial engines driving three-bladed 11-foot 5-inch propellers

Performance: maximum speed 510 miles per hour at 26,000 feet; ceiling, 38,299 feet; range 1,250 miles

Weight: loaded 13,250 pounds (6,000 kg)

Armament: four 20mm cannon; four 1,000-pound or two 2,000-pound bombs

Dimensions: wingspan 52 feet 6 inches (16.00 m); length 46 feet 11 inches (14.30 m); height 12 feet (3.65 m)

Heinkel He 162 *Volksjäger*
Type: single-engine, single-seat jet fighter

Powerplant: (typical) one 1,760-pound (800 kg) static thrust BMW 003A-1 Sturm (Storm) axial-flow turbojet engine

Performance: maximum speed 490 mph (790 km/h) at sea level or 520 mph (838 km/h) or 19,685 ft (6,000 m); range at full throttle 385 miles (620 km); range with six 30-second bursts 369 miles (595 km); initial rate of climb 3,780 feet per minute (1152 m/m); service ceiling 39,500 feet (12,040 m)

Weights: empty 4,520 pounds (2,050 kg); takeoff 5,941 pounds (2,695 kg)

Armament: two 30mm MK 108 cannon (He 162A-1); two 20mm Mauser MG 151/20 cannon (He 162A-2 variant)

Dimensions: wingspan 24 feet 7 inches (7.20 m); length 30 feet 8 inches (9.05 m); height 8 feet 4 inches (2.55 m); wing area 120.56 square feet (11.20 sq m)

Heinkel 280
Type: single-seat, twin-jet fighters

Powerplant: two 1,102-pound thrust (4.9 kN) Heinkel He S8s (He 280V3) or two 1,852-pound thrust Junkers Jumo 004 Orkans (He 280V6) or two 1,323-pound thrust (5.89 kN) BMW 109 003 turbojet engines

Performance: maximum speed 508 miles per hour (817 km/h) at 3,940 feet (1,200 m); rate of climb 3,756 feet per minute (1,145 m/min); service ceiling 32,000 feet (10,000 m); range 230 miles (370 km)

Weights: 3,666 pounds (1,663 kg); loaded 11,475 pounds (5,205 kg)

Dimensions: wingspan 40 feet (12.20 m); length 34 feet 1 inch (10.40 m); height 10 feet (3.06 m); wing area 233 square feet (21.50 sq m)

Armament: three MG 151 20mm cannons

First flight: Mach 30, 1941

Junkers Ju 290A-5
Type: long-range maritime surveillance aircraft/transport

Powerplant: four BMW 802D 14-cylinder radial engines rated at 1,700 horsepower (1,268 kW) on takeoff

Performance: maximum speed, 273 miles per hour (440 km/h) at 19,028 feet (5,800 meters); normal cruising speed 224 miles per hour (360 km/h); climb to 6,096 feet (1,850 meters) in 9.8 minutes; service ceiling (19,685 feet) 6,000 meters; range 3,821 miles (6,150 km)

Weights: normal loaded 9,032 pounds (4,097 kg); maximum overload 9,914 pounds (4,497 kg)

Dimensions: wingspan 137 feet 9 inches (42.00 m); length 93 feet 11 inches (28.64 m); height 22 feet 5 inches (6.83 m); wing area 2,192 square feet (203.60 sq m)

Armament: one 20mm MG 151 cannon in each of two dorsal turrets; one MG 151 in extreme tail; two MG 151s firing from aft waist positions; one MG 151 in front of ventral gondola and one 13mm MG 131 machine gun in rear of ventral gondola

Crew: nine

First flight: August 1942

Lockheed P-38L Lightning

Type: single-seat fighter

Powerplant: two 1,600-horsepower (1194-kW) Allison V-1710-111/113 inline piston engines driving three-bladed, 9-foot (2.74-m) Curtiss Electric propellers

Performance: maximum speed 414 miles per hour (666 km/h) at 25,000 feet (7,620 m); climb to 20,000 feet (6,095 m) in 7.0 minutes; service ceiling 44,000 feet (13,410 m); range 450 miles (724 km); maximum ferry range 2,600 miles (4,184 km)

Weights: empty 12,800 pounds (5,806 kg); maximum takeoff 21,600 pounds (9,798 kg)

Dimensions: span 52 feet (15.85 m); length 37 feet 10 inches (11.53 m); height 9 feet (2.74 m); wing area 327.5 square feet (30.42 sq m)

Armament: one 20mm cannon and four .50-cal (12.7mm) machine guns, plus up to two 2,000-pound (907-kg) bombs or two 1,600-lb (726-kg) bombs and ten 5-inch (127mm) rocket projectiles under wings

First flight: January 27, 1939 (XP-38)

Lockheed YP-80A Shooting Star

Type: single-seat fighter

Powerplant: one 3,850-pound thrust General Electric J33-GE-11 or Allison J33-A-9 turbojet (YP-80A); one 4,600-pound (2,087 kg) thrust Allison J33-A-23 axial-flow turbojet engine (early F-80C); 5,400-pound (2,450-kg) Allison J33-A-35 (later aircraft)

Performance: maximum speed 601 miles per hour (967 km/h) at sea level; service ceiling 46,800 feet (14,265m); range 825 miles (1,328 km)

Weights: empty 8,420 pounds (3,819 kg); maximum take off 16,856 pounds (7,646 kg)

Dimensions: span 38 feet 9 inches (11.81 m); length 34 feet 5 inches (10.49 m); height 11 feet 3 inches (3.43 m); wing area 237.6 square feet (22.07 sq m)

Armament: six .50-caliber (12.7mm) fixed forward-firing nose machine guns plus provision for two 1,000-pound (454-kg) bombs and eight under-wing rockets

North American P-51D Mustang

Type: single-seat fighter and fighter-bomber

Powerplant: one 1,590-horsepower (1,186-kW) Packard V-1650-7 (Rolls-Royce Merlin) liquid-cooled inline engine

Performance: maximum speed 437 miles per hour (703 km/h) at 20,000 feet (6,096 m); initial rate of climb 3,475 feet (1,060 m) per minute; operating radius with maximum fuel 1,300 miles (2,092 km)

Weights: empty 7,125 pounds (3,230 kg); loaded 11,600 pounds (5,262 kg)

Dimensions: span 37 feet 0–1/2 inches (11.29 m); length 32 feet 3 inches (9.84 m); height 13 feet 8 inches (4.10 m); wing area 235 square feet (21.83 sq m)

Armament: six .50-caliber (12.7mm) Browning M3 machine guns with 400 rounds for each inboard gun and 270 rounds for each outboard gun; provision for two 500-pound (227-kg) bombs, eight rockets, or other under-wing ordnance in place of drop tanks

First flight: October 26, 1940 (NA-73X); May 20, 1941 (XP-51); May 29, 1942 (P-51A); November 17, 1943 (XP-51D)

APPENDIX B

USAAF Aerial Victory Credits
over Me 262 German Jets

Date ddmmyyyy	Name	Credit	Ftr Gp	Ftr Sq	Theater	Aircraft Flown
28081944	2 Lt Manford O. Croy Jr.	0.50	78 FG	82 FS	ETO	P-47
28081944	Maj Joseph Myers	0.50	78 FG	82 FS	ETO	P-47
7101944	Maj Richard E. Conner	1.00	78 FG	82 FS	ETO	P-47
7101944	1 Lt Urban L. Drew	2.00	361 FG	375 FS	ETO	P-47
15101944	2 Lt Huie H. Lamb Jr.	1.00	78 FG	82 FS	ETO	P-47
1111944	1 Lt Walter R. Groce	0.50	56 FG	63 FS	ETO	P-47
1111944	2 Lt William T. Gerbe Jr.	0.50	352 FG	486 FS	ETO	P-47
6111944	Capt Charles E. Yeager	1.00	357 FG	363 FS	ETO	P-51
6111944	1 Lt William J. Quinn	1.00	357 FG	374 FS	ETO	P-47
8111944	1 Lt James W. Kenney	1.00	357 FG	362 FS	ETO	P-51

Date ddmmyyyy	Name	Credit	Ftr Gp	Ftr Sq	Theater	Aircraft Flown
8111944	2 Lt Anthony Maurice	1.00	361 FG	375 FS	ETO	P-47
8111944	1 Lt Ernest C. Fiebelkorn Jr.	0.50	20 FG	77 FS	ETO	P-51
8111944	1 Lt Edward R. Haydon	0.50	357 FG	364 FS	ETO	P-51
8111944	1 Lt Richard W. Stevens	1.00	364 FG	384 FS	ETO	P-51
18111944	2 Lt John M. Creamer	0.50	4 FG	335 FS	ETO	P-47
18111944	Capt John C. Fitch	0.50	4 FG	335 FS	ETO	P-47
9121944	2 Lt Harry L. Edwards	1.00	352 FG	486 FS	ETO	P-51
22121944	1 Lt Eugene P. McGlauflin	0.50	31 FG	308 FS	MTO	P-51
22121944	2 Lt Roy L. Scales	0.50	31 FG	308 FS	MTO	P-51
13011945	1 Lt Walter J. Konantz	1.00	55 FG	338 FS	ETO	P-51
14011945	1 Lt Billy J. Murray	1.00	353 FG	351 FS	ETO	P-51
14011945	1 Lt James W. Rohrs	0.50	353 FG	351 FS	ETO	P-51
14011945	1 Lt George J. Rosen	0.50	353 FG	351 FS	ETO	P-51
15011945	1 Lt Robert P. Winks	1.00	357 FG	364 FS	ETO	P-51
20011945	1 Lt Dale E. Karger	1.00	357 FG	364 FS	ETO	P-51
20011945	2 Lt Roland R. Wright	1.00	357 FG	364 FS	ETO	P-51
9021945	1 Lt Johnnie L. Carter	1.00	357 FG	363 FS	ETO	P-51
9021945	Capt Donald H. Bochkay	1.00	357 FG	363 FS	ETO	P-51
9021945	1 Lt Stephen C. Ananian	1.00	339 FG	505 FS	ETO	P-51
15021945	2 Lt Dudley M. Amoss	1.00	55 FG	38 FS	ETO	P-51

Date ddmmyyyy	Name	Credit	Ftr Gp	Ftr Sq	Theater	Aircraft Flown
21021945	1 Lt Harold E. Whitmore	1.00	339 FG	361 FS	ETO	P-51
22021945	Capt Gordon B. Compton	1.00	353 FG	351 FS	ETO	P-51
22021945	2 Lt Charles D. Price	1.00	352 FG	486 FS	ETO	P-51
22021945	Maj Wayne K. Blickenstaff	1.00	353 FG	350 FS	ETO	P-51
22021945	1 Lt Oliven T. Cowan	1.00	365 FG	388 FS	ETO	P-47
22021945	1 Lt David B. Fox	1.00	366 FG	391 FS	ETO	P-47
25021945	Capt Donald M. Cummings	2.00	55 FG	38 FS	ETO	P-51
25021945	2 Lt John F. O'Neil	1.00	55 FG	38 FS	ETO	P-51
25021945	Capt Donald E. Penn	1.00	55 FG	38 FS	ETO	P-51
25021945	1 Lt Milliard O. Anderson	1.00	55 FG	38 FS	ETO	P-51
25021945	2 Lt Donald T. Menegay	1.00	55 FG	38 FS	ETO	P-51
25021945	1 Lt Billy Clemmons	1.00	55 FG	38 FS	ETO	P-51
25021945	1 Lt Carl G. Payne	1.00	4 FG	334 FS	ETO	P-51
1031945	1 Lt Wendell W. Beaty	1.00	365 FG	358 FS	ETO	P-51
1031945	1 Lt John K. Wilkins Jr.	1.00	2 AD		ETO	P-51
2031945	1 Lt Theodore W. Sedvert	1.00	354 FG	353 FS	ETO	P-51
14031945	1 Lt Charles R. Rodebaugh	1.00	2 AD		ETO	P-51
19031945	Maj Niven K. Cranfill	1.00	359 FG	368 FS	ETO	P-51
19031945	Capt Robert S. Fifield	1.00	357 FG	363 FS	ETO	P-51
19031945	Maj Robert W. Foy	1.00	357 FG		ETO	P-51

Date ddmmyyyy	Name	Credit	Ftr Gp	Ftr Sq	Theater	Aircraft Flown
19031945	Capt Charles H. Spencer	1.00	355 FG	354 FS	ETO	P-51
20031945	1 Lt Robert E. Irion	1.00	339FG	505 FS	ETO	P-51
20031945	1 Lt Vernon N. Barto	1.00	339 FG	504 FS	ETO	P-51
21031945	Capt Edwin H. Miller	1.00	78 FG	83 FS	ETO	P-51
21031945	1 Lt Richard D. Anderson	1.00	361 FG	375 FS	ETO	P-51
21031945	2 Lt Harry M. Chapman	1.00	361 FG	376 FS	ETO	P-51
21031945	1 Lt John A. Kirk III	1.00	78 FG	83 FS	ETO	P-51
21031945	1 Lt Robert H. Anderson	1.00	78 FG	82 FS	ETO	P-51
21031945	2 Lt Walter E. Bourque	1.00	78 FG	82 FS	ETO	P-51
21031945	Capt Winfield H. Brown	0.50	78 FG	82 FS	ETO	P-51
21031945	1 Lt Allen A. Rosenblum	0.50	78 FG	82 FS	ETO	P-51
22031945	Capt William J. Dillard	1.00	31 FG	308 FS	MTO	P-51
22031945	2 Lt John W. Cunnick III	1.00	55 FG	38 FS	ETO	P-51
22031945	1 Lt Eugene L. Peel	0.50	78 FG	82 FS	ETO	P-51
22031945	2 Lt Milton B. Stutzman	0.50	78 FG	82 FS	ETO	P-51
22031945	Capt Harold T. Barnaby	1.00	78 FG	83 FS	ETO	P-51
24031945	2 Lt Charles V. Brantley	1.00	332 FG	100 FS	MTO	P-51
24031945	1 Lt Roscoe C. Brown	1.00	332 FG	100 FS	MTO	P-51
24031945	1 Lt Earl R. Lane	1.00	332 FG	100 FS	MTO	P-51
24031945	Col William A. Daniel	1.00	31 FG	308 FS	MTO	P-51

Date ddmmyyyy	Name	Credit	Ftr Gp	Ftr Sq	Theater	Aircraft Flown
24031945	1 Lt Forrest M. Keene Jr.	1.00	31 FG	308 FS	MTO	P-51
24031945	1 Lt Raymond D. Leonard	1.00	31 FG	308 FS	MTO	P-51
24031945	Capt Kenneth T. Smith	1.00	31 FG	308 FS	MTO	P-51
24031945	2 Lt William M. Wilder	1.00	31 FG	308 FS	MTO	P-51
25031945	1 Lt Eugene H. Wendt	1.00	479 FG	434 FS	ETO	P-51
25031945	Maj George E. Bostick	1.00	56 FG	63 FS	ETO	P-47
25031945	2 Lt Edwin M. Crosthwait Jr.	1.00	56 FG	63 FS	ETO	P-47
25031945	Capt Raymond H. Littge	1.00	352 FG	487 FS	ETO	P-51
30031945	1 Lt Patrick L. Moore	1.00	55 FG	343 FS	ETO	P-51
30031945	1 Lt Carroll W. Bennett	1.00	339 FG	504 FS	ETO	P-51
30031945	Capt Robert F. Sargent	1.00	339 FG	504 FS	ETO	P-51
30031945	Lt Col John D. Landers	0.50	78 FG		ETO	P-51
30031945	2 Lt Thomas V. Thain Jr.	0.50	78 FG	84 FS	ETO	P-51
30031945	1 Lt Kenneth J. Scott Jr.	1.00	361 FG	376 FS	ETO	P-51
30031945	1 Lt James C. Hurley	1.00	352 FG	328 FS	ETO	P-51
30031945	2 Lt John B. Guy	1.00	364 FG	383 FS	ETO	P-51
31031945	1 Lt Marvin H. Castleberry	1.00	2 AD		ETO	P-51
31031945	1 Lt Harrison B. Tordoff	1.00	354 FG	353 FS	ETO	P-51
31031945	1 Lt Wayne L. Coleman	1.00	78 FG	82 FS	ETO	P-51
31031945	Capt William T. Bales Jr.	1.00	371 FG		ETO	P-47

Date ddmmyyyy	Name	Credit	Ftr Gp	Ftr Sq	Theater	Aircraft Flown
4041945	1 Lt Robert C. Coker	0.50	339 FG	504 FS	ETO	P-51
4041945	Capt Kirke B. Everson Jr.	0.50	339 FG	504 FS	ETO	P-51
4041945	Capt Nile C. Greer	1.00	339 FG	504 FS	ETO	P-51
4041945	2 Lt Robert C. Havighurst	1.00	339 FG	504 FS	ETO	P-51
4041945	Lt Col George F. Ceuleers	1.00	364 FG	383 FS	ETO	P-51
4041945	1 Lt Michael J. Kennedy	0.50	4 FG	334 FS	ETO	P-51
4041945	1 Lt Harold H. Frederick	0.50	4 FG	336 FS	ETO	P-51
4041945	1 Lt Raymond A. Dyer	1.00	4 FG	334 FS	ETO	P-51
4041945	Capt Harry R. Corey	1.00	339 FG	505 FS	ETO	P-51
4041945	1 Lt John W. Haun	1.00	324 FG	316 FS	ETO	P-47
4041945	1 Lt Andrew N. Kandis	1.00	324 FG	316 FS	ETO	P-47
5041945	Capt John C. Fahringer	1.00	56 FG	63 FS	ETO	P-47
7041945	1 Lt Hilton O. Thompson	1.00	479 FG	434 FS	ETO	P-51
7041945	Capt Verne E. Hooker	1.00	479 FG	435 FS	ETO	P-51
8041945	1 Lt John J. Usiatynski	1.00	358 FG	367 FS	ETO	P-47
9041945	2 Lt James T. Sloan	1.00	361 FG	374 FS	ETO	P-51
9041945	Maj Edward B. Giller	1.00	55 FG	343 FS	ETO	P-51
10041945	Capt Gordon B. Compton	1.00	353 FG	351 FS	ETO	P-51
10041945	1 Lt Harold Tenenbaum	1.00	359 FG	369 FS	ETO	P-51
10041945	2 Lt Walter J. Sharbo	1.00	56 FG	62 FS	ETO	P-47

Date ddmmyyyy	Name	Credit	Ftr Gp	Ftr Sq	Theater	Aircraft Flown
10041945	Capt John K. Hollins	1.00	20 FG	79 FS	ETO	P-51
10041945	Capt John K. Brown	1.00	20 FG	55 FS	ETO	P-51
10041945	1 Lt Willmer W. Collins	1.00	4 FG	336 FS	ETO	P-51
10041945	2 Lt John W. Cudd Jr.	0.50	15 FG	77 FS	ETO	P-51
10041945	F.O. Jerome Rosenblum	0.50	15 FG	77 FS	ETO	P-51
10041945	1 Lt Keith R. McGinnis	1.00	55 FG	38 FS	ETO	P-51
10041945	2 Lt Walter T. Drozd	1.00	15 FG	77 FS	ETO	P-51
10041945	2 Lt Albert B. North	1.00	15 FG	77 FS	ETO	P-51
10041945	1 Lt Robert J. Guggemus	1.00	359 FG	369 FS	ETO	P-51
10041945	1 Lt Charles C. Pattillo	1.00	352 FG	487 FS	ETO	P-51
10041945	Lt Col Earl D. Duncan	0.50	352 FG	328 FS	ETO	P-51
10041945	Maj Richard G. McAuliffe	0.50	352 FG	328 FS	ETO	P-51
10041945	1 Lt Kenneth A. Lashbrook	1.00	55 FG	338 FS	ETO	P-51
10041945	Capt Robert W. Abernathy	1.00	353 FG	350 FS	ETO	P-51
10041945	1 Lt Jack W. Clark	0.50	353 FG	350 FS	ETO	P-51
10041945	2 Lt Bruce D. McMahan	0.50	353 FG	350 FS	ETO	P-51
10041945	1 Lt Wayne C. Gatlin	1.00	356 FG	360 FS	ETO	P-51
10041945	1 Lt Joseph W. Prichard	0.50	352 FG	487 FS	ETO	P-51
10041945	2 Lt Carlo A. Ricci	0.50	352 FG	487 FS	ETO	P-51
10041945	Capt Douglas J. Pick	0.50	364 FG	384 FS	ETO	P-51

Date ddmmyyyy	Name	Credit	Ftr Gp	Ftr Sq	Theater	Aircraft Flown
10041945	1 Lt Harry C. Schwartz	0.50	364 FG	384 FS	ETO	P-51
16041945	1 Lt Vernon O. Fein	1.00	368 FG	397 FS	ETO	P-47
16041945	1 Lt Henry A. Yandel	1.00	368 FG	397 FS	ETO	P-47
16041945	Maj Eugene E. Ryan	1.00	55 FG	338 FS	ETO	P-51
17041945	1 Lt James Zweizig	1.00	371 FG	404 FS	ETO	P-47
17041945	Capt Jack A. Warner	1.00	354 FG	356 FS	ETO	P-51
17041945	Capt Roy W. Orndarff	1.00	364 FG	383 FS	ETO	P-51
17041945	Capt Walter L. Goff	1.00	364 FG	383 FS	ETO	P-51
17041945	F.O. James A. Steiger	1.00	357 FG	364 FS	ETO	P-51
17041945	1 Lt John C. Campbell Jr.	1.00	339 FG	503 FS	ETO	P-51
18041945	Maj Ralph F. Johnson	1.00	325 FG	319 FS	MTO	P-51
18041945	Capt Charles E. Weaver	1.00	357 FG	362 FS	ETO	P-51
18041945	Maj Donald H. Bochkay	1.00	357 FG	363 FS	ETO	P-51
19041945	Lt Col Jack W. Hayes Jr.	1.00	357 FG	363 FS	ETO	P-51
19041945	Capt Robert S. Fifield	1.00	357 FG	363 FS	ETO	P-51
19041945	1 Lt Paul N. Bowles	1.00	357 FG	363 FS	ETO	P-51
19041945	1 Lt Carroll W. Ofsthun	1.00	357 FG	363 FS	ETO	P-51
19041945	Capt Ivan L. McGuire	0.50	357 FG	364 FS	ETO	P-51
19041945	1 Lt Gilmon L. Weber	0.50	357 FG	364 FS	ETO	P-51
19041945	1 Lt Robert DeLoach	1.00	55 FG	338 FS	ETO	P-51

Date ddmmyyyy	Name	Credit	Ftr Gp	Ftr Sq	Theater	Aircraft Flown
19041945	2 Lt James P. McMullen	1.00	357 FG	364 FS	ETO	P-51
24041945	Capt Jerry G. Mast	0.50	365 FG	388 FS	ETO	P-47
24041945	2 Lt William H. Myers	0.50	365 FG	388 FS	ETO	P-47
25041945	1 Lt Richard D. Stevenson	0.50	370 FG	402 FS	ETO	P-51
25041945	1 Lt Robert W. Hoyle	0.50	370 FG	402 FS	ETO	P-51
26041945	Capt Robert W. Clark	1.00	50 FG	10 FS	ETO	P-47
26041945	Capt Herbert A. Philo	1.00	27 FG	522 FS	ETO	P-47

Sources:

USAAF (European Theater) Credits for the Destruction of Enemy Aircraft in Air-to-Air Combat, World War II, Victory List No. 5, Frank J. Olynyk, May 1987.

USAAF (Mediterranean Theater) Credits for the Destruction of Enemy Aircraft in Air-to-Air Combat, World War II, Victory List No. 6, Frank J. Olynyk, June 1987.

USAF Historical Study No. 85, USAF Credits for the Destruction of Enemy Aircraft, World War II, Albert F. Simpson Historical Research Center, 1978.

Combat Squadrons of the Air Force, World War II, edited by Maurer Maurer, 1969.

Air Force Combat Units of World War II, edited by Maurer Maurer, 1983.

Compiled by:

Patsy Robertson, Historian

Organizational Histories Branch, USAFHRA March 2010

APPENDIX C

USAAF Aerial Victory Credits
over Me 163 German Aircraft in ETO

Date ddmmyyyy	Name	Credit	Ftr Gp	Ftr Sq	Aircraft Flown
29071944	Capt Arthur Ferdinand Jeffrey	1.00	479 FG	434 FS	P-38
16081944	Lt Cyril W. Jones Jr.	1.00	359 FG	370 FS	P-51
16081944	Lt Col John Byrd Murphy	1.00	359 FG	370 FS	P-51
7101944	Lt Willard G. Erfkamp	0.50	364 FG	385 FS	P-51
7101944	Capt Elmer A. Taylor	0.50	55 FG	338 FS	P-51
2111944	Capt Louis H. Norley	1.00	4 FG	335 FS	P-51
2111944	Capt Fred W. Glover	1.00	4 FG	336 FS	*P-51*
15031945	Capt Ray S. Wetmore	1.00	359 FG	370 FS	P-51

Source:

USAAF (European Theater) Credits for the Destruction of Enemy Aircraft in Air-to-Air Combat, World War II, Victory List No. 5, Frank J. Olynyk, May 1987.

No Me 163 aircraft AVC located in MTO.

Compiled by:

Patsy Robertson, Historian

Organizational Histories Branch, USAFHRA

Feb 5, 2013

Index